Strategies of Transformation Toward a Multicultural Society

**Praeger Series in
Transformational Politics and Political Science**

The Politics of Transformation: Local Activism in the Peace and Environmental
Movements
Betty H. Zisk

The Latino Family and the Politics of Transformation
David T. Abalos

Mediation, Citizen Empowerment, and Transformational Politics
Edward W. Schwerin

Strategies of Transformation Toward a Multicultural Society

Fulfilling the Story of Democracy

DAVID T. ABALOS

Praeger Series in Transformational Politics
and Political Science
Theodore L. Becker, Series Adviser

Westport, Connecticut
London

Library of Congress Cataloging-in-Publication Data

Abalos, David T.
    Strategies of transformation toward a multicultural society:
fulfilling the story of democracy / David T. Abalos.
        p.   cm.—(Praeger series in transformational politics and
political science, ISSN 1061–5261)
    Includes bibliographical references and index.
    ISBN 0–275–95270–3 (alk. paper).—ISBN 0–275–95271–1 (pb. : alk.
paper)
        1. Multicultural education—United States.   2. Multiculturalism—
United States.   3. Feminism and education—United States.
4. Critical pedagogy—United States.   I. Title.   II. Series.
LC1099.3.A22   1996
370.19′6′0973—dc20   95–37649

British Library Cataloguing in Publication Data is available.

Library of Congress Catalog Card Number: 95–37649
ISBN: 0–275–95270–3
        0–275–95271–1 (pbk.)
ISSN: 1061–5261

First published in 1996

Praeger Publishers, 88 Post Road West, Westport, CT 06881
An imprint of Greenwood Publishing Group, Inc.

Printed in the United States of America

The paper used in this book complies with the
Permanent Paper Standard issued by the National
Information Standards Organization (Z39.48–1984).

10 9 8 7 6 5 4 3 2 1

For Celia with Love

In Loving Memory of
Louis Dorantes
1917–1995

Contents

Acknowledgments

I could not have finished this book without the invaluable help of my wife, Celia. She brought my ideas to life by rearranging and editing them on the computer. But more importantly, she tested my ideas with her insight and a good sense of humor. In addition, Celia often questioned me and in a loving manner challenged me to practice what I knew and taught in theory. Because of my love for my children, David, Veronica, and Matthew, I am inspired to see my students as young men and women who need the same kind of nurturance in the classroom. I am deeply grateful for their love, companionship and friendship. Many thanks to Katherine Olivetti for all of her help and guidance. I also want to thank the members of my extended family, Dick and Mary Scaine, and Jim Palladino and his mother, Lucy Palladino, for all of their support.

Julia To-Dutka taught me much about multicultural education. I listened to her and found that many of her insights helped me and others to see in a new way. We have been friends in a common enterprise as we have worked together to make multicultural and women's scholarship a reality in American life and education. In the various programs that he organized for urban teachers, my friend and colleague David Surrey provided me with many forums to test my ideas. David is one of the most caring professionals that I have met. Danielle Hornett gave me a rare opportunity to share many of the ideas found in this book in a campus setting with faculty, students, and administrators. In addition, I learned from her about the American Indian heritage, not only by what she said, but also by the dignified way in which she went about her work. She is truly an outstanding educator. Alberto Pulido, a young Chicano scholar, has been for me both a friend and a source of inspiration. He is an example of a teacher who embodies in his teaching and scholarship the best of multicultural and gender-fair education.

My students over the years have been a great source of joy and learning. I am especially thankful for Matthew Demian, Darron Redd, Kathy Rosado, Glenda Gracia, Keisha Caine and Kevin Lyles, Gretchen Cole Ueno, Edgardo Ramos, Tinisha Heggs, Stephanie Meredith, Margaret Smith, Gail Thomas, Wanda Roman, Ursula Watson, Jeff Avila, Juan Chavez, Myrna Santiago, Find Findsen, Cherise Harris, Lubna Mustafa, Juan Morales, Jason Van der Walle, Amy Gusick, Doug Carrotozolla, Jessica Ortiz, Elsie Jiminez, Merari Ortiz, Elvis Bernal, and George Maroulakas.

I very much appreciate the support that I received in the writing of this book from my colleagues at Seton Hall University who created for me an environment that allowed me to develop my ideas. They include Phil Kayal, Al Hakim, Dick Adinaro, Rev. Larry Frizzell, Peter Ahr, Chuck Carter, Gisela Webb, Ed Hendrickson, Larry Greene, Carlos Rodriguez, Robin Cunningham, Agnes Wu, Judith Stark, Tony Triano, George and Paula Tzannetakis and Bill Sales. Special thanks to Ms. Renee Cecchino, who assisted me with her fine skills in computer graphics to provide the symbolic drawings for the book. I want to make special mention of Prof. John R. Harrington of the English Department, who died recently. John Harrington was a teacher and colleague who, both as an academic and as a loving human being, made the campus a better place. He cared deeply about his students and his colleagues as well as about the world of ideas. He was one of a kind, and he will be sorely missed. For the past several years, Frank Morales, my Puerto Rican brother, has encouraged me to develop my ideas for a multicultural curriculum. He has helped me in more ways than he is aware with his friendship and affection, and I am grateful for all of his support. But above all, he has performed a great service to Seton Hall by helping to diversify the student body so that it truly reflects a gender-fair and multicultural America.

I cannot thank Manfred Halpern enough for having introduced me to the theory of transformation and especially for having taught me about the four faces of our being—the personal, political, historical, and sacred. It was he who guided me to discover and nurture my own personal creative imagination and intuition, to see politics as what we can and need to do together to create a more loving and just society, to re-envision history as new turning points created by people like you and me, and to acknowledge my own face as a Mexican/Chicano as another manifestation of the deepest transforming source. He has truly touched and deepened all four faces of my being with love and wisdom.

Finally, I would like to thank my editors, Ted Becker and especially Dan Eades, for their encouragement, editing and genuine friendship throughout the writing of the book.

Introduction

The emergence of multicultural diversity as a concrete face of the archetypal story of democracy in our time provides us with a challenge, perhaps for the first time as Americans, to discover our actual past. We now have the opportunity to ask what in our past is fruitful and what is destructive. But before we can ask what in our heritage is creative and what is harmful, we need to know what stories and ways of life currently constitute our society and be prepared to empty ourselves of these partial and truncated dramas and ways of life so that we can create new and more compassionate stories in the service of transformation. Thus this new multicultural aspect of democracy is not about how and why different groups and cultures should be proud of their past. A multicultural society is one that is ready to discover what it is that we need to nourish and what to let go. Above all, we have to be prepared to critique all cultures in our society because all of them are in bad shape. For example, the Latino and African American cultures suffer from a highly destructive machismo that feeds a sexism and patriarchy that is devastating to the women in those communities. The dominant society is caught by the story of capitalism, which is often in collusion with racism to preserve the power of the privileged. We are all in trouble when it comes to facing the inherited stories and ways of life of our cultural past.

For most of our history as a nation, we have not recognized and continue not to recognize each other as full human beings. Recently, during a seminar given at a conference for teachers, an African American woman said to me, "The majority of people in this society continue to see me and the children that I teach as less than human." This assertion brought the discussion to a roaring silence as we all reflected on the impact of what she had said.

The radical nature of this book will consist in searching for the roots of the matter, so that we can together participate in planting and nourishing new archetypal roots as stories, new seeds, new branches that allow each person in all of her and his uniqueness and shared humanity to fully realize the personal, political, historical, and sacred faces of our being. This cannot be done by reforming, by re-establishing, by reclaiming, or by reaffirming the present stories of our society, or by blindly asserting our cultural past; it is accomplished by critiquing, dissenting against, and, in some cases, uprooting the arrogance of *la mission civilisatrice*. De Tocqueville used this phrase when arguing in the French parliament that Algeria should be annexed and made an integral part of France. The French felt that it was their duty to humanity to "Frenchify" the allegedly lesser peoples of the world. Of course it was the French who felt that they knew what was best for others. This same kind of attitude is to be found here in our society when it comes to matters of the curriculum and education in general.

At its best, the multicultural aspect of democracy rejects a narrow ethnocentrism and acknowledges and enhances the fullness of our human-ity—the personal, political, historical, and sacred faces of our being. Thus, strategies of transformation are undertaken to enable each of us from all backgrounds to ask questions about our current society by politically participating in the creation of the kind of history and sacred that we want to be present in our story as human beings living in the United States now. This means that we have hardly begun the process of deepening and redefining the story of democracy in the service of transformation.

Multicultural education enhances and helps to fulfill the story of democ-racy by encouraging each person and each community to come forth in their own being so that each is present and each is heard. For this reason, this is not a book about clever strategies that prepare us to be competitive with the peoples of the Pacific Rim. It is a book about strategies for people like you and me and how we can come to know, critique, and create new archetypal stories and nourish others so that the story of democracy will be fully incarnate in the four faces of our being. Only in this way will people be able to contribute anything valuable to the world.

Often the charge is made that to be multicultural is divisive and that we are in danger of Balkanizing ourselves as a nation. The emergence of multicultural consciousness as a fundamental aspect of democracy is an attempt on the part of many people of goodwill in connection to their deepest sources to turn our society away from the dominant stories that in fact now divide us as a people based on race, gender, class, and other such issues. It is precisely the refusal of the dominant in the United States to see the four faces of the others in this country that so deeply divides us. After all, the powerful turn the poor, who are disproportionately children, people of color, and women, into invisible people who are often considered to be of their very nature inferior. This can be seen from the recent debate on universal health care, in which powerful interests were ready to deny the poor the kind of health care they needed. The marginalized groups may by some twist of fate produce some "good ones" who are offered the concession of assimilation into the ranks of the powerful. Women and people of color can, and are, promoted into the system, but at the expense of their own heritage. If they prove to be disloyal by attempting to improve the lot of women and communities of people of color as a whole, they are quickly exiled to lesser positions or fired. Those who are seen as the most defiant can be killed. Even the *New York Times* warned us about the most dire consequences for the excluded when on its editorial page it agreed with members of the African American community who saw the spectrum of genocide in the slow response of the government to the spread of AIDS in the black community. The dominant refuse to see the personal faces of their victims; these fringe people are depoliticized except when they vote as the powerful want them to. Their culture and stories or history are wiped away so that they become people who are taught only the story of the powerful; their sacred face is obscured since the lords who inspire the powerful do not acknowledge them.

If we are to reject the stories of the dominant that are inherently undemocratic, since they violate the reality of many of our citizens by denying their humanity, what will we put in their place? As a nation we have to ask ourselves how we can create fundamentally more compassionate, loving, and just relationships and stories by which to live our lives. To do this we all must have the right and ability to participate in the process of uprooting destructive stories that cripple the powerful and the powerless alike.

But how will we know when we are in fact creating fundamentally new and better relationships and stories? I propose to demonstrate that of the very nature of our humanity, we all have four fundamentally different normative choices by which to participate in the task of building a new society. All of our relationships and stories are practiced in the service of one of these four ways of life: emanation, incoherence, deformation, and transformation. As human beings we all have the right and ability to choose between these underlying four ways of life. Each way of life provides us with a normative choice for understanding, living, and structuring life. But only in the service of the way of life of transformation as the core drama of life are we able to participate critically, creatively, and lovingly with the fullness of our being to bring about the fundamentally new and better in all aspects of our life. Therefore we can know the quality and deeper value and meaning of a particular story, such as the archetypal story of democracy, by asking the question: In the service of what way of life am I enacting this relationship, this specific story of my and of our collective life? The Declaration of Independence is grounded on the inviolability and equality of each individual person. I interpret this to mean that at its best, the story of democracy in the service of transformation declares that each of us has a unique face that allows us to create a new environment together with others so that politically we can bring about a more human turning point in a new history. This turning point will break the repetition of victimhood and affirm the inherent sacredness of all groups and individuals in our community.

To further explain and develop the above I will present in Chapter 1 a theoretical context within which, in subsequent chapters, we will be able to examine the current situation in U.S. society and to propose strategies of transformation in society and culture. One of the key areas that affects us all is education. Two of the more important alternatives to violence are politics and education in the service of transformation. I therefore plan to show how we can as a nation affirm each of our citizens by beginning with our schools and especially the curriculum. I want to do this not only by explaining but by actually helping to create a new concrete manifestation of the archetypal story of democracy, multicultural diversity. This face of the story of democracy is still in the making. Each of us can and needs to participate in helping to shape this new emergence from our creative depths. Once a theory of transformation has been set forth I will in Chapters 2 and 3 apply theory to practice so that the reader can clearly see key aspects of the theory of transformation, such as the core drama of transformation, the four faces of our being, the four underlying archetypal ways of life, and the archetypal stories and relationships by which we live and shape daily life. These conceptual and theoretical dimensions will be made real and concrete by providing copious examples from multicultural literary works and scholarship. By analyzing the lives of characters drawn from literature and history, I intend to throw light on the stories and relationships that people like you and me have inherited and that we often unconsciously live and repeat. In the process of doing this the four faces of our being—the personal, political, historical, and sacred—will be shown as belonging to the very nature of our humanity.

An integral part of the struggle for democracy in our society, together with the multicultural, is the issue of women's rights. Consequently, in

Chapter 4 I will spell out the relationship between the multicultural face of democracy and the feminine as the inherent principle of liberation and transformation that underlies the whole of the democratic story.

We must not be naive as to the difficulty of the fight to continue the transformation of the democratic story in our nation. We have to know not only the strategies of the dominant, who wish to hold on to power and privilege, but also strategies by which to bring about the fundamentally new and better. Strategies for teaching and choosing between deformation and transformation are necessary. Thus, in Chapter 5, strategies for practicing and teaching multicultural and gender-fair education from the perspective of transformational politics will be articulated. Questions like the following will be addressed: How does a teacher here and now make a personal decision to participate together with her or his colleagues to bring about a new and better kind of democracy for our wider society through multicultural and gender-fair education? What kinds of resources are available? Is it necessary to develop new teaching methodologies? Do I have to wait for the dean or the school board to approve before I start new lesson plans or new courses? What kinds of assignments can I give that will lead to a multicultural and gender-fair consciousness? How can I do this when I am already swamped with so many other demands made by the school district, the Department of Education, my department, my chairperson? Are there now courses being taught from the perspective of transformational politics that are multicultural and gender-fair, and how are they actually taught? To deal with these practical concerns of teachers, examples of course outlines and assignments will be provided in the Appendix so that teachers can see how courses are structured to meet the requirements of their discipline and simultaneously be infused with a multicultural and gender-fair perspective.

The emerging multicultural and gender-fair face of the archetypal story of democracy will not become a reality unless people like you and me participate as colleagues and fellow citizens to bring it about. My hope is that this book will make a significant contribution to this effort. You and I are together linked in a common cause that will demand that our personal face be fully present, so that together with others, we can create a political environment wherein we can shape a new history that honors the deepest sacred in each of us.

Strategies of Transformation
Toward a Multicultural Society

CHAPTER 1

Setting the Context:
A Theory of Transformation

Theory allows us to see.

—Albert Einstein

As a young student at the University of Toronto, I vividly remember wishing to take a course that could provide me with insights into the relationship between politics, philosophy, science, literature, history, and religion. I felt that so many of my classes showed almost no connection to the rest of my studies or to my personal life. Looking back, I now realize that what I was hoping for was some kind of a matrix, a context, perhaps a paradigm, a perspective on reality that would enable me to see how the lives of individuals were interconnected. This search for a philosophical network had much to do with my awareness that so much of my life was not related to my studies. I often felt that to be a scholar, a dedicated academic, one had to learn to separate one's personal life from the world of scholarship. I didn't know where to go with such confusion. But as a young Mexican born of immigrant parents with no formal schooling, I had a burning desire to succeed in the world of education. I felt instinctively that it was my only way out of a very dangerous world.

One of my teachers suggested that I begin with a favorite author as a starting point that would serve as the center of an emerging spiral. From this initial point I could follow the successive turns of the spiral as an intellectual journey that this author would open up for me. I was quite taken by this imagery of the spiral as a continuing process that would allow me to link and see the relationship between different courses of studies and to see my journey as a search to understand the context of our lives. I mentioned to this guide that my most challenging author was Dostoevsky. So that is where I began my search to understand the context of my life.

As I read *The Brothers Karamazov*, I could see how Dostoevsky related Russian culture and history to religion, how he dealt with issues of class, ethnicity, and gender, hope and despair, faith and meaninglessness. Above all, I was impressed by the insights he provided on the deeper aspects of what it meant to be human. Because of my own struggle with poverty and ethnic and racial humiliation, I had wanted to see a world that was so optimistic that it was unreal. Dostoevsky reminded me that we all had to face the darker aspects of our own depths, as Raskolnikov did in *Crime and Punishment*. But especially in *The Brothers Karamazov*, he had shown me how it was possible for one individual to be wracked with the doubts of Ivan, the lust of Dimitry, and the search for the sacred through Alyosha. I immediately identified with Alyosha since he was the young monk and I was a seminarian. It was Dimitry, the womanizer, and Ivan, who had no faith, who threatened me because they reminded me of the macho male culture from which I had escaped. But as I read more of Dostoevsky I knew that this simplistic dichotomy between good and evil served only to obscure and to trivialize the real message.

It was a rude awakening for me to see that all three of the brothers—Dimitry, Ivan and Alyosha—and all that they represented were within me. I was at once liberated and afraid of this new knowledge. I was upset because I thought that by getting away from the old neighborhood and the corrupting powerlessness of poverty, I had freed myself from violence, raw sexuality, and the sense of dread that comes with belonging to a community relegated to the margins of society. However, I felt relieved by this new understanding because in some intuitive way I knew that I no longer had to deny so much that was in me but that I did not know how to integrate into my life. Nevertheless, this uneasy wound persisted. I was split between wanting to be the person above it all, so that I could continue to succeed academically, and the person who wanted to return to the depths of my experiences, since so much of me was still grounded there.

My search for a context, for a new setting that would allow me to be whole, led me away from dogmatic answers that denied the growing ambivalence within me. I wanted to be able to affirm everything that I felt without necessarily agreeing with it. But it was me, with all of my contradictory feelings that I wanted to accept in order to begin the task of separating what was to be redeemed and what discarded. It was because I could not with a sense of integrity confront the problem of sexuality except as temptation and evil that after seven years I decided to stop studying for the priesthood. All of my idealism had gone into this aspect of my journey. For a time it served an extraordinarily rich purpose. I discovered real fathers who cared about me and loved me in a way that I had never known. This love and encouragement helped me to study, read, and write well, analyze, do very well academically, and be a fine teacher. My ego needed this kind of success. But it was my deeper self that was being repressed. I had through the seminary experience responded to the needs of a period of my life, but now it was time to go back to the sources that had been bypassed and forgotten.

After leaving the institutional study of the priesthood, I continued to search for connections. Intellectually I understood my dilemma very well. What I did not know or understand was how to heal the split between the various aspects of my life. There was a parallel intellectual struggle: I remained unable to integrate the various worlds of academic discourse to my satisfaction. In the midst of this struggle I got married, finished my M.A. in theology at Marquette, and accepted a teaching position at Seton Hall University in New Jersey.

After two years of teaching, my journey took me to Princeton Theological Seminary, where I returned to finish my doctoral studies. After searching through the catalog at Princeton University and through the advice of a fellow student, I decided to enroll in a politics seminar on modernization taught by Professor Manfred Halpern. I was to learn later that this was the first time that Halpern had taught this seminar. Even more important, this course represented a turning point in his own personal and academic life. Just prior to teaching the seminar, Halpern had begun to despair because the prevailing social science and philosophy could not explain why inherited relationships and ways of life were dissolving all over the world and what alternative we had in the face of this great breaking—and where the fundamentally new and better comes from.

In this course, we were introduced to a new theory of transformation that allowed us to ask new kinds of questions about human relationships. Although some students were skeptical, we concluded that Halpern knew the tradition of politics so well that he was guiding us away from the usual study of stability in the structures and functions of a society because it did not really tell us anything about real people in the daily quest to know and see what it is that we need to do together to create a more human and just society. We were encouraged to see how the lack of connections between the personal, political, historical, and sacred faces of the people involved in our study of modernization led to breakdown. What fascinated me was the insight into the interrelationship between these four aspects of our lives and the connection between academic disciplines.

I had previously read many of the authors who we studied or who were recommended in the seminar. But now I read them for the first time, because previously I had no idea where these authors were taking me. Others I had read because they were required and still others were considered power authors or books, in the sense that anybody who is anybody had read and analyzed such-and-such a book. I now had the general theoretical context that I lacked before. As a result of this new perspective, I rediscovered many of my favorite books and authors. But above all, what was so intellectually and personally rewarding was the assertion and understanding that we could test this theory with our own experiences. This was not a theory about "those people" over there but about you and me, us and them. In addition we could test and participate in the creation and development of this theory. This was not about an Ivy League professor pursuing a career by developing a school of thought that became his or her exclusive intellectual property; this was about students and professor working as colleagues to apply theory to practice. Thus we all came to understand that modernization is not westernization, or secularization, but transformation, the creation of the fundamentally new and better in all aspects of our lives.

But perhaps the most outstanding experience of this seminar was the personal affirmation that I received as a Mexican/Chicano/Latino Catholic male. I did not have to leave anything of myself behind, even in this prestigious academic university. Everything was valuable because it all had to do with understanding that transformation, in order to be authentic, had to have a personal and sacred face as well as a political and historical one. As a result I could and did affirm that my search for intellectual and personal wholeness was real. I came to understand that the story of my sexual and identity struggles had a political face that had to do with others wanting to control my identity as a means of determining my loyalty. I rediscovered my Catholic background by realizing that there had always been present a transformative story, the story of the counter-tradition of transformation that was often obscured by those who arrested the transformation in the first act and scene in what is a three-act drama. To see where my own Catholic experience had gotten lost as the result of the story of uncritical loyalty, and of how this story could be rejected and replaced by the drama/story of transformation as exemplified in the life, death, and resurrection of Jesus was something that nobody had ever told me.

I also succeeded in re-envisioning my Mexican/Chicano heritage with all of its primal energy, which had so threatened my quest for deliverance. The repressed aspects of my self could now be experienced so that I could heal the split between my conscious ego's desire to achieve respectability and the deeper, sacred sources of my own unconscious pulling me beyond this to the experience of the wholeness of my being.

I had entered into the realm of archetypal relationships, stories, and ways of life. I came to understand that all of our concrete relationships and stories derive their deeper origin, meaning, and significance from underlying patterning, sacred sources called archetypes. We know only appearances, only the superficial, only symptoms when we remain unaware of the underlying causes of all reality. The deepest of these archetypal realms consists of four ways of life: emanation, incoherence, deformation, and transformation. The first three ways of life are all fragments of the most important story that you and I can live, the story of transformation. As mentioned earlier, this is a three-act drama that you and I need to journey time and again in order to respond to new problems in life. No transformation is ever once and for all. We live in a world of continuous creation, and the real question is whether the creation is for good or ill. However, as human beings we are free to stop and arrest the journey of transformation, sometimes for centuries, by getting caught in stories that prevent us from leaving Act I, Scene 1. One example of this is the story of uncritical loyalty that prevented me from being critical of a way of life that told me that there was no longer any reason to search since the truth was given to us once for all by God. I believed in this story, in this way of life of emanation, which restricted my relationships to seeing myself as an extension of more important people, who had the right to command me, with whom I could negotiate for better benefits, and who gave me an intellectual filter by which to keep out any dangerous ideas.

As a result, the four faces of my being were shaped as follows. My personal face was repressed because my ideas and needs were not important when compared with the demands of authority figures who were wrapped in a mysterious shroud. My political face was dominated by a desire to be totally, even blindly loyal so that I had no right to question and thus initiate change. Historically, my face was dominated by the inherited past, which I had no right to challenge. Thus, I could not be the agent of new stories or turning points but only the recipient of a dead past. My sacred face was filled with the blush of sin, shame, and guilt whenever my anger caused me to momentarily break through the repression in which I was held and held myself.

I wrote my doctoral dissertation, "The Breakdown of Authority of the Roman Catholic Church in the United States," under the guidance of Manfred Halpern. Twenty-five years ago, I was able to see that the collapse of the Catholic Church's authority was due to the inability of people to live authentically. I knew through personal experience that repression permeated this community. The theory of transformation enabled me to see this personal dilemma for myself and millions of Catholics as a political, historical, and sacred issue as well. With this new theoretical perspective, I returned to teaching, prepared to help students realize where we got lost in the story of transformation, and more important, how we together could intervene in the story to end destructive archetypal stories for the sake of creating fundamentally more loving and compassionate dramas by which to live our lives.

Now that the reader is getting to know me and my struggle for transformation, it is in this personal vein that I now wish to continue to tell the story of the theory of transformation. As I introduce new aspects and concepts, I hope to make them more accessible by giving concrete examples to put the theory, so to speak, on solid ground. After all, what is crucial for any theory is for you and me to be able to apply it to practice to see if in fact it helps us to see our reality more clearly. In this way a good theory is like a good teacher. The finest teachers never put anything in us; they guide us by providing us with the concepts, the words, that will help us to name what has always been in us. Above all, the theory of transformation will enable each of us to tell our own story. The story of transformation is our unique, individual story as well as the story of humanity. Thus to seek and find our own self is also to search and find the humanity of the other.

The theory of transformation that helped me so much to understand my own life as well as the wider world around me shall serve as our grounding and our guide as we re-envision, reinterpret, and re-create the American experience. Our theory allows us to participate in the most important story of our lives, the core drama of transformation. This participation allows us to choose between partial and biased ways of life or transformation as a way of life that allows us to bring together the fullness of the personal, political, historical, and sacred faces of our personal and societal lives. By applying theory to practice we will be able to see the nation in motion as its members struggle to re-create a new multicultural identity as a new concrete face of the archetypal story of democracy in the service of transformation.

I was always puzzled by the concept and meaning of culture and didn't know if this was the realm of anthropologists, sociologists, or historians. I considered culture to be some amorphous mass that somehow or other covered people with a particular identity. Lately I have come to see culture as a network of stories (stories always meaning archetypal dramas) that provide people with a cosmos of meaning. All of us are raised with and socialized into stories that give us the necessary attitudes and skills by which to become the members of a society. But what is also so important to understand is that these stories are not just entertainment; they are above all sacred stories that can possess us if we are not conscious of them. The stories are archetypal; that is, as mentioned above, they have an underlying forming source that gives them their deeper meaning. Thus in daily enacting the culture and thereby the stories of our lives, we are also giving concrete expression to those deeper underlying sources called archetypes.[1]

We are coming to understand that culture and the new emerging face of the story of democracy that we call multicultural is grounded in deeper, sacred, forming forces. People like you and me give a new expression to what it means to be human by coming to know, critiquing, and transforming our stories. People of color, women, men, and individuals from all backgrounds are manifesting the four faces of our being by making a personal decision to tell a new story that was rendered invisible. Through our political face we together can and need to give shape to an environment in which we become aware of and are free to critique our stories. Together we can create a new turning point for our nation, a new history and a new aspect of the story of democracy, multicultural diversity, that is an affirmation that each of us has a sacred face as a manifestation of the deepest of all sacred sources. Most of us were never told that each of us by virtue of our humanity has these four faces by which we shape daily life. Furthermore, we were seldom taught about the human propensity to enshrine cultures once for all and the challenge to keep them alive and open so that they can be constantly renewed and transformed through our conscious participation. People too often simply become a part of the culture but most often lose their ability to critique the stories by allowing themselves to be made into uncritical participants who carry out pre-programmed behavior. In this way cultures take on a life of their own and we become the mere recipients rather than the persistent creators of our cultures.

THEORY AS OUR PARTICIPATION IN SACRED STORIES

The word "theory" can be intimidating because for many, theory is taught as a set of abstract principles that are difficult to understand and/or put into everyday language and practice. What freed me from this fear of theory was that I came to understand the original Greek meaning of theory. *Theoria* was not an abstraction; it was a participation in a sacred story that had to do with how the life, death, and resurrection of a god affected the lives of the community.

This realization of *theoria* as the sacred re-enactment of the drama of transformation helped me to make the connection to the understanding of archetypal stories as the deeper, sacred meaning of all of our concrete stories. Some sacred sources remain partial, and our anxiety leads us to join with them. Others succeed in achieving transformation and urge us from within to undergo the same passage of transformation: to be born, to die, and to be resurrected. What is more important is the recognition that we are invited to live and participate in the story of transformation. It is we who inherit archetypal stories and fail to move on by remaining stuck in the journey and never getting beyond the first act of this three-act journey by preserving our stories unconsciously. But through transformative action, we can enter into rebellion against them in Act II, Scene 1 and in the second scene of Act II uproot the destructive stories and send them into the abyss. We create new and better stories in Act III, Scenes 1 and 2 that allow us to shape a more loving, just, and compassionate society in the service of transformation.

For me, theory came to mean knowledge and participation in the story and process of transformation. Thus in this book, theory will be reinterpreted, re-envisioned, and, I hope, re-experienced and applied in a personally concrete way in the context of our political, historical, and sacred faces as our participation in the birth, death, and transformation of sacred stories.

The theory that will be described and applied in this book was developed by Professor Manfred Halpern.[2] It is an extraordinary theory in its ability to tell an old, yet new story that allows us to see the intimate connection between the personal, political, historical, and sacred underlying deeper meaning of our lives. Furthermore, this theory will give us an opportunity to understand and participate in the most important story of our life, the story of transformation as the core drama of life, wherein we choose between four ultimate ways of life—one of which ends in destructive death. The reader will be provided with concrete examples, most of which are taken from multicultural and women's literature, so that we can understand the four ultimate ways of life. Since the emerging multicultural story is about real people like you and me, we shall have the opportunity to participate in constructing new and personal manifestations of more just and loving stories and relationships. To understand what is meant by archetypal ways of life, stories, and relationships is to know something crucial about how to shape a new and more compassionate multicultural story in U.S. society.

Next, this theory will enable us to understand and analyze the archetypal stories or dramas of our life that affect us as citizens of a changing nation, particularly the nascent multicultural story, together with other stories such as capitalism, tribalism, patriarchy, democracy, transforming love, possessive love, and matriarchy. Finally, it will present a means of critiquing and changing the reality of our lives from a clear and compelling normative perspective.

Good theory provides us with an interrelated set of testable generalizations that fulfill the following requirements: It must allow us to deal with problems that are central to all human relations, formulated in terms and concepts that are not culture-bound. Such a theory must allow us to use the same concepts and interrelated hypotheses for intrapersonal, interpersonal, and intergroup relations.

I propose to provide the outlines of the theory of transformation here and to use it in the struggle to analyze and develop strategies of transformation toward a multicultural society in the United States or elsewhere in the world. This theory, I hope, will help us understand how the relationships and stories connecting us as Americans are being used creatively and/or destructively. The theory can enable us to see that we fail to achieve the meaning of our lives by remaining arrested in Act I of the story of transformation, wherein we unconsciously live the story of uncritical loyalty to the inherited dominant stories of a white, male, Anglo-Saxon culture. Moving to Act II, Scene 1 but then becoming caught in rebellion in the story of capitalism as the pursuit of self-interest is to remain a partial self. Exiting the journey by turning to the fundamentally worse alternative of violence, which results in personal, political, historical, and sacred destruction, is deformation. Our only viable alternative is that of transformation in Act III, wherein we make concrete a way of life committed to the persistent creation of fundamentally new and more loving sacred stories.

At stake here is our willing and creative participation in the *story* of transformation. This story arises out of our *experiences* of transformation. Once we have experienced transformation, we do not believe in it, that is, turn it into a dogma. Instead we must risk faith, meaning that we risk trust in experiencing this journey in this particular case, in regard to this particular problem. Transformational theory is above all *participation* in the drama of the life, death, and resurrection of sacred sources in ourselves and in the stories of our lives. What is so compelling and truthful about this theory is that people can live it and test it with their own experiences. It helps us to make sense of our own lives and to see how the whole of our experiences hangs together. Let us begin then, in providing our theoretical and conceptual framework by retelling and re-envisioning the story of creation and the story of transformation.

RETELLING THE STORY OF THE CREATION OF THE COSMOS: THE HEART OF THE MATTER IS THE STORY OF TRANSFORMATION

According to this creation story, which contradicts the account of creation as told in the Book of Genesis, the deepest source of all sources, what Meister Eckart called the god beyond god, created first of all and again and again the most important story of life: the archetypal story of transformation. This three-act drama must be enacted again and again because the source of all sacred sources is still creating the universe.[3] From the beginning, creation was intended to bring forth the fundamentally new and better. The story of transformation as the heart of reality requires participation in all of its three acts between the deepest source and us, the concretely created. Our deepest source is not perfect, that is, finished. The source of all continues to create. Neither our sacred source nor we are perfect. So together with the deepest sacred, we break and relink again and again in order to re-emerge in a new and better unity. This is another way of saying that we and the source of all sources can continually live and journey through the story of transformation. But this participation demands freedom to say yes or no. Who are the participants? We are, since we are the only creation able to persist in transformation without a preprogrammed specific outcome.

Other key participants are archetypal, sacred forces. Why sacred forces, plural? We could not feel deeply attracted to Act I, the service of the way of life of emanation, and be seduced to remain in it and to arrest and consolidate it unless an archetypal, sacred force or lord was also free to say no and to separate itself from the story of transformation and hold us there. Similarly, we could not break away from the seductive security of Act I and then get caught in Act II, unless an archetypal source, the god of incoherence, could separate itself from the core drama of transformation and hold us there. We could not be sucked into the abyss of deformation unless an archetypical force, symbolized by Satan, had the power to pull us down as we give in to fantasies of superiority based on gender, nation, race, or religion to cover our insecurity.

Why do we need these archetypal forces that can frustrate the story of transformation created by the source of all sources? This is not a puppet play. The story of transformation has to offer us and the archetypal forces the capacity and freedom to say no and yes to this story, which constitutes the heart of creation. Therefore, the lord of emanation arrests the story in Act I, and we can be overwhelmed and continue to repress our feelings and doubts in order to allow Act I to remain a viable container. We cannot act at all without archetypal sources to pattern our actions, but neither are archetypal forces complete without us. For this reason we have to ask always which god, or archetypal source, inspires me.

All archetypal forces in the story of transformation are free to act once they have been created by the deepest source of our being. Some of these sacred, archetypal sources repress their knowledge of the deepest ground of our being so that it is difficult for us to hear and understand when the voice of the god beyond god reaches out to us in order to further transformation. For example, according to the Mayan Book of Creation, *The Popol Vuh*, some gods became jealous of human beings because "they could see all things," and so they blinded human beings.[4] Evil came into the world when we and the archetypal force symbolized as Satan betrayed the drama of transformation and moved into consciously creating destructive death or deformation by exiting from the story.

The deepest source of our being began creation by creating the story of transformation because only that story fulfills the need for persistent transformation. But the source of all sources gave us and archetypal sources the freedom to prevent or to participate in fragmentation and destruction. Still, evil is not a necessary byproduct of freedom or transformation. We can choose to move through the story together with the deepest ground of our being again and again without exiting from the drama and descending into the abyss of deformation, which makes life fundamentally new but worse. To practice transformation is to continuously say no to the archetypal lords who enchant us in emanation, enchain us in fragments of power in incoherence, or suck us into the abyss of deformation. We need to free ourselves from these sacred sources, to be filled anew by our deepest sacred source. The deepest sacred source does not stand by passively but enters the drama again and again. But the god beyond god cannot command transformation; therefore the ground of our being needs our participation to renew and widen transformation.

In this drama all of us can participate in the structure of the story of transformation. Increasingly, in the modern age the most important choice is between deformation and transformation. To choose to make life fundamentally more loving and compassionate is to participate with each other, and the god of transformation that leads us to be renewed by the deepest ground of our being.[5]

There is a marvelously redemptive aspect to the story of transformation, which consists in our ability to realize in what story we were caught and in what way of life we enacted a decision. We are now free to reject the destructive stories and ways of life and to choose more just and loving relationships in the service of transformation. This participatory nature of transformation prevents us from losing precious time by punishing ourselves because of hurt pride, guilt, or anger. We are now empowered to put an end to our guilt by creating alternatives in such a way that we simultaneously accept responsibility for what was done and decide to do something to heal the injury that was caused by living destructive stories.

This great blessing of the story of transformation is due to the inherent mercy of the source of sources. It is a witness to the inherent dynamic of the structure of the universe, one based on love. It is never too late, either for ourselves or for others. For this reason we must not freeze ourselves or others in cultural stereotypes because it violates the very nature of the universe, which is a constant invitation from the ground of our being to dry up our tears and to get on with the task of co-creating the universe.

To conclude, we know that there were different and lesser gods present from the beginning of the creation, but only in the story of transformation would human beings have a necessary role in creation. It is a necessary part because the source of all sources, which has no concreteness, needed human beings to give creation a concrete face. This necessary co-creation between the source of sources and human beings made us the object of jealousy to the lord of a final and fixed truth, because this source of emanation could dominate only in the realm of a once-for-all creation. We are both sacred and concrete; we have four faces. Through us the sacred has real feet on the ground and can continue to create. But the fullness of this co-creation can take place only if we realize our inner sacredness by embarking on the journey of transformation.[6]

THE THREE ACTS OF THE CORE DRAMA OF TRANSFORMATION

The deeper, underlying patterning force of the story of transformation is the only way of life in the service of which we have the freedom and wholeness to participate in creating more just and compassionate aspects of our life.

Telling the story of this drama tells us something we are rarely told: How in actual practice can we transform ourselves? How can we actually find a fundamentally better way and test it by translating it into practice together with our neighbors?[7]

The story/drama of transformation is a journey that has three acts.[8] There are no deeper acts of life than the three acts of this drama (see Figure 1). When we arrest life, and therefore our journey, in one of these acts before we reach the third act, we stunt and contain our life in a fragment of the story of transformation. Because it is only a fragment of life, it leaves us as partial selves, fragile, wounded, and angry, no matter how much power we may accumulate within it.

We always begin in Act I, Scene 1. In that scene, we are still caught up in the enchantment of overwhelming and mysterious forces that now possess us. This is symbolized in Figure 1 by the enclosed, enigmatic squiggle. Our lack of wholeness, our partial self, is symbolized by the half-moon. Because we are acted upon and not actors in our own right, the one-way arrow symbolizes our state of dependency.

Because we are devoted to conforming to established archetypal stories that we have inherited, we can arrest our lives here and turn this scene into an entire way of life in the service of emanation. This is an underlying way of life in which we consistently experience feelings of sin, shame, and guilt whenever we begin to ask fundamentally new questions. The resulting stability keeps the dominant group in power. We therefore repress essential aspects of our being or else experience legitimized oppression by the powerful.

Figure 1
The Core Drama of Transformation

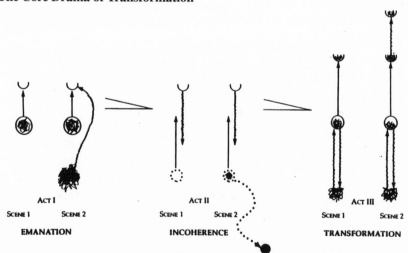

Act I		Act II		Act III	
Scene 1	Scene 2	Scene 1	Scene 2	Scene 1	Scene 2
EMANATION		INCOHERENCE		TRANSFORMATION	

This symbolic drawing and the interpretation provided in this chapter are intended, together with the intuitive understanding of the reader, to point toward a deeper and fuller understanding of the drama of transformation. This understanding will unfold over the course of the book.

THE WAY OF LIFE OF EMANATION

The deeper and larger context within which traditional societies lived the stories of their lives and enacted their repertory of relationships was the way of emanation, arrested in Act I, Scene 1 of the core drama of transformation.

Politics in the service of emanation (for example, in the service of a fixed faith or tradition) holds us within containers in which all we can and need to do together is already codified and ritualized, and declared to be no longer a problem except for the skill and intensity with which we affirm, elaborate, deepen or refine what we are already performing together.[9]

In this way of life a person is told that we have found all the truth once and for all. For example in the novel *Siddhartha*,[10] Siddhartha's father could not understand why his son wanted to leave home because everything had been revealed to them in the Brahmin culture. The father believed that the way of his fathers had answered all the questions of life once for all. Emanation is a way of life in which a moment of truth or a lie masquerading as the truth has become frozen, distorted, or corrupted. Because of this understanding, Ku'oosh, the medicine man in *Ceremony*,[11] did not know how to change the ceremonies, so he failed to cleanse the young warriors who had been infected by new forms of death. Because we cannot ask fundamentally new kinds of questions to respond to new forms of deformation, this way of life is everywhere in the world being questioned and undermined.[12]

Any attempt to leave the way of life of emanation arrested in Act I, Scenes 1 or 2 means breaking with the inherited concrete manifestations and underlying archetypal relationships in such a way that it will lead to a change of relationships for self and others. This is clearly heresy and dangerous to a cosmos blessed once and for all by the god of emanation. In the past people were killed for such thoughts and behavior, which appeared to the orthodox to be the demonic come to life. It has always been dangerous for people living in closed societies to practice the heresy of personally contacting the sacred so as to participate in continuous creation. Betonie, the medicine man who plotted the new forms of death in *Ceremony*, was disliked by his people because he insisted on listening to new voices that allowed him to respond to destructive death with new and better ceremonies. Life for too many of the people was arrested in Act I of the core drama as the will of an all-powerful lord.

In the following pages, we shall be looking more closely at this limited repertory and some of the archetypal dramas, which will allow us to see actual daily behavior. We shall go beyond mere descriptions of the breaking of the concrete, inherited manifestations of archetypal relationships practiced in the service of the dying way of emanation, and the rejection of other sacred stories to consider how we might transform such incoherence. However, as long as the inherited relationships and stories in the service of emanation in Act I remained in effect, we did not have the ability to cope with new forms of change and conflict. We were all socialized to favor continuity and collaboration with the status quo; change meant the terror of insecurity and injustice. Because of this too often we remained limited and partial selves who could not respond to new problems.

In this manner the journey is made heretical. We therefore live the inherited stories of our lives as final and ultimate because they are the outer flow of the revelation of a mysterious and overwhelming source of power. People are reluctant to depart; they are arrested in their flowing forth from the deepest source of our being. The lord of the way of life of emanation impoverishes all of us and the deepest source because now there will be an emphasis on continuity and cooperation with the status quo. We are forbidden to create conflict or change. Our justice is security; the cost is the sacredness within our selfhood. Because we arrest our entire lives here, we turn Act I, Scene 1 into an entire way of life. Emanation is a way of life in which we live all of our inherited stories as the final will of an all-powerful lord. This is the source that inspired Celie in *The Color Purple*[13] not to fight but to survive, that compelled Tita to accept her mother's commands in *Like Water for Chocolate*[14] as if they were God's will, that caused Lindo Jong's despair that at such an early age her life was already determined by others in *The Joy Luck Club*,[15] and that inspired Sara to see her father as a lord who could not be resisted in *Bread Givers*.[16] This is the sacred source that kept Cleofilas in *Woman Hollering Creek*[17] fatalistic while her husband abused her.

Cut off from our deepest source, caught in the embrace of this orthodox lord, we cannot develop a new consciousness, creativity, or new linkages to others or shared goals. We are actually stillborn. This is the lord of the sociologists of religion. These sociologists study this lord of institutionalized religion without knowing it. As a result, they study only a lesser sacred source because they do not know about the realm of the deepest, underlying sacred, forming source. Thus they marvel at the power of religion to perform functions for society. This process is given an ultimate justification by the lord of emanation allied with the lord of power. Together they uphold the state to possess the minds and bodies of its citizens. These are the gods that Marx and Freud rejected, assuming that they had thereby rejected all of the sacred. Our story will allow us to reject these lesser lords who seek to be "the" god and to identify the deepest source and choose between creative and destructive sacred sources.[18]

The way of life of emanation, arrested in Act I, Scene 1, is fragile precisely because of the structure of the story of transformation. This is a cosmos of persistent creation, which means living the story of transformation again and again. We can only realize transformation in regard to one aspect of our life at a time; transformation is never total. For millennia, women and men have listened to their deepest inner source, which gave them the courage to go against the officially sanctioned stories and ways of life of their societies. These men and women of the counter-tradition, which is at least 2,600 years old, held the following in common: they recognized the deep incoherence in their society. To get out of incoherence they realized that they had to end previous forms of emanation. As they looked for alternative ways to shape life, they discovered archetypes, that is, the underlying patterning forces of which all concrete relationships and all concrete stories in which we live our lives are manifestations. They came to see the world as a cosmos of continuous creation and therefore saw transformation as our personal participation in that process. They then saw the connection between our personal, political, historical, and sacred faces as essential to participating in continuous creation. All were radical because they sought to go to the root of the issues by searching for the ultimate source of the fundamentally new and better.

Some of those who explored the theory and practice of transformation were: Heraclitus (sixth century B.C.), Lao-Tse (sixth century B.C.), Buddha (died 483 B.C.), Plato (died 347 B.C), Jesus, Moses Maimonides (died 1204), al-Farabi (died 950), Ibn Arabi (1165–1240), Meister Eckhart (1260–1327), Jacob Boehme (1575–1624), Giordano Bruno (1548–1600), Goethe (1749–1832), William Blake (1757–1827), the early Hegel (1770–1831), the early Marx (1818–1883), C. G. Jung (1875–1962), and in our own time the women and men who are practitioners of liberation theology in Latin America, Asia, and Africa. Most of these pioneers developed their theoretical and practical understanding of transformation in terms of the four faces of our being: personal, political, historical, and sacred. Some practitioners of the counter-tradition emphasized more faces of our being than others, while some neglected several faces of our being. For example, Marx failed to deal with the personal and sacred faces of our being, and Jung did not recognize the political and historical faces of our being. All of the above men and women of the counter-tradition made great contributions to our understanding of the theory and practice of transformation. But they failed to explain how to free ourselves on the deeper level from archetypal dramas, ways of life and lesser sacred lords that now possess us.

As did all of these members of the counter-tradition, many of us also came to realize that there are two scenes in Act I. Scene 2, symbolized in

Figure 1 by the darkness, represents the source of the fundamentally new from which emerge, like snakes, temptation, heresy, doubts, intuitions, ideas, and experiences that are beyond the official voice of conscience. We are filled anew with sacred forces from the depths. But we cannot yet know in the second scene which sacred sources inspire us. The inspirations that come to us from the depths are not always to the good. Other lesser lords seek to substitute themselves for the deepest source of transformation. These partial lords can succeed in arresting the drama and holding us permanently in one scene of the drama of transformation. Therefore, it is our task to struggle with and analyze the forces that emerge as the sources of the fundamentally new and to determine whether they are possessive, destructive lords, or the deepest transforming sacred. It is this inner voice, inspired from the depths, that undermines the effectiveness of the repression. Increasingly we suspect that there is something more, an unrealized aspect of our lives that must be explored. To take these feelings and insights seriously is to make the conscious decision to leave Act I, Scene 1, and to break with the significant others who have held us there. The threat, challenge, and opportunity of the inner voice is what people as famous as Einstein and Newton responded to. A new paradigm always begins as a mixture of joy and threat, heresy, or a radical departure from the normal.

The way of life of emanation is everywhere dying, because people are no longer willing—or able, in the face of so much breaking of established values, ideas and relationships—to deny their own experiences, ideas, and hopes. However, some will make the choice to repress the new. We owe much to those who are seen as deviants, heretics, outsiders, and troublemakers. I vividly remember my mother referring to me as a *malcriado*, a sassy brat, a son *sin respeto*, without respect, who should be filled with *vergüenza*, shame, for daring to question her, the Catholic Church, or God. In *The Color Purple*, Celie initially repressed her inner voice, symbolized by Sofia, in Act I, Scene 2. Celie was threatened by Sofia because Sofia represented everything in a woman that Celie was not. For this reason she said to Harpo, "Beat her." Celie later repented when confronted by Sofia.[19]

When this arrested fragment of life breaks, people who have lost or feel that they are losing the seeming security of acting as the outward embodiment of a mysterious source are tempted towards deformation—promising to lead us to a great restoration, but it leads to destructive death.[20]

To preserve the way of life of emanation arrested in Act I, the powerful often resorted to deformation to defend their world. Those who listened to their inner voices were often killed, as during the Spanish Inquisition, because they refused to accept a truth given once for all. There are five ways to treat persons who are threats to the final truth of the official container: (1) They can be isolated and made invisible; (2) society can make them pariahs, inferior people who are allowed only to do the menial in life; (3) those judged to be like the superior may be adopted as "honorary" members of the elite and thus allowed to assimilate as a reward for not being like the rest of "those people"; (4) if a person withdraws his loyalty to the dominant elite that gave him/her privileges, he or she may be cast out, exiled, excommunicated; (5) the allegedly inferior can be exterminated by war, exploitation, forced exile, and starvation.

In a strikingly similar manner, Iris M. Young speaks of a kindred story when she writes of the five faces of oppression: the marginalized, the powerless, the exploited, the victims of cultural imperialism, and those subject to systematic violence.[21] This creation of the archetypal drama of oppression in the service of deformation began as an attempt to preserve the way of life of emanation. Emanation cannot accept fundamentally new consciousness, creativity, new forms of justice, linkages to outsiders, and most important, the notion that anybody could receive any new inspiration from the depths. To prevent these eruptions of the sacred, more and more force and violence must be used to protect the one "truth." This promise to restore the glory of the past and to bolster a deteriorating story that possessed us and held us in the first act of the story of transformation helps us to understand the phenomenon of a David Koresh, the emergence of fascism in Russia, the emergence of neopatriarchy, and fanatical movements that wish to restore the old racism as in South Africa by seeking to create a separatist white state.

Thus to take Act I, Scene 2, that is, our doubts and intuitions, seriously is to take courage and enter into Act II, Scene 1, wherein we break with our parents, religious upbringing, vision of the world, the established stories of the dominant culture, and enter into open rebellion. As symbolized in Figure 1, in Act II, Scene 1, the security of the enclosed container is now fragmented, and we are free to continue on the journey of transformation. But having entered into Act II, we are also free to arrest the journey and institutionalize rebellion into the whole way of life of incoherence in the service of which we enact stories and a culture that organizes the competition for power. This is where we are currently as a culture as we enact the story of the market society or capitalism. This story puffs us up with a sense of freedom, of being able to do whatever we want but with the realization that we live in a hostile world. Rather than continue the journey, many begin to create fortresses in a world that they do not understand. It is very important to say here that this is not only a rational, personal choice on our part; we have not become "secularized" merely by rejecting the lords of emanation. Other sacred forces are present.

The source of incoherence, the lord of power, also does not want us to live the story of transformation. This source replaces the lord of orthodox truth. There is only power and self-interest with no other meaning to life. This way of life takes us over and has an emanational hold over us that we cannot understand. There is a sacred source present in the depths but because the sacred is relegated to outmoded superstitions, we can no longer name what drives and obsesses us. Therefore, we get trapped in stories that possess us and turn us against each other in a perpetual competition that turns our relationships into contests of mutual suspicion and fear.

At best we can agree on procedures that keep us from assaulting each other as we struggle with each other in the name of self-interest. The language and the deeds of love and compassion are not welcome in the public realm.[22] To overcome our vulnerability we seek power, which of course increases our anxiety. There is no security. We turn this attempt to organize insecurity, without being able to name it, into a whole way of life of incoherence.

THE WAY OF LIFE OF INCOHERENCE

The relationship of incoherence breaks open the way of life of emanation arrested in Act I, Scenes 1 and 2. But if the relationship of incoherence, which was necessary to polarize the members of a group frozen in inherited patterns, becomes permanently arrested in Act II, Scene 1, it then becomes another way of shaping life, the way of life of incoherence. The relationship of incoherence, standing in the presence of others and not knowing what to say or how to relate, is intended to open up new possibilities to travel through the core drama in order to achieve a new kind of wholeness and life. However, if we remain permanently fixed in our anger, the polarization initiated by the relationship of incoherence becomes arrested as a whole way of life, the way of life of incoherence.

Politics in the service of incoherence takes account of the fact that in the modern age, all our concrete inherited forms of relationships are breaking, but therefore builds fortresses in a desert it cannot overcome. The guardians who would contain us within these fragments insist upon removing much of what we can and need to do together from what they define as politics. They treat politics solely as an arena for contests of power. They seek to give their histories the appearance of final legitimacy (as if they were the true heirs of faith and tradition) in order to justify the exclusion from this arena of all fundamentally new issues and encounters which do not serve their already established power. Hence they compel most people to accept politics as the acknowledgment of dependency upon the powerful and to deny the value and importance of their own miseries and joys.[23]

The relationship of incoherence means that a person stands in the presence of her way of life, her culture, her relatives, and her self, and can no longer relate in the expected manner according to inherited patterns. But rather than allow the relationship of incoherence to lead to a fundamentally new and more loving way by entering Scene 2 of Act II, in order to empty herself of destructive, inherited archetypal stories, she now settles for less, learns to live with incoherence, arrests the core drama in Act II, Scene 1, and thereby turns the relationship of incoherence into the way of life of incoherence.

The relationship of incoherence in the way of life of emanation was always a sin because it constituted a rejection of the final revelation of the truth. In the way of life of incoherence we have entered into a new deeper drama or story of our life. This is a story that holds together around the reality of constant rebellion and insecurity. We cannot count on any absolute meaning or the loyalty of anyone. The past is regarded as superstitious, powerless, old fashioned, or foolish. To realize the American dream one must become like the dominant and accept its values, especially the pursuit of power, which arrests everyone in Act II, Scene 1 of the core drama.

This loss of self and the accompanying rejection of others and their own sacred sources means living with incoherence, arrested in Act II of the core drama. The only certainty now is the insecurity of knowing that nothing is secure or lasting. Because in this way of life we cannot know or acknowledge any ultimate meaning or value or love, we have to get what we can while the going is good. This anxiety feeds a constant need to compete. Success is always limited to organizing the incoherence so that the powerful can protect themselves from the powerless and assert their right to become more powerful fragments.

Because we come to believe that only power can alleviate the terror that we experience, we are taken over by the story so that it has an emanational hold over us. This is because as an archetypal way of life, incoherence is part of the deepest realm of underlying sacred forces. But since it is only a fragment of the story of transformation, we cannot discover our wholeness while held in its embrace. There is no way out of this story unless we enter into incoherence in order to break with incoherence as a way of life. Now we have the opportunity to free ourselves from the story of power and to create the fundamentally more compassionate and just by practicing transformation. In this way incoherence becomes the necessary step toward transformation.

Those attempting to preserve their power in the way of life of incoherence often resort to violence in the service of deformation because they are caught, in spite of all of their alleged secularism, by a new sacred lord that inspires them to believe that they have the right to be rich and the others are to be their servants. The irony of this is that a group that has cast off the so-called superstitions of their past and that prides itself on its rationality has been possessed by a new sacred force, the lord of deformation. This sacred source of deformation does more than arrest the journey; the whole journey is now put at risk not only for themselves but for all.

EXITING THE CORE DRAMA: THE WAY OF LIFE OF DEFORMATION

The way of life of deformation is that context within which life is made fundamentally new but worse. It is the exit from the core drama into the abyss. This way of life diminishes our humanity and cripples our capacity.[24]

The ways of life of emanation and incoherence are fragile and ever vulnerable to leading us to destructive death in deformation. The whole of life from the perspective of the core drama is intended to be a persistent process of creation. Therefore incoherence is bound to increase manifest in the experience of broken connections that previously bound us together. In the arrested way of life of emanation, some parents and spouses decide that there is only one way: the use of physical, psychological, or financial violence to force the rebellious wife or children to return to the old ways. But a wife or children cannot go back to a container that is now demystified; the subjection previously exercised and blessed by god, because it was part of the legitimacy of the way of life of emanation, is now considered illegitimate. In Act I, in the service of emanation, what gave subjection its legitimacy is that we believed that we deserved the punishment, given the rules of the game that were broken and accepted by all. The appropriate amount of submission restored us to good standing in the family and the proper order of things.

Now, however, this cosmic view has collapsed so that what was once considered acceptable is now seen as unbearable and untenable. But it should also be said here that violence was always an acceptable part of the strategy to preserve the way of life of emanation. Therefore the relationship of deformation and as a way of life was available as an ally to maintain the container of emanation. Wives were beaten as a matter of right for men. It was not necessary for a woman to be in open rebellion to be struck. The greatest and ever growing danger in these circumstances is that the hidden resentment of the husband will erupt in an irrational manner in the form of violence. Albert in *The Color Purple* advised his son Harpo to beat his wife just to let her know who is boss. Albert felt that it was his right as a man and as a husband to beat Celie and her duty to accept this violence. In this way both Albert and Celie colluded in practicing the relationship of deformation as victim and victimizer. By practicing the relationship of deformation, Albert was exiting the core drama and living in the service of deformation in regard to the story of patriarchy. Soon the way of life of deformation threatened to destroy him physically and psychologically.

After Celie left, Albert turned to violence against himself in a more direct way; he became suicidal. This is deformation because it makes life fundamentally worse. Albert was frustrated in his inability to hold onto his male ego, which was inextricably related to life in Act I in the service of emanation. To bring down the container of final truth was to destroy the facade of his partial self. To maintain his fragmented self, Albert increasingly turned toward the abyss of violence and thereby exited the core drama. While caught in this descent, Albert was painfully aware that something was wrong but he did not know what to do except to try to restore what had been lost. He failed to intimidate Celie. His refusal to go forward through the core drama exposed the wounded nature of his partial self. Partial selves are essentially people who have arrested their lives in the truncated ways of life of emanation and incoherence. People living within these ways of life are constantly in anxiety due to the fragility of these ways of life. Why is this so? When Act I is arrested as the way of life of emanation, people must guard against any new inspirations from the depths because this way of life tells them that there can be nothing new under the sun. Since we cannot escape our depths, the underlying realm of sacred sources, this attempt to prevent the emergence of the fundamentally new has failed and will continue to fail.

People dedicated to this arrested way of living cannot allow any new feelings within themselves or in those around them. People must continue to repress, deny, and destroy new ideas, feelings, intuitions, and stories that question their way of life. The logic of this means that people are prepared to constantly violate themselves and others in order to keep their family and world intact. This inability to acknowledge crucial aspects of their lives constitutes the danger of being a partial self. To preserve a stunted identity in a truncated world, the road to violence opens up again and again. For this reason, to question is seen as an act of disloyalty that demands a swift retaliation.

In regard to the core drama, those who remain arrested in Acts I or II due to loyalty to others and repression of self or the desire for power are profoundly threatened by those others who do not accept or who are excluded from participating in the life of the society. In Act II, arrested as the drama of incoherence, the greatest fear is the loss of or inability to gain power. Anybody who gets in our way is expendable. Power of its very nature cannot be shared. This drama possesses our soul such that we are not free to be compassionate or loving.

The fragility of repression that leads us to be disloyal to ourselves in the way of emanation and the obsessive pursuit of power in the service of incoherence tempts the true believers and the powerful toward increased violence. This makes life fundamentally worse and turns history toward the abyss.

The poor and excluded also face the reality of deformation in the public realm. The number of teenage addicts, children born with AIDS, school dropouts, the unemployed, and the homeless is growing at an alarming rate in the country. Fully 39 percent of all Latino children, 45 percent of African American children, and 20 percent of all children in the United States live in poverty. Poor children from all backgrounds are becoming an endangered species. A society permeated by the ways of life of incoherence and deformation creates an environment that turns people into faceless persons who often respond with violence to assert their presence.

It is clear that we have to be aware of the deeper underlying sacred forces, especially when they urge us toward violence when the two ways of life of emanation and incoherence are threatened. Since we have only broken with our actual antagonists in Act II, Scene 1, we continue to remain vulnerable to the lord, to the way of life and to the archetypal story in the depths that gave others their mysterious hold over us. Thus in *Bread Givers* it was not enough for Sara to empty herself only on the level of the concrete of her actual father, Reb Smolinsky. She had to experience a deeper breaking, but this time critically and consciously, by emptying her soul in Act II, Scene 2, of the archetypal story of patriarchy and the deeper way of life of emanation, which inspired and gave mysterious power to her father. Sara must say no to the archetypal story and to the way of life of emanation or else she will merely repeat in her life what she had rejected. At the end of the novel Sara attests to the presence of this sacred story, which continues to haunt her because she has not yet freed herself of its power:

Just as I was beginning to feel safe and free to go on to a new life with Hugo, the old burden dragged me back by the hair. . . . I suddenly realized that I had come back to where I had started twenty years ago when I began my fight for freedom. . . . I thought I could escape by running away. And now I realized that the shadow of the burden was always following me, and here I stood face to face with it again. . . .

But I felt the shadow still there, over me. It wasn't just my father, but the generations who made my father whose weight was still upon me.[25]

It is because we do not understand the power of these sacred stories, the ways of life in which they are enacted, and the necessity of emptying ourselves of them that we repeat history, that is, the same stories of our lives. In my own story, as a Mexican/Chicano male I was inspired by the culture to dominate women under the guise of protecting them. One of the reasons that I left home was that I seriously disagreed with this domination of women, legitimized by the story of patriarchy in the service of the way of life of emanation arrested in Act I, Scene 1. I did not like the way that my father had controlled my mother and I objected in Act I, Scene 2 to the manner in which my older brother and godfather related to women. My parting shot as I rebelled and entered Act II, Scene 1 was that I would never be like them. As a result of education and travel, I thought that I had left the story behind me. But at that time I still believed that it was enough to break with specific patriarchal males. I knew nothing of the world of the deeper, underlying archetypal, sacred stories and ways of life that possess us, especially if we remain unconscious of them. Nor did I have any awareness of the deepest source of transformation with which I could create a new and more loving life. Because I had merely broken with the actual concrete actors of this story in Act II, Scene 1 but had failed to empty myself on the deeper level in Act II, Scene 2 of the story enacted in the service of emanation that gave them their power, I woke up one day and realized that I was just like them. But once we have emptied ourselves in Act II, Scene 2, symbolized in Figure 1 by descending broken lines, we free ourselves from unbearable archetypal dramas and send them, not ourselves or others, into the abyss at the exit from the core drama: "We now free ourselves in Act III, Scene 1 to hear anew from the deepest source of our being—and in the second scene of Act III we try out in practice with our neighbors to see if our new vision is in fact fundamentally better."[26]

THE WAY OF LIFE OF TRANSFORMATION

The way of life of transformation is the most crucial story in the universe of human relations. The other three ways of life are truncated fragments of the story of transformation, which cannot provide us with the necessary vision, imagination, or creativity to respond to our problems. To live in the service of transformation is to persist in continuous creation of the fundamentally new and more loving by journeying through the core drama again and again. The structure of the universe makes sense only if there is a source of the fundamentally more just and compassionate.[27]

The fundamentally new and better cannot come from frozen, orthodox religious institutions and their lords because they have spoken once for all. We must point to the deepest of all sacred sources, which can guide us to form a more compassionate and inclusive world. Our participation as sons and daughters of the deepest sacred is necessary to transform the personal, political, historical, and sacred faces of our lives.

Acting in the service of transformation in Act III, Scenes 1 and 2 of the core drama means rejecting the inherited and assimilated stories of uncritical loyalty, power, and deformation in our lives so that we might choose the story of life—creating and nourishing fundamentally new and better relationships. To journey through the story of transformation as the core drama of life is the vocation to which all of us are called. Anybody who prevents this journey for herself or for others violates a sacred process. A decisive breakthrough has been accomplished when we realize that our greatest freedom is that we can become conscious of the different stories and relationships in which archetypal forces manifest themselves and prepare ourselves to choose some, reject others, and participate in creating new archetypal stories. This kind of participation can take place only in Act III, Scenes 1 and 2. In this last act of the core drama of transformation, we are empowered as individuals to cooperate with the source of all sources in order to share in the continuous work of creation.

The story of transformation is radically different. This sacred story needs and demands our participation. To empty ourselves three times over in Act II, Scene 2, that is, of our actual concrete antagonist, of the underlying story that the oppressor practiced, and of the way of life in which the other held me, is to prepare ourselves to be filled anew by the source of sources in Act III. The way of life of transformation provides the only matrix within which we can express the capacity, freedom, and wholeness of being both in our concrete creation and in our sacred depths. Thus we can fully realize love and justice. The source of sources is free to continuously re-create the world only when we are prepared to participate in its transformation. The deepest ground of our being continues to pour forth creation and invites us to join as co-creators of the universe.

The experience of wholeness and of participation in Act III, Scenes 1 and 2 is symbolized in Figure 1 by the deepest source of transformation that is now open to us. The ascending and descending arrows represent mutual participation with the deepest source in the new creation represented by the sphere. Within this sphere of wholeness, in contrast to our half-mooned existence in Act I, Scene 1, we are now a source free to create a more loving and just alternative in all aspects of our life. Hence the arrow now comes forth from us as an actor in the drama of transformation. In Act III, Scene 2, the new creation that we have helped to bring into being is not the end; this is a cosmos of continuous creation. Thus, Figure 1 at Act III, Scene 2 shows another creation coming forth from the previous transformation.

Having experienced transformation in at least one aspect of our life, we begin anew in Act I, Scene 2, wherein the sources fill us with new intuitions. But now we are prepared to refuse the lesser lords that would arrest us once again in a fragment of the drama of transformation and to respond to the deepest source of transformation by asking the question: In the service of what way of life and sacred source am I now being inspired? Each inspiration from the depths needs to be tested by going through the drama of transformation in response to each new problem. In regard to children who begin in Act I, Scene 1, we are now prepared to be their guides so that we do not entrap them in Act I as a permanent enclosure. Act I, Scene 1 is transformed into a merciful container by preparing them through loving support to begin the drama of transformation as the most important task in their lives. In this way the inheritance of the next generation is not a fixed body of previous transformations, now hardened into dogma, but their own experience of the drama of transformation.

Thus the world is imperfect, the deepest sacred source is unfinished. Everything is in process; everything is a performance. The first two lords of emanation and incoherence seek to arrest the journey and, in the case of the lord of deformation, to have us exit into the abyss. Our choice must be the deepest source of transformation which invites us to flow, to transform time and again.

ARCHETYPAL ANALYSIS: PARTICIPATING IN THE LIFE AND DEATH OF SACRED SOURCES AND STORIES

This theory of transformation is grounded on an archetypal analysis that allows us to know both the concrete and its origins in underlying patterning sources. To apply and practice this kind of analysis is to become conscious of the full panoply of human capacity and its actualization. This theory helps us to see beyond the concrete, specific realities of our daily lives to comprehend those forming underlying realities known as sacred, or archetypal forces. Archetypes are the necessary form by which all concrete realities manifest themselves. We are constantly acting out archetypes; these archetypes or sacred forces move through us and in us.

Thus to do archetypal analysis is to grasp the underlying meaning of the stories of our lives. This approach is unique in the social sciences in claiming that by the very nature of our humanity, all of us share in these sacred depths. But we were never taught that archetypes as sacred sources die and new ones are born. Therefore, we did not know how to free ourselves from the dying and destructive faces of the sacred so that we could participate with the deepest source of transformation, to grow new and more loving stories. People can struggle against both the destructive, concrete manifestations and the underlying archetypal sources in order to choose and enact more compassionate and just relationships and stories.

To tell archetypal stories or create new ones is to participate in the core drama of life, the story and journey of transformation. Discovering archetypal stories is more than a story or a plot. It is the drama of the intertwining of the human and the divine. To be involved in the story of transformation is to participate in the creation, nourishment, and destruction of sacred stories and sources. To reject a way of life or story of our life is not only to break with an external concrete manifestation but to descend into the deeper depths and to recognize that all of our stories are sacred because the gods are within us. The gods and the sacred permeate our lives.

If we see theory only as rational categories and abstractions, we miss the real drama in the underlying plane—the life and death of sacred sources, the creation and re-creation of ultimate meaning. Our task is therefore not to stand by passively as the gods command us but to struggle, to wrestle with them until we discern their and our true identity.

A THEORY OF HUMAN RELATIONSHIPS ENACTED WITHIN DIFFERENT ARCHETYPAL WAYS OF LIFE

As we have seen, our analysis is firmly grounded on a theory of transformation that asserts that there is a structure to the universe provided by the core drama of our lives, the story of transformation. The story of transformation consists of three acts; within the matrix of these three acts we enact archetypal ways of life, the stories of our lives and archetypal relationships. The theory of transformation sees the encounter between self, other, and the sacred with respect to concrete problems as the most fundamental dialectic in human life. According to this view, the quality of the connections between individuals, groups, families, ideas, and our personal and sacred sources gives us the capacity to simultaneously be free to change yet continue our connections to others, to be able to conflict yet cooperate, and to work toward a more compassionate justice for all.

Our first worldwide breaking consists precisely in the breaking of the concrete, inherited manifestations of archetypal relationships and the dying of the way of life of emanation. (Increasingly, in our own time the way of life of incoherence is also proving to be fragile as we confront many kinds of problems that cannot be resolved by the pursuit of power and calculated self-interest.) Everywhere in the world, societies and cultures founded on an ultimate truth and on ways of doing things as god's will are being undermined and subverted. This collapse of meaning and purpose gives rise to a profound terror that opens up both horrible and creative possibilities.

The concrete manifestations of inherited archetypal relationships and stories enacted within the way of life of emanation are breaking because they can no longer give us the capacity to respond to the flow of life, to the changes that demand a new kind of self, a renewed relationship to those around us, and a mutual creation with our underlying depths. This way of life cannot allow any new consciousness or creativity because the final revelation has been provided for the people. Figure 2 depicts a symbolic representation of the nine archetypal relationships by which we shape daily life. Figure 3 shows the four ways of life within which we enact these relationships.

Figure 2 is a mandala symbolizing nine archetypal relationships: emanation, subjection, isolation, buffering, direct bargaining, autonomy, incoherence, deformation, and transformation. These are the patterns by which we shape daily life and live the stories of our lives. We and those around us encounter difficulties when the concrete, inherited manifestations of these underlying patterns no longer give us the ability to deal with the five issues of daily human performance: continuity, change, collaboration, conflict, and the just use of resources. In regard to the five faces of capacity, each relationship differs in its ability to connect us to new consciousness, creativity, linkages to others, shared justice with others and the ability to reach the deepest source of our being. Each concrete form of an archetypal relationship gives us a different ability to cope with these five issues of performance and the five faces of capacity.

The repertory of archetypal relationships available to people has usually been limited by the societies in which they were raised to one dominant and two or three subdominant relationships in dealing with most problems of life. For example, Lindo Jong in Amy Tan's novel, *The Joy Luck Club*, was living in the way of life of emanation in Act I, Scene 1 of the core drama. Lindo was limited to the use of four relationships: emanation, subjection, buffering, and direct bargaining. As we will explain below, these four relationships are the officially sanctioned relationships that sustained and maintained the realm of emanation. In the container of emanation, Lindo, like most Chinese women in Confucian China, was socialized to relate to

Figure 2
Nine Archetypal Relationships

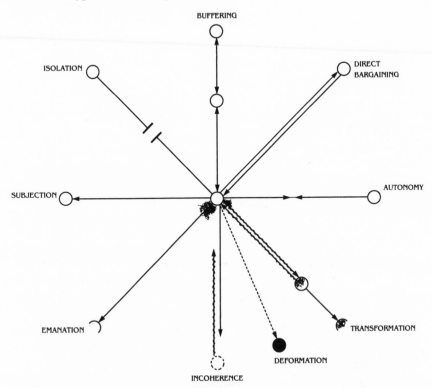

her elders in only these four ways. These four patterns of relating provide people with a maximum of continuity and cooperation and shield them from conflict and change. The benefit, or justice, rendered by these relationships is that they provide security, but at the cost of not being able to speak about one's own desires if these contradict the society's norms. Lindo entered into rebellion when she found it unbearable to continue to see her life as merely an extension of her husband, with her life arrested in Act I, Scene 1 of the core drama of life. The price of this security was too high because it meant continuing to repress the four faces of her being and her desires. Therefore Lindo sought a change of relationships so that she could experience a new kind of justice—accepting and living her own desires.

These relationships will be fully explained with examples taken from multicultural and women's literature in this chapter and throughout the book. Our goal is to understand how to take the concrete, inherited manifestations of these nine archetypal patterns into our own hands so that as they break we can create new concrete combinations of these archetypal

Figure 3
Four Archetypal Ways of Life

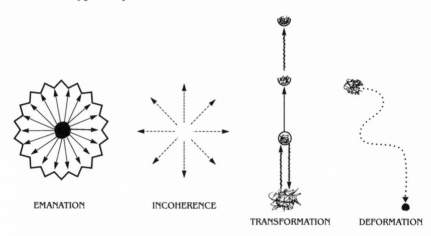

EMANATION   INCOHERENCE   TRANSFORMATION   DEFORMATION

patterns that restore to all of us the capacity to change our lives and society. We can identify patterns that have to be struggled against by naming them clearly as patterns that, in their present concrete form, cripple the human capacity to re-experience self, other, and our creative sources.

Having given this introduction, let us consider in depth the nine relationships that are available to us and by which we pattern daily life. Within our discussion of the nine encounters we shall also return to the story of transformation and of choosing among archetypal stories enacted within the four ways of life.

What are the archetypal patterns of relationships that link the lives of all of us? From one moment to the next, our theory sensitizes us to the realization that our task is to deal with constant change. Our lives are always in the process of creation, nourishment, destruction, and re-creation. This perpetual process of change is given shape by the nine specific archetypal relationships, and they in turn are given their deeper meaning by the archetypal stories and the four archetypal ways of life within which we enact relationships. Practiced within a particular story and way of life, each of our nine archetypal relationships has its own capacity to relate ourselves to self, to the other members of our society, and to problems.

NINE ARCHETYPAL RELATIONSHIPS

For all encounters between self and other in all recorded human history and in all societies, there exist only nine forms of relationship that give people the capacity to deal simultaneously with continuity and change, collaboration and conflict, and the achieving of justice. The hypothesis that there are nine and only nine archetypal forms applies to all intrapersonal, interpersonal, and intergroup relations. It applies to all groups, from family or affinity groups to political parties or nations and to the human species as a whole. This hypothesis applies to relations between individuals and groups, whether formal or informal, stable or fluctuating. It applies to our relations to concepts, symbols, ideas, values, feelings, norms, and problems. This hypothesis also applies to our connection to those sources of energizing and forming which we may call transpersonal, which others have called the unconscious, the sacred or god. This hypothesis applies to all encounters in all of recorded history and in all human societies. Because this hypothesis applies to all such human experiences, all readers already possess sufficient factual information to test this hypothesis.[28]

Let us explain the nine forms of encounter enacted in the service of four different ways of life. To be able to tell which relationships are allowed by a particular society tells us what any person or group is free to express and what they are forced to repress. Very few persons are free to experience all nine relationships. No current society encourages or even allows the free use of all nine relationships. Thus, they discourage our full human capacity.

EMANATION

This is an encounter in which one treats the other solely as an extension of one's self. The other accepts the denial of his/her own separate identity because of the mysterious and overwhelming power of the source of this emanation—a yielding which is rewarded with total security. All of us began life as children without power adequate to meet the other. We therefore necessarily yielded our identity to the mysterious and overwhelming power of our mother until we freed ourselves to risk losing total security. However, some fathers or mothers seek to retain all members of their household as emanations of themselves. Others treat their property or their employees in this way. Many individuals remain eager to submerge themselves as emanations of another—of a political movement, a dogma or a lover.[29]

The relationship of emanation is the most prevalent relationship even in modern times. It points to an unexamined, unconscious, uncritical relationship to a mysterious and overwhelming source that contains us and within which we live our inherited stories. Indeed, we are not even conscious of archetypal stories. We may see emanation manifested in the lives of Lindo Jong, Celie, and Cleofilas, who see themselves as women as a mere extension of husband and family. They saw themselves as the expression of their husbands' personality without any autonomous jurisdiction of their own. Lindo Jong, Celie, and Cleofilas were raised in inherited stories, especially patriarchy, in which they were trained to believe that the limits of their lives were determined by men.

It is a relationship in which people agree to collaborate with whatever intensity or passivity is required for collaboration at the price of repressing conflict. Both parties are willing to achieve continuity by implicitly accepting or rejecting change solely at the demand of another, and hence granting mysterious and overwhelming power to the one in exchange for total security for the other.[30] Emanation keeps people firmly ensconced in Act I, Scene 1 of the core drama of transformation. But later in this chapter we shall see that emanation is not in itself destructive; there are crucial distinctions to be made among encounters of transformation. The relationship of emanation can be enacted in profoundly different ways depending on which of four different ways of life it serves. For example, in the service of transformation, emanation can be used temporarily to nurture the young; the flow of emanation can then be broken to allow for emergence rather than containment.

SUBJECTION

In the relationship of subjection both self and other are fully present, but in reality both are denied a full identity of his/her own. The relationship is still asymmetrical; it still rests upon the experience of overwhelming power. But this power, which was mysterious in emanation, becomes naked in subjection—naked in its source, imposition, and resistance.[31]

We see subjection when the dominant culture sets the curriculum in schools and the teacher demands that children speak English at all times, in the father or husband who solely controls the spending of the family's finances. We see subjection when the protagonist in Ralph Ellison's *Invisible Man* is ordered to go to New York City by Bledsoe, the president of an all black college in the South.[32] Subjection exists whenever I control others as a means to my own end, whether I base this control on the naked power of standards of efficiency or simply on the power of the gun.

In subjection, conflict is no longer repressed but suppressed. Too often in their own education, people of color and women remain conscious of their inability to step forward freely to tell their own stories. Collaboration is based on explicit rules defined solely by the dominant culture. The powerful everywhere often combine emanation and subjection when relating to the less powerful. Thus, most new Americans are still prepared to relate to authority figures in this country with the same deference and respect they gave in their homeland. The dominant group therefore assures continuity and change in accordance with their power. Justice involves an exchange of the right of survival for the powerless in exchange for their acceptance of the supremacy of power of the other. Almost always, especially in regard to matters of educational policy, members from diverse backgrounds who were not considered to be part of the elite survived by giving up their right to create conflict or change on their own in regard to matters of the curriculum so that their children would not be hurt.

BUFFERING

This encounter is managed by intermediaries. Buffering is carried out by a mediator, broker, or by a concept. Buffering allows for change by permitting indirect and occasional conflict and collaboration with a mediator on behalf of others who cannot speak for themselves.[33]

In *The Color Purple*, Shug was a very important mediator for Celie in her struggle to free herself from an abusive husband, Albert. As in all societies, Celie used buffering as it is perhaps most often exemplified by mediating her own experiences through a socially acceptable filter of habits and stereotypes, such as never contradicting a man because it is bad luck. Justice in buffering means obtaining some change and conflict that achieves a certain amount of self-determination through the intervention of a third party. Thus because of her influence with Albert, Shug was able to achieve considerable periods of free time for Celie as she explored her sexuality. The problem here is that our freedom relies on the ability and skill of the mediator. Our self-determination is therefore limited and we can become too dependent on others.

ISOLATION

In this relationship, individuals or groups agree upon one way of collaboration—to refrain from demanding anything of each other. Both sides here collaborate in avoiding all conflict intended to lead to change in, with or by the other. Justice, in comparison to emanation and subjection, means a degree of self-determination— but at the price of not attempting to affect change in the others. Isolation in this use of the term cannot be achieved unilaterally. It demands collaboration. The attempt to isolate without an agreement to avoid conflict, change or new forms of justice provides incoherence, not isolation.[34]

Patriarchal males such as Albert in *The Color Purple*, César in *The Mambo Kings Play Songs of Love*,[35] and Tomas in *Lucía*,[36] who possessed their wives in the relationships of emanation, assumed that their spouses would always want to be near them because they were the source of emanation that gave the women their reason for living. Albert was shocked when Celie wanted to leave him because he thought that without him she would fail. Thus the threat of isolation was used to emphasize a woman's condition of dependency. But as we shall see later in the book, women became painfully aware that they had no right to be alone. Their anger helped them to use the relationship of isolation to break the patriarchal container that had prevented them from transforming their lives.

DIRECT BARGAINING

In this form of encounter, individuals and groups create conflict and collaborate with each other directly. Justice does not only consist in the better bargain that one side or the other may achieve, but above all what is won with this relationship is the reciprocal capacity to seek a better and more advantageous bargain as, from moment to moment, the balance of power changes.[37]

By means of gifts or favors, the less powerful often create or maintain a sense of indebtedness between themselves and the powerful. The one who provides the favor is often heard to say: "You owe me one." Direct bargaining is present in that form of rebellion when one remains angrily present while refusing to bargain precisely in order to improve one's bargaining position. As is clearly shown in *Like Water for Chocolate*, women knew that the way to get a better bargain from men was through the bargaining power of sex and food. In exchange for these services, their husbands often relented and allowed them certain favors. But the use of direct bargaining was always one of the most effective ways to head off real transformation. When a man sensed that his wife was becoming danger- ously close to rebellion, he could resort to offering her a better deal within the story of patriarchy. By giving her a new car, a man could lead a woman to feel guilty that she could ever question his love. Thus too often women went back to normal, that is, to the story, relationships and way of life that caused the problem. In this way the story of male dominance was reformed, or made easier but not done away with.

AUTONOMY

This is an encounter in which each self and other is entitled to claim an autonomous zone of jurisdiction based on some explicit principle of law, custom, status, value or competence that both share. The individual or group whose zone of autonomy has been effectively reduced may as a consequence have to consider changing behavior. . . . Justice in the encounter of autonomy is the reciprocal right of each to sustain or enlarge their autonomous zone of jurisdiction. Autonomy is the form of encounter which allows us to be fellow-citizens, to separate yet keep in constant tension the three branches of government, to charter the limited liability corporation, to create autonomy yet collaboration among professions, scholarly disciplines, and bureaucracies. The encounter of autonomy allows large numbers of individuals and groups to collaborate on a sustained basis in connected roles, for each claim can be challenged in order to be joined or subdivided, or a principle found to add more connections in the chain.[38]

The relationships of autonomy and direct bargaining are the most powerful patterns in official U.S. society. They are necessary to survive in this country. Autonomy in the service of incoherence on the personal level demands aggressive, calculating individuals who know how to advance their interests by enlarging their area of jurisdiction or who know when to defend their zone of autonomy against another bureaucrat who seeks to redraw the area under his jurisdiction to include theirs. The relationship of autonomy on the societal level is enacted when the rights of parents to participate in the education of their children is involved. The struggle between the community and teachers is often a question of autonomous jurisdictions of the certified experts and the parents. On the personal level, it is a young student going to university and becoming a teacher so that she can achieve economic autonomy and other rights based on explicit contractual principles. Women were not allowed to exercise this relationship for much of recorded history. To keep women dependent, even when they worked outside the home, a woman was often required to hand over her check.

INCOHERENCE

Incoherence in our theory is that form of encounter in which self and other face each other in the same place and at the same time but are unwilling or unable to agree upon how, simultaneously, to manage continuity and change, collaboration and conflict, and the achieving of justice between them. Incoherence is not a residual category for purposes of classification, but obviously an experiential alternative to the other forms of encounter. It is the experience of discontinuities rather than continuity; of change, yes, but unintended, uncontrolled change; of conflict without shared rules, leading to injustice for both self and others.[39]

In *Like Water for Chocolate*, Tita was so angry with her mother when her nephew Roberto died that she rebelled against her mother. All of the inherited relationships that connected Tita and her mother to each other were shattered. Tita no longer saw her mother as the source of her mystery in emanation; she refused to accept her commands in subjection. She rejected the rationalizations that her mother knew best, as in buffering, and there was no room for negotiating a new arrangement, as in direct bargaining. Consequently, Tita and Mama Elena stood in the presence of each other and could not agree on how to relate—the relationship of incoherence. In *Bread Givers*, Sara sought privacy, isolation, and personal freedom by enacting the relationship of autonomy by moving to New York without her father's permission. Father and daughter stood in the presence of each other and were unable to agree on which relationship to use. Sara listened to her inner voice in Act I, Scene 2, and entered into rebellion in Act II, Scene 1. She broke with the person with whom she was previously linked in emanation in Act I, Scene 1. The only legitimate way to leave home was to be like her sisters, who were handed over from one emanational container, the family, to another, the new family of the husband and marriage. From the perspective of the core drama, this meant that Sara's sisters never really left their father in Act I, but simply married their husband/father and remained in Act I. Bessie, Masha, and Fania knew what they were doing and made a conscious decision to repress their own voice in the second scene of Act I in order to remain in Scene 1 as a mere extension of their father/husband's life.

When Sara left home without this ritualized process, it was truly an act of incoherence. It was a sin from the perspective of the way of life of emanation. All of the psychological artillery of sin, shame, and guilt was used by Reb Smolinsky to attempt to restore Sara to her senses. Sara missed her father and loved him but she would no longer accept him at the expense of her own life. Reb Smolinsky argued: If you love me, marry Goldstein, become a real woman (that is, a wife and mother), come home again, back to the "normal" way things used to be in Act I, Scene 1, the dying way of life of emanation.

The result was that Sara and her father were no longer able to relate. They related in different worlds and meant fundamentally different realities in their use of the word "love." They lived in different ultimate ways of life and in different acts of the core drama. The relationships of emanation, subjection, buffering, and direct bargaining enacted in the service of emanation were broken; to the repertory were added the relationships of isolation, autonomy, deformation, incoherence, and transformation.

DEFORMATION

Deformation is a relationship in which we make connection with a particular person, object, idea, or feeling which from that first moment deeply moves us into the road to destructive death. We have been feeling depressed for so long that we take cocaine to get a high; we join with a group of white supremacists to defend the purity of our neighborhood so that we feel for the first time that we really do belong here. This is not a relationship of emanation but in fact a sacred source that is demonic.[40]

It is easy to confuse this relationship with emanation because it carries such a mysteriously overwhelming power. In truth it is pseudo-emanational, a fake emanation because it is in the guise of emanation.

The presence of this relationship means that we are on the road to destructive death in key aspects of our life. For example, when Reb Smolinsky slapped Sara in order to hold her in the container of emanation, he went beyond the relationship of subjection. Reb saw his life and everything he lived for threatened. He wanted not only to punish Sara but to cripple her. He could not respond to this new demand on the part of his daughter as a partial self arrested in the way of life of emanation. His terror could be alleviated only by responding to two fundamentally opposing inspirations: to create a truly open relationship and risk himself for the sake of Sara and himself or to crush Sara as the person who meant the end of his repressed self. This latter choice brought Reb to the brink because he thought that without the world as he knew it, he would die. What he refused to see or accept was that his world was already being dismantled.

We can be inspired anew at any time to stop and break with any archetypal relationship, to empty our selves of any archetypal story, any way of life. However, this requires our connecting to a more powerful sacred source than those that lead us to destructive death. It requires a source powerful enough to help us empty ourselves of both the concrete and the archetypal bonds that enchant and enchain us.

TRANSFORMATION

The relationship of transformation is an encounter in which one's consciousness is no longer the mere embodiment of an external source of emanation but has become conscious of those sources in the depths which constitute the archetypal dramas and stories of our lives. To enact this relationship is to keep alive a conscious awareness of alternative dramas of relationships being created, nourished, petrified, destroyed or recreated; a creativity that empowers us to be acted upon as well as to act, and thus woo new combinations into being; a linking with others that is at once knowing and loving; a justice which is participation in becoming and being.[41]

People who create a new sense of self, who break inherited relationships and reject in Act II, Scene 2 the archetypal stories in the service of emanation, incoherence, and deformation that possessed their souls, have enacted the drama of transformation. They create new linkages to others previously forbidden to them and alternative stories of their life based on mutuality. In Act III, Scene 1, people are inspired by a new vision of how to shape life anew. In the second scene of Act III, this new intuition is put into practice. This new-found wholeness enables people to enact not only all eight relationships (excluding the ninth relationship of deformation, which cannot be enacted in the service of transformation) but an infinite number of concrete manifestations of each relationship. This is what is meant by participating in the process of creating, nourishing, and destroying in order to create and transform time and again.

However, what looks like transformation can be distorted because it is in reality reformation. Transformation in the service of emanation is not possible; the very logic of emanation as a way of life precludes the emergence of the fundamentally new as the worst heresy. Change that may be called transformation is reformation when a person alters his personality in order to be more loyal to his lover, church, hero, or mother. Transformation is frustrated as reformation in the way of life of emanation when a woman becomes the first doctor in her family's history but did not choose to practice medicine and became a doctor only to remain loyal to her parents' wishes.

This is not a transformation because it was performed in response to the question: How can I ultimately show uncritical loyalty to mysterious others? Such a person is really arrested in Act I, Scene 2 because she was inspired to become someone new but responded in this scene of the core drama by becoming a better extension of someone else. She thus returns to Act I, Scene 1 with even more intensity. Transformation always means the creation of fundamentally more loving and just alternatives in all aspects of our life. Transformation will be further discussed as a way of life later in this chapter.

The nine archetypal relationships do not stand alone. Each derives its deeper meaning and value from a wider matrix, a way of life of emanation, incoherence, transformation, or deformation. The four ways of life determine the quality of our stories and relationships. Consequently, eight archetypal relationships are neither negative nor creative in themselves; only deformation is always destructive. Their quality or ultimate meaning is given to them within the way of life in which we choose to enact them. Emanation, incoherence, deformation, and transformation as archetypal relationships differ from emanation, incoherence, deformation, and transformation as ways of life. We shall always specify which we mean, the relationship or the entire way of life.

No archetypal relationship is ever enacted in and for itself. It gains its larger content, meaning and purpose by virtue of its contributions to, and derivation from, a larger context. The largest of the contexts—ways at once of asking, seeing, understanding, organizing, working, suffering, and enjoying human relationships—we call archetypal ways of life. Just as it is possible to discover and demonstrate that there are only nine archetypal relationships, so it is also possible to discover and demonstrate that all particular and concrete ways of life in human history are manifestations of four ultimate choices. These are the ways of life of emanation, incoherence, deformation and transformation. Therefore no archetypal relationship, including these four, can be enacted except in the service of one of these four ways of life.[42]

INITIATING THE PROCESS OF TRANSFORMATION

The process of transformation takes place first in the individual's depths. The archetypal source that crippled us and used our ego as its incarnation is now rejected in Act II, Scene 2 so that we are prepared to be renewed by the sources. But each of us as a person has four faces: the personal, political, historical, and sacred. Thus, when we reject a particular father or lover or ruler, there is a political dimension. Our ego, which also incarnates the body politic (the archetypal way of life that shapes the meaning and purpose of both our personal and political history), therefore says no not only to a person but to the official politics, gods, and story of that society. Only a person can choose to be political. Our personal face is necessary to choose a new turning point in the creation of a new history; the deepest source of our being knows us only as a unique and individual person.

Therefore we cannot settle for only personal transformation. We have to reach beyond our personal lives to the political and historical networks that severely limit our capacity. To resist the racism in one's personal life requires also a struggle against structural deformation in a society that continues to cripple others and to threaten the tenuous personal liberation achieved. We must be political, that is, do what we can and need to do together to liberate ourselves with others from the dramas of control and power that are justified in the wider society in the concrete and in the depths, by sacred forces. To cast out demons in society and history means to create a new turning point by struggling with both the immediate concrete tyranny and its underlying forming source, and ultimate ways of life.

By rejecting the inherited ways of life and the stories of our lives, we enter into the relationship of incoherence in Act II, Scene 1. We break with the official personal, political, historical, and sacred faces of our being. But we cannot create a new history or politics once for all. That is the failure of utopian politics. Although we have experienced transformation in regard to a particular problem, we will have to make this choice again and again as new problems emerge. This prevents us from stereotyping, from establishing a new orthodoxy, or from declaring that the revolution has been won. We cannot stereotype because at every moment we must test each relationship, each drama, and ask: In the service of what way of life am I helping to give concrete form to these archetypal forces? It follows from this that no previous incarnation will be authentic once for all; we must persistently choose, nourish, break, and create so that we can shape life anew.

Authentic self love means loving others as myself. Our neighbors might still be largely involved in the fragments of the crippled way of emanation, the pursuit of power in the service of incoherence, or ways of deformation. However, it is not possible to create a new body politic or society without our community. This reality demands the next step in our process, creating strategies of transformation. To enact as individuals and in groups new concrete manifestations of eight of our nine archetypal relationships and archetypal dramas enacted in the way of life of transformation is to create a new politics and a new history. Enacting new relationships and stories in our lives as more loving and just faces of our underlying sources is the meaning of justice relevant for our times. It means to enact ways of relating, living, and being that were not there before. This is our new-won freedom in Act III, Scenes 1 and 2—not only to choose among existing archetypal dramas but to create new ones that will do justice to ourselves, others, and to the source of sources.

This kind of participation is utterly democratic because it is available to each person. This theory is committed to awakening in each of us the capacity we have to tell a new story with personal, political, historical, and sacred implications. For this reason we need guides who have themselves experienced the process and therefore can help to awaken it in each of us. When any one of us enacts a transformation, we have made a personal breakthrough and created a new kind of politics by changing our environment for the better. Only in the service of transformation are our depths, our consciousness, our creativity, links with others, and justice kept in lively tension with the changing realities of life, for in the way of life of transformation, the concrete realization of transformation is never experienced as a final solution. To enter into the relationship of transformation becomes the final moment of a particular turn on the spiral process of transformation. The next turn will inevitably reveal new suffering, threats, joys, and opportunities, moving us down or up this spiral. To live in the service of transformation is therefore persistently to experience an archetypal process of breaking relationships, moving into incoherence, and entering into the relationship of transformation anew. Through this same process, chains of emanations are turned into links of transformation.[43]

The politics of blind loyalty in the service of emanation arrested in Act I of the core drama, the rapacious entrepreneurship in the arrested way of life of incoherence in Act II, and the permanent crippling of others by entering the abyss as a result of exiting the core drama are consciously rejected and replaced with the love and commitment of Act III, to include all others, to practice compassion and organize aggressively to empower all of us to redirect the use of our society's resources. This means to enact new forms of eight archetypal relationships in the service of transformation, to participate in uprooting the inherited and destructive archetypal dramas/stories of our lives.

This freeing of ourselves of destructive social and political dramas allows us to initiate a new history wherein for the first time people are empowered, for example, to create together new forms of the relationship of autonomy, no longer in the service of incoherence in which we seek to enlarge the domain of our personal power but now in the service of transformation: unions, task forces, rent strikes, co-ops, political parties, and immediately accessible affinity groups that nurture and care for the sick, old, and dying such as the recent creation of caring communities among gays to defy the isolation and powerlessness of those suffering from AIDS. History takes now an upward turn in the spiral of life.

Our guide throughout this way of transforming life is not a master or tyrant who commands but a sacred source, the god of transformation, who invites and calls us to be participants on a common journey that will result in transforming the personal, political, historical, and sacred faces of our lives. To be aggressive, to step forward urgently in this way of life allows us to end the repression, suppression, and murder of self and others both physically and psychologically. Transforming the self, others, the world, and the sacred takes decisive and courageous steps in the service of love and compassion.

It is a great blessing that we can discern between the ways and stories of life and destruction; we are not predetermined to remain locked into a strategy of power or death. Yet to choose strategies of aggressive response in the service of transformation will require a constant choice and willingness to enact a transforming solution to each particular problem. The three ways of emanation, incoherence, and deformation, because of their wounding of the self, turns us into impotent and partial selves. In contrast, the persistent call to take the journey of transformation in regard to new problems is witness to the indispensability of our loving and personal participation as whole persons. Without our involvement as practitioners of transformation, the source of all sources will not be able to have a more just, loving, concrete, and sensual face.

Throughout the pages that follow, we shall give numerous examples of the strategies used in multicultural and women's literature to practice transformation. Any good theory must help us see and understand what we have been living but have not fully understood. To re-envision our lives through a theory of transformation based on reflection and action exposes the threat of our present situation as well as its promise, if we choose to live what most of us have intuitively known in our deepest depths.

NOTES

1. David T. Abalos, "The Personal, Political, Historical and Sacred Grounding of Culture: Some Reflections on the Creation of Latino Culture in the United States from the Perspective of a Theory of Transformation," *Old Masks, New Faces: Religion and Latino Identities*, vol. 3, Anthony S. Arroyo and Gilbert Cadena, eds. (New York: Bildner Center, CUNY, 1995).

2. Manfred Halpern is currently writing *Transformation: Its Theory and Practice in Personal, Political, Historical and Sacred Being*. I have gained greatly from having read the chapters of his manuscript in the writing of this book. For applications of the theory of transformation, see David T. Abalos, *The Latino Family and the Politics of Transformation* (Westport, Conn.: Praeger, 1993) and *Latinos in the United States: The Sacred and the Political* (Notre Dame, Ind.: University of Notre Dame Press, 1986).

3. Halpern, *Transformation*, Chapter 1.

4. Miguel Leon Portilla, ed., *Native Mesoamerican Spirituality* (New York: Paulist Press, 1980). For an explanation of the *Popol Vuh* from the perspective of transformation, see also David T. Abalos, "Rediscovering the Sacred Among Latinos: A Critique from the Perspective of a Theory of Transformation," *Latino Studies Journal* 3: (May 1992).

5. Manfred Halpern, "Why Are Most of Us Partial Selves? Why Do Partial Selves Enter the Road into Deformation?" Paper delivered at the annual meeting of the American Political Science Association, Washington, D.C., August 29, 1991.

6. Ibid.

7. Manfred Halpern, "Toward an Ecology of Human Institutions: The Transformation of Self, World and Politics in Our Time." Paper delivered at a national symposium, "Beyond the Nation State: Transforming Visions of Human Society," College of William and Mary, September 24–27, 1993.

8. Halpern, *Transformation*, Chapter 1.

9. Ibid., Chapter 3.

10. Hermann Hesse, *Siddhartha* (New York: Bantam Books, 1971).

11. Leslie Marmon Silko, *Ceremony* (New York: Penguin Books, 1986).

12. Halpern, *Transformation*, Chapter 3.

13. Alice Walker, *The Color Purple* (New York: Washington Square Press, 1982).

14. Laura Esquivel, *Like Water for Chocolate* (New York: Doubleday, 1992).

15. Amy Tan, *The Joy Luck Club* (New York: Vintage, 1991).

16. Anzia Yezierska, *Bread Givers* (New York: Persea Books, 1975).

17. Sandra Cisneros, "Woman Hollering Creek," in *Woman Hollering Creek and Other Stories* (New York: Random House, 1991).

18. Halpern, *Transformation*, Chapter 13.

19. Walker, *The Color Purple*.

20. Halpern, "Toward an Ecology."

21. Iris M. Young, *Justice and the Politics of Difference* (Princeton, N.J.: Princeton University Press, 1990), pp. 39–65.

22. Halpern, *Transformation*, pp. 13–14.

23. Ibid., Chapter 4.

24. Ibid., Chapter 5.

25. Yezierska, *Bread Givers*.

26. Halpern, Transformation, Chapter 1.

27. Ibid.

28. Ibid., Chapter 7.

29. Manfred Halpern, "Four Contrasting Repertories of Human Relations in Islam: Two Pre-Modern and Two Modern Ways of Dealing with Continuity and Change, Collaboration and Conflict and Achieving Justice," in *Psychological Dimensions of Near Eastern Studies*, eds. L. Carl Brown and Norman Itzkowitz, eds. (Princeton, N.J.: Darwin Press, 1977), p. 62. Much of the summary and many of the quotes from Halpern's theory are taken from this source and from Halpern's *Transformation*, Chapter 7.

30. Halpern, "Four Contrasting Repertories," p. 64.

31. Halpern, *Transformation*, pp. 9–10.

32. Ralph Ellison, *Invisible Man* (New York: Vintage Books, 1972).

33. Halpern, *Transformation*, p. 12.

34. Halpern, "Four Contrasting Repertories," pp. 77–78.

35. Oscar Hijuelos, *The Mambo Kings Play Songs of Love* (New York: Harper and Row, 1990).

36. Humberto Solas, *Lucia*, produced in Havana, Cuba, 1968.

37. Halpern, *Transformation*, pp. 13–14.

38. Halpern, "Four Contrasting Repertories," pp. 78–79.

39. Halpern, *Transformation*, p. 18.

40. Ibid.

41. Ibid.

42. Ibid, Chapter 7.

43. Ibid.

CHAPTER 2

Applying the Story of Transformation to Practice: Images of the Sacred and the Political in Literature

Why is it that we have been blessed from time to time with a book, a novel, a poem, a film that we found it impossible to put down or to forget? Such occurrences have inevitably left us profoundly affected. We go back to such treasures and mine them time and again because the author has succeeded in telling our story, in rendering the "deep story" that touches the ground and roots of our being. This kind of awakening through the creative act of others is for us at once both a political and sacred moment. In her brilliant book *Justice and the Politics of Difference*, Iris M. Young, the feminist philosopher, taught me that the struggle for justice in literature as well as in economics must not fall prey to the paradigm of distributive justice.[1] Yes, we must provide more for the poor and distribute jobs, goods, and services more equitably. Of course, the conflict over the curriculum means distributing the works of women and people of color in the curriculum. But the real issue is that somebody else is determining that this community deserves so much more or that this group has earned several units of study in the curriculum. In other words, the real issue is the structure of decision-making that determines which groups are considered worthy. As long as others have the final say, it strengthens the oppression of the recipients who are dependent on the largess of others. Rousseau taught us in the eighteenth century not to be intimidated by constitutions. We must always ask who wrote the constitution and for whose benefit.[2] To fail to ask questions that expose the structural decision-making is to perpetuate the oppression and domination of groups that are being evaluated.

For someone to tell my story is a rewarding experience, but there is a political result. I am now awakened in my deeper person so that I want to participate by completing my story. This is to come forth as a full person out of the shadows and to refuse to be invisible. But my story and your story are also the story of a people, a group to which you and I belong. Why was I hesitant to speak? Why did I not know the story of my group? Why could I not identify myself as a valuable member of a society who also happened to be the member of a specific group? Such questions lead to the awareness and consciousness of another story: the dramas of oppression, exclusion and tribalism. That I discovered something of my humanity through the stories of others is no small matter. But not to have had the opportunity to share and tell my story or to know myself through the stories of my group is to have experienced a form of distributive justice in education and culture that silenced me.

PREGNANT WITH OUR OWN STORIES

People of color and women were provided with universal stories, true for everyone and therefore, it was alleged, fully human. But this kind of universality veiled the ascendancy and the hierarchical status of a dominant group. The group's rendering of the truth was supposedly neutral and universal. Everything was self-evident. We all studied T. S. Eliot, Shakespeare, Milton, Mark Twain, John Steinbeck, and William Faulkner. From time to time distributive justice meant allowing Emily Dickinson, Ralph Ellison, and Richard Wright. But Elaine Pagels has taught us, using the words of Jesus from the Gospel of Saint Thomas, "If you bring forth what is within you, what you bring forth will save you. If you do not bring forth what is within you, what you do not bring forth will destroy you."[3] This statement is very much in agreement with Leslie Marmon Silko, who wrote that each of us is pregnant with our own stories:

> Here, put your hand on it
> See, it is moving.
> There is life here
> for the people.
>
>
> And in the belly of this story
> the rituals and the ceremony
> are still growing.[4]

The essence and heart of the stories are that they are an ongoing creation by which we heal ourselves and respond to the destruction that surrounds us.

The distributive justice paradigm in literature meant that people of color and women were violated and subjected to oppression, not because American literature and Western civilization courses were evil in themselves but because they were considered by the dominant culture as the *only* view of the world, the only story worth telling. The result of such socialization was that the stories of women and people of color were discredited, went untold, stopped providing healing and wholeness. These groups were forced to seek wholeness vicariously, living their lives through others, which denied the validity of their lives. To be different became something ugly and disruptive.

Underlying the literacy of the culture was a hidden curriculum. The universal curriculum became a form of cultural imperialism. "Neutral" stories were really destructive. Many began to believe that they had no story, culture, memory, or imagination, that is to say, no self worth sharing. This silences people and depoliticizes them. The silent (*silenced*) student becomes the silent (*silenced*) and passive citizen. To be silent assumes choice. However, there was no choice because people were shut up against their will and thereby violated.

And yet only some of the stories continue to be told, retold, and lived. The message of the culture mirrored in the schools and in the decisions as to who gets to write books (tell their stories) is that some people are not as valuable. From this kind of indoctrination, it is taken for granted who does research, who runs the corporation, who runs for office. It is all part of the natural state of affairs. But if the powerful erred from time to time, there is always a way to correct such mistakes by distributing some justice to the aggrieved interest group so that they can go back to their invisibility.

Thus, the inherited stories of U.S. society, such as the market society, romantic love, the conquering hero,[5] patriarchy, competence, and even tribalism came to be seen as neutral, universal, natural, and, if not necessarily good for all, at least as inevitably part of our daily lives. To question these stories was to be un-American.

But politics is more than official contests for power. If politics is what we can and need to do together, we were being told that the political reality was to let others tell the story of our nation. This is all that we could do and that needed to be done to shape an environment because the smartest and brightest revealed to us the only story in town.

These stories are not only political; they are also sacred stories.[6] There are stories that wound us, enable us, enchant us, and puff us up. We all live inherited dramas that often go unexamined because they are part of "reality." What I mean by the sacred is a mystery that moves and shapes our lives decisively in the depths. There are competing sacred sources within each of us. Some sacred sources have a destructive and others a creative face. It is part of our task to determine which sacred sources are involved in our stories. For this reason it is not enough to simply tell, analyze, or intellectualize our stories. Since our stories are rooted in sacred sources, they can possess us. There is a process, the journey of the story of transformation, that allows us to name the story, break with the story keepers, empty ourselves of that lord who blesses the story, and choose our own lord as the creative principle in telling a fundamentally new and better story.

The images that emerge of the fundamentally new are the archetypes that are in the process of dying, birthing, and nourishing. These images or archetypes are the necessary underlying, sacred forming sources that come forth in individual persons who are free to respond to them and to articulate them in the creative act. It was Ibn Arabi (d. 1240) who taught us that each person has a creative imagination and his or her own lord.[7] I would elaborate by saying that each of us has to have the political space to contribute, to participate in building the world, to create a society by telling her or his story. Not to be able to do so is to violate the person and to deny the archetypal story of democracy upon which our nation is grounded. To find one's voice and to be able to speak, write, paint, act, teach, and administer is a personal, political, historical, and sacred participation in the story of democracy.

LITERACY AS LIBERATION: DISCOVERING ONE'S OWN VOICE

This understanding of the sacred and the political dramatically alters our view of what it means to be literate and the underlying meaning of literature. As we have seen, the stories of some have been interrupted, suppressed, and silenced by the stories of others. This experience of oppression has made many "illiterate," that is, been made ignorant, incapable of telling, cut off from their own tongues, voices, images, stories. Therefore, authentic literacy must mean liberation. Literacy does not and has never meant the mere act of connecting letters and identifying such an aggregate with a particular object such as t-r-e-e, which spells and points out that green and brown, soft and hard, tall object. Literacy means being able to name the world by also listening to and engaging the world in a relationship. Humberto Solas's revolutionary film, *Lucía*, depicts the emergence of women during three historical periods. In the final piece of the trilogy, Lucía identifies literacy with a personal, political, historical, and sacred act of liberation. The first words that she writes are: "I am going; I am not a slave," which she addresses to an abusive husband.[8] To name, to define, to identify is to participate. It also means first of all to experience and name one's self as the center of consciousness that knows and engages the world around us as a series of relationships, or stories in motion.

MULTICULTURAL AND FEMINIST LITERATURE

To better understand how to develop strategies of transformation in the re-creation of the story of American democracy, I wish to tell something of the relationship between the sacred and the political through the images of women's literature and multicultural literature, the archetypal stories or dramas of communities of people whose story has not been told. My personal political passion as a Chicano/Mejicano/Latino first helped me to understand how my silence as a scholar, teacher, and writer regarding my own background was not freely chosen. I was silenced by a distributive justice mentality active in the realm of schooling, publishing, and awarding tenure and credentials in general. But if my voice was silenced, so were those of others. The common experience of oppression can be healed only by the mutual experience of the liberating event of the story of democracy in the service of transformation.

Since the 1960s, our society has been experiencing a revolution of consciousness, a revolution made by previously excluded, "illiterate" groups that have now rediscovered the story of democracy that was always there, although the political opportunity to bring their voices and stories to the table was missing. Women and communities of people of color—Native Americans, Latinas and Latinos, African Americans, Asian Americans, gays and lesbians, the differently abled, and senior citizens—have with one voice declared that they are here. Together they are transforming the story of democracy in our time. Others have shaped the environment as if these groups were not important. The recognition and acceptance of diversity rejects the old liberal views of fairness and equality based on the assumption that all people are really the same. To honor difference is to enable people to come forth with their unique capacity that they can now contribute for the enrichment of the whole in a truly democratic society.[9]

Returning to our critique of distributive justice, the literature and scholarship of people of color and women is not just an add-on, a concession or form of behavior modification. This is a movement that intends and by the very nature of its integrity will transform American democracy and society.[10] Structural change is taking place; the structures of privilege and oppression are being questioned, demystified, and undermined. This is the heart of the fight over the curriculum. A new story is being woven and told that seeks to replace the story of cultural tribalism. And since all of these stories are sacred dramas that profoundly touch our lives from the depths, many see the resultant changes in American culture, politics, and education as a disaster—a disaster for their story, which justified and upheld their privilege and power.

To read the new literature and scholarship of Toni Morrison, Sandra Cisneros, Henry Louis Gates Jr., Oscar Hijuelos, Edward Said, Alice Walker, Amy Tan, Leslie Marmon Silko, Adrienne Rich, Iris M. Young, Gloria Anzaldúa, to mention only a few, is to witness a shift in paradigms. This is more than just a fight, another fad, or an argument over shared American values, or the curriculum of accepted scholarship and privilege. What we are witnessing here is a truly remarkable emergence of creativity, talent, and energy that is the culmination of thirty years of struggle. A paradigm shift, an opening up of the "deep stories" of the creative depths, means a new gestalt, a new stance, a new vision, a transformation. The new concrete face of the story of democracy that is emerging is one of multicultural and gender scholarship. As a result the old containers of politics, culture and education are simply being overwhelmed.

This new scholarship primarily consists of people from a diversity of backgrounds and women telling their story as a personal, political, historical, and sacred act. Women and previously excluded communities, especially but not only of people of color, are creating, defining, and naming themselves precisely by becoming literate, and in the process are redefining American democracy. It is for this reason that others who have been setting the agenda are alarmed. The powerful, although at times unconscious of their domination, have built their identities on the assumption that the "others" would remain marginal people. Thus, even people of goodwill know that it is not just power that is at stake but also their very sense of self and the national identity as a whole. Transformation means leaving behind untenable containers, venturing into dark and unknown waters, taking a leap of faith and risking that there will be something, indeed, someone more human and loving on the other side.

I learned in physics and chemistry as a high school student that a mixture will forever be a juxtaposition of elements, such as iron filings and sand. But a chemical reaction changes the molecular makeup such that when two elements interpenetrate, a third and new reality is present that was not there before. Yet the specific, unique, original identity remains within the whole so that the gas or element is not annihilated but gains a new and wondrous reality. This is the ecstatic equilibrium involved in multicultural and feminist literature. It is a new face of the underlying story of democracy coming forth through novels, poetry, art, drama, music, scholarship. Why do I call it ecstatic? Because it actually *ex/stare* stands outside of the ordinary, the taken-for-granted world. It is an equilibrium because it contains, at times painfully so, the opposites of continuity and change, of conflict and cooperation, of the masculine and the feminine, the human and the divine. The shaman, the curandera, midwife, prophet, and storyteller have always been such a carrier of the sacred and therefore willing to stand apart in dissent, to polarize, awaken, and threaten because something new is coming.

It is in the literature of women and people of color that a new journey, a context, a historical, concrete expression of the archetypal story of democracy is emerging within which we encounter the new images of the sacred and the political. Let us now consider some literary works that exemplify the emerging concrete images of the sacred and the political story of democracy within the theoretical and conceptual framework of the story of transformation.

THE NEW VOICES: CREATING THE ALTERNATIVE

I would now like to provide examples of images of the sacred and the political drawn from the works of women and multicultural literature. In these pieces of creative imagination, the authors are creating in a fundamentally new way the story of democracy as our nation's collective journey of transformation.

The Four Faces of Our Being

In *The Persian Letters*, written by Montesquieu in 1721, we are given hints of the coming revolution. Roxane, Uzbek's favorite wife in his harem, declares her liberation in an astonishingly modern manner.

How could you have thought that I was naive enough to imagine that I was put in the world only to adore your whims? That while you pampered yourself with everything, you should have the right to mortify all my desires? No! I might have lived in servitude, but I have always been free. I have rewritten your laws after the laws of nature, and my spirit has ever sustained itself in independence.[11]

This statement is further evidence that transformation is not "modern" but has existed in the form of a counter-tradition in all historical periods and in all cultures and civilizations. At the heart of this declaration is a four-fold revolution. In raising the specter of resistance, Roxane has made a decision to reject repression and choose the emergence of her personal face. Furthermore, she has thrown off her second inherited face, the politics of uncritical loyalty, by vehemently rejecting the social and political structures that gave men permission to appropriate her life. She has chosen a politics of love and self expression. The third face of Roxane's being, the historical, has been dramatically altered because she will no longer live according to the laws and patterns of men but by new laws of nature, which meant creating a new history centered in liberation. Finally, like Alice Walker, Amy Tan, Sandra Cisneros, Adrienne Rich, Gloria Anzaldúa, and Virginia Woolf, Roxane declares the grounding for this new-won personal, political and historical revolution: It is in her spirit that Roxane finds the strength to resist the destruction of her life. This source as the grounding of our being is precisely the realm of the archetypal, the underlying deeper self that constitutes the sacredness of each of us.

Thus, as the journey of transformation is undertaken time and again, what is at stake is the radical recasting, reshaping of the four faces of our being. With each journey, one more aspect of our life becomes whole, as we are healing ourselves. These four faces of our being are always present: the personal, political, historical, and sacred. Each of our stories has these four faces and each of our faces and of our stories is fundamentally changed when we complete one more journey of transformation.

William Attaway's *Blood on the Forge* provides an excellent pedagogical blessing by which to highlight the utter emptiness of revenge. To seek revenge is to be captured by the consciousness of the story of the oppressor. Revenge is a form of rebellion that is utterly powerless to create a new and better story. By attempting to gain revenge by hurting others, we ourselves become death. This characterizes the failure to empty ourselves in Act II, Scene 2 of the archetypal drama, that way of life in which the drama was enacted, and the sacred source that inspires the drama and way of life. Not to purge ourselves in this deeper manner means that we are rebels who, when faced with a challenge, are so fragile that we are doomed to repeat the story and consciousness of the oppressor.

Big Mat and his brothers were forced to leave Kentucky and a certain lynching because Big Mat had severely beaten the riding boss, a poor white. In Pennsylvania they seek a new life. Like Luis in *La Carreta,* Big Mat has left agricultural serfdom, but his anger keeps him permanently polarized in Act II, Scene 1. Unless Big Mat also empties himself of the story of racism, the way of life of emanation that justified his marginality, and the lord of emanation that filled him with sin, shame and guilt, he will not be able to create a fundamentally new and better life. In fact, Big Mat's anger is used by the mill owners and their surrogates, the sheriff and law enforcement personnel, who in a brilliant stroke of co-option make him a deputy sheriff.

Since Big Mat seeks revenge and believes that even God has cursed him, he chooses a new god; a powerful and angry Big Mat is now the avenging angel. He makes himself into the new concrete manifestation of the story of racism. He is now the riding boss, and acknowledges this, as he kills one of the white strikers: "There was no riding boss over him now. . . . He was exalted. A bitterness towards all things white hit him like a hot iron. Then he knew. There was a riding boss—Big Mat. Big Mat Moss from the red hills was the riding boss. For the first time in his life he laughed aloud. Laughing crazily, he held the man by the neck."[12]

This demonstrates the bankruptcy of rebellion. Big Mat not only fails to empty himself of the story of tribalism/racism, the lord of deformation, and the way of life of deformation, he now becomes the oppressor, the person who descends into the abyss and makes life fundamentally worse by practicing deformation. Big Mat became possessed by the story of tribalism, the way of life and god that he hated in white people. This demonstrates how deadly rebellion is and how it always ends in making life worse for everybody.

In Leslie Marmon Silko's *Ceremony*, Tayo struggles with the same dilemma as Big Mat and Luis. He is confused by his dual identity.[13] Tayo returns from World War II without his cousin, Rocky, whom he had promised his family he would bring back safely. He is in the process of going mad. As the story unfolds we learn that Tayo is filled, like Big Mat, with the story of tribalism and oppression. He feels the pain of invisibility, the anger of inferior treatment the seduction of assimilation, the dilemma of excommunication, and the horror of possible extermination. Through the help of an American Indian shaman, Betonie, Tayo is guided through the injustice and terror of Act II, Scenes 1 and 2 into the wholeness of Act III, Scenes 1 and 2.

The novel makes it decisively clear that people must *choose* to take the journey and be willing to pay the consequences: "How far are you willing to go"; "it has never been easy." Tayo is in the process of rejecting the container of the white world that has made him marginal, that practiced cultural imperialism against the American Indians, violated and humiliated him, exploited him and his people, and numbed him with the corrupting sickness of powerlessness. In the persons of Emo, Harley, and Pinkie, he has seen the deadly impact of the five faces of oppression and the five faces of tribalism. He hates this story of oppression/tribalism, the destroyer gods who inspire this drama. Betonie provides him with a ceremony of cleansing, a fourfold test, and a call to take the journey. This is the heart of Act II, Scene 2. Tayo must empty himself not just of white men but of the sacred source that he knows as the destroyers who inspire their story of tribalism as the only viable response. Tayo successfully confronts the fourfold challenge of Betonie's vision, but the destroyers make their last effort to ensnare Tayo in the revenge that destroyed Big Mat: "The end of the story. They want to change it. They want to end it here, the way all their stories end, encircling slowly to choke the life away."[14]

The destroyers want to end not only Tayo's journey but the story and the journey of transformation itself so that there will be permanent night, perpetual death, with no sunrise and no resurrection. Thus Tayo's journey is not only a personal struggle but a political, historical, and sacred passion/passage as well. Tayo's journey is everybody's, yours and mine: "He cried the relief he felt at seeing the pattern, the way all the stories fit together . . . the old stories . . . the story that was still being told."[15]

Competing sacred sources and stories of transformation and deformation were vying for Tayo's soul: "Tonight the old priests would be praying for the force to continue the relentless motion of the stars. But there were others who would be working this night . . . swallowing the universe endlessly into the black mouth . . . outlining the end in motionless dead stars."[16]

Tayo clearly and decisively chooses not to return to the world of oppression and tribalism through an act of deadly revenge; this choice is Tayo's final passage from the story of tribalism, the inspiration of the destroyers and the sickness that there is only the way of life of deformational repetition: "The witchery had almost ended the story according to its plan; Tayo had almost jammed the screwdriver into Emo's skull. . . . Their deadly ritual for the autumn solstice would have been completed by him."[17]

Having emptied himself and vomited out the poison of revenge and oppression, Tayo dreams that he is going home. Home meant for Tayo a return to his deeper, sacred self, nurtured by the deepest sources: "the transition was complete."

The novel ends with a prayer:

> It is dead for now.
> It is dead for now.
> It is dead for now.
> It is dead for now.
>
> Sunrise,
> accept this offering,
> Sunrise.[18]

Alice Walker and Sandra Cisneros actively create through their work new understandings of what it means to be a woman of color. In her short story "Woman Hollering Creek," Cisneros challenges a five-hundred-year-old legend/story/myth.[19] In cities throughout Latin America, and especially in Mexico, there is a haunting story of a woman who wanders the streets at night crying, "Mis hijos, mis hijos," seeking her lost children. There are various interpretations of this story. Some say it is the violated and abandoned women of Latin America; others say it symbolizes the unforgettable trauma of the conquest and the loss of Native American Indian identity. I believe that Sandra Cisneros is deliberately challenging this central myth of a violated womanhood/identity/culture and attempting to create a new history and sacred story for women and people of color. Cisneros is rejecting "la llorona," the woman crying and overwhelmed with grief, because this image of an abandoned woman stereotypes excluded groups, and especially women, as permanent victims. In the title, a woman hollering, in Spanish is "la gritona," the shouter, the protester, the dissenter. This is a fundamental departure from the woman who cries out but who also submits to her fate. In "Woman Hollering Creek," Cleofilas makes a political move by leaving an abusive husband; in so doing she breaks a historical pattern and initiates a new story for Latina women. She also asserts the sacredness and value of a woman's life. Virtue is no longer submissiveness as the lords of emanation demand, but the call of the journey is an invitation from the god of transformation to begin a new life.

Similarly, Celie in Alice Walker's *The Color Purple* becomes aware of an inner voice—not conscience, which is the voice of the established order—through the voice and resistance of Sofia.[20] Sofia represented for Celie another way to be a woman. Celie's total domination by Albert became the natural order in the way of life of emanation. Consequently, Celie was startled by Sofia's "heresy," since no matter how unhappy Celie was, she had grown comfortably numb in her selflessness. It was too painful to feel, think, and fight. Like Tayo, Celie was ready for a guide to show her the way. This person arrived in the unlikely person of Shug, her husband's lover. Shug and Celie become lovers. The refreshing thing about this relationship is that neither Celie nor Shug seek to hurt Albert but to affirm their own lives. Shug succeeds in awakening Celie's personal face.

Still Celie hesitated, remaining cautious in Act I, Scene 2. What made her relationship untenable and unbearable was her discovery of the extent of Albert's cruelty; he had kept Nettie from her all these years by hiding Nettie's letters. Celie quickly breaks with Albert and enters Act II, Scene 1. Like Tayo, Celie is about to fulfill the inspiration of the destroyers by killing Albert. This act of revenge would, as in the case of Big Mat, have ended the journey, and Celie would have become as cruel as her oppressor. Celie successfully empties herself of the archetypal story of patriarchy in the service of emanation at the dinner table scene in which she announces that she is leaving for good. The anger created here is no longer for revenge but is necessary to generate the energy to break away, to polarize in order to create a new and better life.

Her new life begins with a prayer: "I'm poor, I'm black and I may be ugly and can't cook, a voice say to everything listening. But I'm here. Amen, say Shug, amen, amen."[21]

Celie experiences the wholeness of Act III, Scene 1, in regard to her new-found sense of self: "I am so happy. I got love, I got work, I got money, friends and time."[22] But transformation is an ongoing, continuous process. Celie's relationship to Albert and Shug is unresolved. We soon learn that she has become dependent upon Shug and that she feels betrayed when Shug chooses to leave with a new lover, Germaine. This new incoherence is successfully dealt with when she comes to realize: "Shug got a right to live too. She got a right to look over the world in whatever company she chooses. Just cause I love her don't take away none of her rights. . . . My job just to love her good and true to myself."[23] With this realization and her acceptance of Shug upon her return, Celie enters into Act III, Scene 2. She becomes a guide to Shug by reaching out to her with her political and historical face, thus creating a mutual relationship with her that allows both of them to create a new history together.

Alice Walker has been criticized for being too hard on the African American male. *The Color Purple* is a classic and brilliant example of how to transform the oppression of patriarchy into mutual love. Celie remains open to Albert; she feels that she is responsible for Albert. When she sees his change and willingness to enter into a new relationship, Celie is ready but quickly rules out a sexual relationship. It is Albert who guides her through her depression when Shug leaves. Celie reciprocates by initiating a creative partnership with Albert tailoring made-to-order pants and shirts. Thus Celie guides Albert and Albert escorts Celie through her depression as loving friends who enact in Act III, Scenes 1 and 2 the story of transforming love.

But the greatest contribution from the perspective of the theory of transformation and Walker's commitment to the transformation of both men and women is found in the relationship between Albert and Harpo. This episode reveals an extraordinary insight into how crucial it is to intervene, interrupt and uproot destructive archetypal stories. It demonstrates that it is possible to get out of the abyss of deformation. It is clear from the novel that Albert had been crippled by his father, who refused to give him permission to marry Shug. As an act of rebellion, he descended into deformation by openly humiliating and betraying his wife while he carried on an open and scandalous sexual relationship with Shug. Possessed by the same logic of this revengeful archetype, Albert's first wife was killed in the presence of her children by her lover.

Albert's response is a revelation to us that breaking with a hated father does not free us from the archetype of the father. Albert had merely polarized, rebelled against his concrete father but he had not emptied himself of the archetype of the father and the way of life of emanation. To protect his identity, forged by the drama of patriarchy and the way of emanation, he turned against his own son and used violence in the service of deformation. Albert did to Harpo what his father had done to him. Harpo, in his turn, even though he is not close to his father, seeks his approval by beating Sofia. Harpo's children are doomed to be raised with the same wounding, deforming patriarchal drama. In this way, at least four generations are crippled by the same story.

But the spirit intervenes. Alice Walker gives a marvelous portrayal of redemption from our perspective of transformation. After Celie, Shug, and Mary Agnes leave for Tennessee, Albert is devastated because his male ego had been built around the oppression of women. Now that he has nobody to control, he has no purpose in life. He won't eat, won't work, stays in bed, and lives like a pig. He wants to die. This is another rebellion, since it is an attempt to gain revenge by killing himself. He is controlled, possessed by the sacred drama of patriarchy, the logic of which tells Albert that without a submissive woman he is nothing. Harpo intervenes, and in an achingly beautiful and tender way rescues his father: "Mr. _____ would be all cram up in a corner of the bed. Eyes clamp on different pieces of furniture, see if they move in his direction. You know how little he is, say Sofia. And how big and stout Harpo is. Well, one night I walked up to tell Harpo something—and the two of them was just laying there on the bed fast asleep. Harpo holding his daddy in his arms."[24] As a result of this risk on Harpo's part, Albert decided to live and began his transformation by returning all of Nettie's letters to Celie. Harpo emptied himself of the archetype of the father in Act II, Scene 2 by fathering his own father and created an alternative relationship that allowed both men to be whole in Act III, Scene 1 and to become mutual guides to each other in Act III, Scene 2.

To do this he had to become a friend to Albert and have faith in his own ability as a person to reach out toward another human being. This sign of love between two men, father and son as mutual friends, restored Sofia's love for Harpo. Sofia had left Harpo because she refused to live the inherited drama of patriarchy. Now Harpo responds: "I ast Harpo do he mind if Sofia work. What I'm gon mind for? he say. It seem to make her happy. . . . Well you got me behind you, anyway say Harpo. And I loves every judgment you ever made."[25] This is precisely the way history is interrupted by personal decisions that reject the old politics of patriarchal domination and that result in new patterns of mutuality becoming the new history of the family. This is finally a personal and sacred event because Harpo comes forth as the destroyer of old patterns and the creator of a new drama—transforming love that only equals can enact.

Anzia Yezierska also tells us the story of patriarchy as a form of oppression in her novel, *Bread Givers*.[26] Sara's father, Reb Smolinsky, sees men as the center of creation; women can reach God only through men. In this emanational container, Smolinsky practices the five faces of oppression. Why does he resort to such cruelty against his own daughters and wife? As mentioned earlier, the stories of our lives lived out in the service of emanation and incoherence are always vulnerable and fragile. In the way of emanation in Act I, everything must be done to repress the fundamentally new from whatever quarter. New ideas, friends, feelings, intuitions are always heretical because Act I holds us in the enchantment that everything is God's will and has been given once for all. In the way of life of incoherence arrested in Act II, Scene 1, power is fluid and unpredictable. We live in constant fear that what is ours will be taken away. Thus we build fortresses in a desert of competing partial selves. To protect the seamless web of belief and eternal truth or the insecure world of power, authorities feel justified by the gods of emanation and incoherence to treat the infidels and competitors as invisible, inferior, assimilated as the better ones, excommunicated as heretics, or finally, exterminated as the ultimate threat. If one's loved ones stray from the truth, they too must be punished, cast out, or even killed lest they corrupt the rest.

Sara's three sisters, Mashah, Fania, and Bessie, are forced to marry their father's choice. Sara sees this and resists. Her sisters make conscious decisions not to respond to their inner voices, the anger and depression they feel, in Act I, Scene 2. They repress these feelings and accept life in the patriarchal drama as inevitable. We are reminded again that these are sacred stories that possess us because this is not a case of intellectual liberation. We have to descend into the deeper story of our life there to struggle and to empty ourselves not only of our actual enemy but of the archetypal story and way of life that gives our concrete oppressor its mysterious hold over us.

Sara is assaulted by her father as she confronts his cruelty and unequivocally states that the old world had made its last losing effort to hold her back. She leaves her father and mother and enters into the desert of Act II, Scene 1. Sara comes forth in amazing ways, discovering new aspects of herself. She is tested by two men, who are new concrete manifestations of the archetype of the father. She resists and transforms as a whole person as she successfully graduates from college, the first in her family to do so. Sara has overcome the story of the wounded self. She has entered into Act II, Scene 2 and emptied herself of a destructive personal face that makes it possible for her to achieve the transformation of becoming a whole person in Act III, Scene 1. In the second scene of Act III, Sara enacts her political and historical face by becoming a guide to her students. But each of us is a bundle of connections. Sara must still empty herself in a more complete way of the archetypal story of patriarchy not only by freeing herself from the destructiveness of her father but by entering into a mutually rewarding relationship with a man or the masculine within herself. This she encounters in the person of Hugo Seelig, with whom she succeeds in creating a mutually open and loving relationship.

At this point her own father re-enters her life and threatens to return her to the inherited and crippling patriarchal drama. But Sara has made great strides. Her relationship to Hugo is a clear indication that she has success-fully emptied herself of the archetype of the father in Act II, Scene 2. Transformation is very demanding; because it is never total, we can only experience it in relationship to one aspect of our life at a time. Now Sara is asked to do it again with her father. She is very conscious of the fact that she is locked in a historical, personal, political, and sacred drama that is ongoing: "Just as I was beginning to feel safe and free to go on to a new life with Hugo, the old burden dragged me back by the hair. . . . And now I realized that the shadow of the burden was always following me."[27]

As the novel ends, it is also clear that Sara's father has no intention of changing. He remains in Act I, Scene 1 until the end: "In a world where all is changes, he alone remained unchanged—as tragically isolate as the rocks. All that he had left to his life was his fanatical adherence to his traditions."[28]

Thus the novel, and Sara's ongoing struggle, ends with ambiguity, with much left to do. And yet this is what the four faces of our life in the service of transformation are all about—always taking the next step in responding to new personal, political, historical, and sacred challenges.

PLAYING IN THE DARK: LISTENING TO THE SOURCES IN THE CRUCIBLE OF LIFE

The beauty of multicultural and feminist writing is that it is bold and free enough to step beyond the usual boundaries. We can have dialogues across cultures, genders, historical, and religious barriers. Therefore, I would like to carry on a dialogue between Alan Paton and Toni Morrison. Alan Paton, a white South African, wrote a truly courageous and utterly subversive book in *Too Late the Phalarope*.[29] In this novel he had the insight to do what Toni

Morrison so brilliantly discussed in her book, *Playing in the Dark*.[30] Morrison has given all of America a gift of a self portrait. Her main thesis is that as Americans, we can come to know ourselves in what we have been denying or repressing. As we "play in the dark" side of our lives, great secrets that have been cut off from us can now be integrated in the sense of healing our brokenness so that we can become whole. Morrison asks how it was possible for American authors to write as if there was no Africanist presence. Using many examples, she demonstrates that constant presence in the very absence of the African person.

In his writings, but particularly in *Too Late the Phalarope*, Alan Paton documents the cost of racism/tribalism/oppression, which deny the story of democracy by repressing the significant others in our lives and relegating them to the darker realms. In this novel, Pieter, the protagonist, has a silent and awkward relationship with his father. We soon learn that Pieter is two men—both strong and sensitive. His father hates the gentleness in Pieter: "For the truth was that he had fathered a strange son, who had all his father's will and strength, and could outride and outshoot them all, yet had all the gentleness of a girl . . . and a passion for the flowers of the veld and kloof. . . . Had he been one or the other . . . his father would have understood him better, but he was both."[31]

Slowly but inexorably, Paton takes us into the inner workings of the Van Vlaanderen family and into the most intimate details of their private lives. As a political novelist Paton is really exposing the soul of South Africa as it is tormented by its refusal to acknowledge its dark side: the black South African. It falls to Pieter to explore the hidden side of South African life and culture. He is attracted to a black woman, Stephanie. He cannot explain this attraction and is horrified by it. Like Julie in Rousseau's *La Nouvelle Hèloise* and Celie in *The Color Purple*, he does not want to listen to his inner voice, which is always heretical and can bring down the world. At one point Pieter wishes that he were like his friend Moffie, who dropped an injured woman in dismay once he realized that she was Malay or colored. He would be safe then from his own emotions, that is, his dark side.[32] But Pieter is not safe—he cannot block it out nor can the Afrikaner people continue to repress the cost of violence.

So great is the cost of repression in the story of tribalism in the service of deformation, that it means on the personal level killing crucial aspects of one's own personal face in order to continue violating others. Politically, it means excluding whole groups of human beings from the necessities of life, which involves the use of armed force, death, and violence. Historically, as these patterns and the story of deformation continue, life becomes fundamentally worse. The sacred face of the Dutch Reformed Calvinist

Afrikaner is the lord of nothing that justifies his oppression of "those others."

This drama's crushing logic is brought to a tragic reality when Pieter is asked by his father to accompany him on a picnic so that together they might find the phalarope, an elusive South African bird. As the father excitedly spots the bird, he points it out to Pieter. Pieter cannot see the phalarope. His father touches him so that he can guide him to where the bird is flying. But Pieter is unnerved and unmanned; he wants to cry.[33] His father never touched him. Why? Because his father believed that affection and touching and the muck of emotion were really signs of weakness. Who can afford to be weak in the presence of the black nation? To control black people, Pieter's father killed the gentleness in himself; but by so doing he also destroyed his ability to reach out and love his own son. Mr. Van Vlaanderen killed himself and those around him because he paid the price, perhaps unwittingly, but nevertheless the cost of being privileged, the oppressor, the wolf, the violator.

This is one of the saddest books that I have ever read. It spells out without mercy the destruction of the oppressor and the oppressed. Throughout the novel we are told that this is a nightmare of cosmic proportions, the political and historical story of a people in danger, and not just a personal and sacred drama. "And darkness came over the grass country, and over the continent of Africa, and over man's home and the earth, and over us all. And the sun went down, and never rose again."[34]

The members of the counter-tradition throughout history have always taught that the process of transformation that applies to the individual is also the journey of whole cultures and nations. Thus, time and again Paton ends a chapter with phrases such as: "And I write it all down here, the story of our destruction."[35]

The only hope is the coming of the light to the dark that was repressed. Pieter is betrayed, arrested, and exiled. His prominence in society forced people to ask: If this happened to one of our brightest and best, then what have we done? His father dies, representing the old dispensation, and the feminine as love comes forth as his mother lifts the shades and reopens the doors ordered shut so that Pieter's father could close out the world and create the *kraal*, or circle of defense, against the truth. But Pieter goes to his fate feeling guilty and confused. Like Luis in *La Carreta*, he believes that the tragedy was his fault; he was the deviant. Therefore, feelings of individual guilt and failure that are not shared by the society at large preserve the structural neuroses of the drama of racism as a form of tribalism.

Toni Morrison's hope is that if we risk playing in the dark, Americans will not see individual transformation as enough. Rather, the agenda of the whole nation must be to acknowledge its dark and terrifying but also its creative underside. By so doing, this society might come to realize the need to include what was repressed so that the coming together of the opposites of the light and dark will produce a new and more loving society as we re-create the story of democracy.

In the language of the theory, America and South Africa as societies must travel the journey and relive the story of democracy in the service of transformation. Together we must leave behind racist containers, listen to the darkness of the inner voice in Act I, Scene 2, and break with those practicing tribalism and oppression in Act II, Scene 1. But unlike Pieter, we must not see transformation as an issue of individual kindness dispensed at whim. This is the liberal game, which leaves the system of oppression intact and even strengthened. What is necessary is to enter Act II, Scene 2 and to let go the whole drama of racism, which means the structural and undemocratic privilege of the dominant group. Unless this happens, we will continue as in Paton's novel to place the welfare office in the old butcher shop, where the hook to hang the carcass still hangs to receive its victims. This means that liberalism continues to justify the dominant group's privilege while seeking to defuse the rage of racism. If the dispossessed continue to protest, they are regarded as ungrateful and deserve the consequences of their refusal to accept the largess of the dominators. Violence is ultimately justified to protect the dominators' privilege and property because the dispossessed resisted being bought off: "It is their own fault; after all that we have done for them" are the charges. Thus, due to the fragility and dishonesty of the ways of life of emanation and incoherence, liberals enter into deformation; they maim and kill to keep what is theirs. For this reason liberalism is actually a rebellion; it is a response to growing incoherence but it refuses to respond to the unrest by structural change. It cannot do this because the structure of privilege is a sacred drama that possesses our soul; by its very logic the drama cannot be given up, only made more or less powerful. For this reason people committed to transformation must empty themselves of the drama of privilege, of the fragile ways of life that can only spawn benevolent dictators or violent tyrants, but not honest and moral persons. In Act II, Scene 2, the demand of the journey is to let go the entire drama, that is, the whole structure, to create a more loving and just alternative in Act III, the story of democracy in the service of transformation.

The works of women and people of color provide us with very powerful images of the sacred and the political as they retell for our time the story of democracy as our journey of transformation. Like Silko's Betonie in *Ceremony*, the best storytellers plot the new forms of destruction that make life fundamentally worse so that they can respond with the stories and the ceremonies of transformation. This is simultaneously a personal, political, historical, and sacred act of the creative imagination, which means that each of us must not only be hearers of the story but be in turn inspired to tell our story. In this way, our personal, creative imagination is free to forge a new political environment that initiates the entry of our stories as another face of the sacred into history as a fundamentally more loving reality. This is what the archetypal story of democracy is all about.

CONCLUSION

All of us, in the final analysis, are like Celie, the heroine of Alice Walker's superb novel. In telling the story of Celie, Walker describes a woman who persisted and eventually resisted the domestic violence of her patriarchal husband. Because she had the courage to break the connections that were destroying both of them, Albert was also given a new opportunity to discover the meaning of his own life. But this is not just Celie breaking with Albert, or Pieter struggling with repression in *Too Late the Phalarope*, not just Doña Gabriela and Juanita outwitting the jaws of the mechanistic system of racism in *La Carreta*. Neither is it Tayo alone saving himself and his people from the death of physical and spiritual drought in *Ceremony*, or only Sara Smolinsky struggling against the patriarchal father in *Bread Givers*, or just Sandra Cisneros's Cleofilas liberating herself from the story of patriarchal abuse in *Woman Hollering Creek*, or only Attaway's three brothers in *Blood on the Forge* standing alone against the deformation of exclusion and exploitation. It is all women and men from all cultural backgrounds unveiling themselves and telling their stories; it is a new people coming out of Egypt into the parting of the ways as they embark anew on the journey that was given to us from the beginning by which to transform our lives. It is African Americans, Latinas, Latinos, Asian Americans, American Indians, European Americans, and women as women dealing with the daily transformation of their lives as they struggle to hold together the story of democracy and their authenticity in these days of deep troubles. It is the sacred discovering that it has a brown, white, red, black, yellow, feminine face. It is, in the end, each of us leaving behind the security of the known and rowing across a dark river with a deep and abiding faith that when we reach the other side, there will be a fundamentally more loving and compassionate reality to receive us. This is a reality that we cannot know or grasp ahead of our arrival because it is a new creative union of the feminine and masculine, of men and women of all cultures fulfilled by the coming together of differences in a new and sacred democratic union.

NOTES

1. Iris M. Young, *Justice and the Politics of Difference* (Princeton: Princeton University Press, 1990).

2. Marshall Berman, *The Politics of Authenticity* (New York: Atheneum Press, 1972).

3. Elaine Pagels, *The Gnostic Gospels* (New York: Random House, 1979), p. xv.

4. Leslie Marmon Silko, *Ceremony* (New York: Penguin Books, 1977), p. 2.

5. Manfred Halpern, "A Theory of Transformation and the Archetypal Drama of the Conquering Hero. Paper presented at the annual meeting of the American Political Science Association, San Francisco, September 1, 1990.

6. Manfred Halpern, "The Human Being in the Image of God: A Cosmos of Creative Participation" in his unpublished manuscript, *Transformation: Its Theory and Practice in Personal, Political, Historical, and Sacred Being.* See also David T. Abalos, "Rediscovering the Sacred Among Latinos: A Critique from the Perspective of a Theory of Transformation, *Latino Studies Journal* 3:2 (May 1992).

7. Henri Corbin, *Creative Imagination in the Sufism of Ibn Arabi* (Princeton: Princeton University Press, 1981).

8. Humberto Solas, *Lucía*, produced in Havana, Cuba, 1968.

9. Young, *Justice*, pp. 15–38.

10. For a further elaboration, see David T. Abalos, "Multicultural and Gender Inclusive Education in the Service of Transformation," *Latino Studies Journal* 2:1 (January 1991), pp. 3–18.

11. As quoted in Berman, *Politics*, p. 30.

12. William Attaway, *Blood on the Forge* (New York: Monthly Review Press, 1987), pp. 285–86.

13. Silko, *Ceremony*.

14. Ibid., pp. 231–32.

15. Ibid., p. 246.

16. Ibid., p. 247.

17. Ibid., p. 253.

18. Ibid., pp. 261–62.

19. Sandra Cisneros, *Woman Hollering Creek and Other Stories* (New York: Random House, 1991).

20. Alice Walker, *The Color Purple* (New York: Washington Square Press, 1982).

21. Ibid., p. 187.

22. Ibid., p. 193.

23. Ibid., p. 236.

24. Ibid., p. 201.

25. Ibid., p. 246.

26. Anzia Yezierska, *Bread Givers* (New York: Persea Books, 1975).

27. Ibid., pp. 295–97.

28. Ibid., p. 296.

29. Alan Paton, *Too Late the Phalarope* (New York: Charles Scribner's Sons, 1953).

30. Toni Morrison, *Playing in the Dark* (Cambridge, Mass.: Harvard University Press, 1992).

31. Paton, *Too Late*, pp. 2–3.

32. Ibid., pp. 125–26.

33. Ibid., p. 213.

34. Ibid., p. 215.

35. Ibid., p. 3.

CHAPTER 3

The Four Faces of Our Being
in Multicultural and Women's Scholarship

Not every artist is a special kind of human being, but every human
being is a special kind of artist.
                              —Meister Eckhart (c.1260–1327)

Each of us can participate in discovering which stories in our society are
being practiced, how to uproot them if necessary, and how to create
fundamentally new and more compassionate stories. Indeed, culture is not
a mechanical handing on of values and stories, but rather the evaluation and
transformation of these stories as we move from one generation to the next.
That is because these are not just stories; they are sacred stories because
they are grounded in underlying forming sacred sources, the realm of
archetypes. All of our stories are enacted and lived in the context of deeper,
underlying archetypal ways of life—the ways of life of emanation, incoherence, deformation, and transformation, which will now be further elabo-
rated. As we have seen, the only story and way of life that demands our
conscious, critical participation is the story of transformation. Thus the
quality of our life and work will be determined by the way of life in which
we live the archetypal stories of our society.[1]

At stake here is our guidance of ourselves and others not merely to inherit
a cultural past but to actually create history. Whenever a culture or a
community stops taking responsibility for the archetypal stories they live,

when they unconsciously repeat and re-enact them, such a society becomes ahistorical.[2] Thus, the past and history are not synonymous. To simply repeat inherited stories is to live as if we were amnesiac. We have lost personal involvement and the right to participate. The past is what shaped us to be who we are, but history is more than just living and repeating a story or a common cultural inheritance. To be historical means making a personal, political, and sacred decision to create new turning points that make life fundamentally more human and just. Our stories possess us whenever we merely inherit them and live them unconsciously. We need to be participants in the uprooting, creation, and nurturance of archetypal stories.

THE FOUR FACES OF THE STORIES OF OUR LIVES

We and the stories of our lives have four faces: the personal, political, historical, and sacred faces. These four faces of our being change dramatically when we practice them in the service of the four underlying ways of life. These sacred forces are called archetypal not because they are eternal and perfect but because they are the necessary underlying forming sources for all of concrete reality.[3] But it is not only the power of the sacred force of our stories that explains their great hold over us. As we have seen in Chapter 1, the presence of these underlying sources points to far more sacred, deeper, and powerful forces than our allegedly secular culture is willing to acknowledge. The quality and meaning of our stories and of the four faces of our being are determined by these deeper underlying sacred dramas in whose service we create and live our stories. There are four archetypal, underlying ways of life in the service of which we concretely enact the stories of our life: the ways of life of emanation, incoherence, deformation, and transformation.

The three ways of life of emanation, incoherence, and deformation are actually arrested fragments of the core drama of transformation. Only this one sacred drama, the story of transformation, does not possess us because it needs our conscious, critical, and political participation. This underlying drama of transformation constitutes the core of the cosmos of being human. We call the story of transformation the core drama because each time "we move ourselves and advance with our neighbors successively through the three Acts of the drama, we reach the heart of life—a wholeness of all four faces of our being that leads to love and justice for the problem at hand."[4]

The four faces of the stories of our lives will now be applied to help us to analyze and understand multicultural and women's literary works as concrete faces of the archetypal story of democracy. This new scholarship represents a new and emerging culture and a redefinition of American democracy.

CREATING A MULTICULTURAL AND
GENDER-INCLUSIVE SOCIETY

The world has changed since Conrad and Dickens in ways that have surprised, and often alarmed, metropolitan Europeans and Americans, who now confront large non-white . . . populations in their midst, and face an impressive roster of newly empowered voices asking for their narratives to be heard.[5]

Henry Louis Gates, Jr. taught me how important it is to see literacy as crucial in the creation of the self. Literacy in this sense means telling one's own story. In his study of slave narratives, he found that the struggle for literacy was a demand to be seen as a self, a civilized person, a member of the human race, a creator of history for one's people, and as a protest against the inhumanity of slavery. The motto of these slave narratives, as well as that of the history of African Americans in this country, can be said to have been: "I write myself, therefore I am."[6] In regard to the four faces of our being, Gates points out that each person is unique, but we also have a political face that unequivocally demands that what we can and need to do together is shape an environment that includes all people and thereby end the invisibility inherent in all forms of oppression. We also enact our historical face by creating a new turning point that allows ordinary people to shape a new and better life. The inspiration for this creativity emerges from our deepest sources, which demonstrates that each of us has a sacred face.

In a manner similar to Gates's work, Humberto Solas demonstrates in his film, *Lucía*, as we have seen in Chapter 2, how Lucía achieves literacy at the very moment of her declaration of freedom from a patriarchal marriage.[7] With her first words Lucía begins to tell her story, and her words lead to action. This is what authentic praxis is all about—the theory and practice of transformation.

In multicultural and women's literature there is a clear breaking with the old, established stories of the curriculum that wounded so many by making them invisible and a move to create new stories that weave a richer and more complete history of our nation and culture. The poverty of the present curriculum is in what it leaves out. The emergence of previously excluded stories points us to the creation of a new ethos of inclusion, participation, mutual respect, affection, and recognition of otherness while celebrating our common humanity. What is really happening here is that we are redefining and re-creating in a new concrete way the archetypal story of democracy. As a nation we are still growing into democracy as part of the great experiment.

Sandra Cisneros deals with themes found in the writings of Toni Morrison, Amy Tan, Alice Walker, Anzia Yezierska, and Adrienne Rich, to mention only a few. What is so very powerful about these authors is that they assess and reject the destructive stories in their own racial and cultural background as well as the wounding stories of this society. They realize that the heart of the matter is to create a new culture out of those stories that are conducive to transformation in all cultures. To better understand this process, let us consider an inherited story that has played a crucial role in all cultures, the drama of patriarchy. This is a cultural story that most of us, from whatever cultural heritage, have experienced but seldom understood on a deeper level. It is not enough to say no to patriarchy or to any other story of our life because the stories of our lives are sacred stories that possess us if we remain unconscious of them. They are archetypal dramas. And archetypes, as we have seen, are the necessary underlying forming sacred sources of all concrete reality. The experience of patriarchy is the concrete manifestation of an archetypal drama. To struggle with particular patriarchal fathers, husbands, or bosses is only the beginning. We also have to confront the deeper story, the archetypal roots of the story in underlying sacred sources. Almost always we confront only the concrete face of the archetypal story of patriarchy in our actual fathers. Because we have failed to engage the story on the deeper, sacred level, it continues to manifest itself generation after generation.

When Cleofilas in *Woman Hollering Creek*[8] refuses to continue the story of patriarchy in her life, as a Latina/Mejicana/Chicana, she takes on the ahistorical tyranny of the inherited past that she was socialized into in Act I, Scene 1 in the service of emanation and initiates the most fundamental story of her and our lives, the core drama of transformation. In resisting the physical abuse of her husband that tradition had told her was her personal fate, her political duty to uphold, her historical heritage, and God's way of testing women, Cleofilas leaves Act I, in the service of emanation, and enters Act II, Scenes 1 and 2. She rejects not only this particular man and this concrete story but the underlying legitimization of her oppression, the story of patriarchy, which has deeper sacred roots because it draws its possessive strength from the sacred drama of the way of life of emanation.

By saying no and leaving, she manifested a new self, the emergence of a woman who dared to be a person. She practiced a new political face by rejecting the social and political structures that gave a man the right to assault her, even in this country. By leaving she created a new turning point for herself and other women that decisively stated that they would take responsibility for a new history; the sacred was no longer found outside of her but within herself. Cleofilas learns that to create a new history, a new story, and therefore a new democratic culture, it is necessary that our historical face be penetrated by a fundamentally new, more just and loving, personal, political, and sacred face.

A woman discovers her voice by choosing to create a new *herstory* based on the value of the lives of women. She is grounded in this great refusal and affirmation by her new feminine and sacred face. But Cisneros is writing this new woman into history as a Mexican American woman. Thus, whatever issue she faces from her past and in her present situation or wherever she finds herself in this country, Cisneros wants this new woman to be free to practice the fullness of the democratic story by protesting and creating a new and more compassionate story in all aspects of her life.

In a similar vein Gloria Anzaldúa dares to be disrespectful with an inherited past in Mexico and the United States that denied the importance of the lives of women. The title of her book underlines this challenge: *Making Faces (Haciendo Caras)*.[9] One of the most disrespectful things that you could possibly do in a traditional Latino family was to show your feelings to people in authority, especially your parents. In all of her writings, Anzaldúa practices a politics of resistance, rebellion, and disrespect. She consistently resists the stories of patriarchy, racism, and homophobia. Her criticism of multicultural education, if it is only another ploy to bring back the melting pot, is a challenge that has to be taken seriously.

Tayo, the protagonist in *Ceremony*,[10] whom we met in Chapters 1 and 2, is the prototype of the person of color caught in the agony of double consciousness described by W.E.B Dubois. Tayo is the son of a Native American woman and a white man who journeys to create the four faces of his being in a society that does not honor the stories of people of color. Before he can create the personal, political, historical, and sacred faces of his being, Tayo has to deconstruct the inherited story of tribalism and the denial of his worth that he received from the wider society. According to the logic of the story of tribalism, there are only five ways by which the allegedly superior can treat "those others": as invisible, inferior, assimilated "honorary whites," excommunicated ingrates, or dangerous enemies worthy of extermination.

Throughout the novel Tayo vomits, symbolizing the struggle to purge himself of the poison of self-hatred inherent in all forms of tribalism and domination. At one point, Tayo cuts the wire that prevents him from reclaiming his stolen inheritance left to him by his Uncle Josiah. As Tayo fights to free the cattle, he becomes conscious of his reluctance to admit that they were stolen by white men, because as everyone knows, only brown people steal. As he cuts the wire he realizes that it is like stripping away the lies that held his mind and heart captive.[11] On his journey Tayo realizes that this is not just a personal task but a search for the means to end the drought that is devastating the land and the soul of his people. It is not only from our personal and sacred bodies or faces that we have to empty the poison of the story of tribalism; by reaching out toward others we enact our political and historical faces by fighting together to create a new and better present and future for the whole community.

One of the saddest books that I have read is Oscar Hijuelos's, *The Mambo Kings Play Songs of Love*.[12] It is the story of two brothers, each in his own way searching for the feminine. They represent men as children who are lost, fumbling, looking for love when as patriarchal men they are afraid of intimacy. Cesar delights in the conquest of women throughout the novel, but he dies in utter loneliness. Hijuelos seems to be saying that the current domination of Latina women by Latino men is bankrupt. We need to reject the traditional domination by men in male/female relationships. Rather than defining masculinity on the basis of power and control, it can be redefined to be an aggressiveness, that is, a stepping forward urgently to protect the humanity of the community in this country, which is suffering not only from patriarchy but also from racism and capitalism, which are incapable of providing equal access to opportunity.

In René Marques's *La Carreta*,[13] the journey of transformation takes a detour as a family wanders from its Puerto Rican roots. It then finds the right path again as the Puerto Rican women, symbolic of the feminine principle of liberation, rediscover the return to the sources of transformation. Luis, the oldest child, represents a whole generation of lost Puerto Rican youth, who are like orphans, looking for their mother or origins: "*Como un cabrito buscando a su mama.*" Luis is desperately searching for a source of love, nurturance, renewal, and redemption. As the play opens the family, all except *el viejo*, the old man, is leaving the land that their ancestors worked for generations. The grandfather chooses to remain behind as a guardian and witness to the transformative potential of the Puerto Rican soil and heritage that has been obscured by the cultural imperialism that Iris Young calls one of the five faces of oppression.[14] In reality the family, like Puerto Ricans in general, has been displaced from the land by economic and political factors beyond its control. But Luis has already abandoned the land as useless as he turns to *el misterio de la maquina*, the mystery of the machine or technology, the system that will provide success and meaning to their lives. They are on their way to San Juan in *la carreta*, the oxcart, to seek a better life.

But the urban experience, together with the encounter with the story of market society, or capitalism as the machine, is a disaster. Members of the family lose their way: Juanita turns to a world of fantasy, is raped, and has an abortion; Chaguito, the youngest son, turns to crime and goes to jail; and Doña Gabriela, the mother, is increasingly disheartened as she sees the members of the family lose their way. Luis cannot find permanent work; he sums up their sense of loss by stating: "Estoy como sin raíces," I feel rootless; "No encajo en ningún sitio," I can't catch on anywhere. To escape this despair they leave for the United States without Chaguito, who remains imprisoned.

In New York the family further deteriorates. Luis is caught in a web of self-hatred as he tries to assimilate and to fulfill the role that others have designed for him. His mother, Doña Gabriela, "Ya no regana," no longer scolds because her spirit has been broken. She has lost her authentic voice. Juanita becomes a prostitute and openly scorns the values of the past. Luis is trapped in a job with no future. In the final scene of the play, Luis is destroyed by a machine, "entrapado," trapped and ripped apart.

The play is a story about people who journey away from their roots and pursue someone else's story. It was a machine, a faceless bureaucratic system, that devoured the emotions, hopes, and joys of Luis so that he lost his desire to live. Luis failed to empty himself of his belief that if you are totally loyal to a system, it will reward you. He replaced love for the land with the exploitation of the factory. He either could not or did not want to see that he was being victimized by colonial forces, both cultural and economic, and convinced himself that it was his own fault; he was the deviant, the neurotic, the failure. In this way the system is excused and continues to wound and kill. But at the conclusion of the play, Juanita is shocked by Luis's death into the realization of what impersonal systems do to all of us. Juanita and Doña Gabriela decide to return to Puerto Rico to bury Luis, to empty themselves of the stories of capitalism and tribalism in Act II, Scene 2 and to return to their sources of renewal in Act III, Scenes 1 and 2: "Y hundiré mis manos en la tierra colorada," And I will bury my hands in the red earth and they will be strong again.[15] At this point Juanita makes a remarkable personal, political, historical, and sacred statement that shows us the four faces of our being in the service of transformation:

This has nothing to do with returning to the land to live like dead people. Now we know that the world does not change by itself. But that we are the ones who must change it. We are going to live like people with dignity, as our grandfather used to say. With our heads held high. Knowing that there are issues for which we must fight. Knowing that as God's children we are all equal. And my children will learn things that I never learned, things that they don't teach you in school. In such a way we will return to our barrio! You and I, mama, standing strong as we were before on our own land, and Luis resting in peace in the land."[16]

Finally, I would like to consider a more recent work, Laura Esquivel's *Like Water for Chocolate*.[17] Laura Esquivel's novel (also made into a very successful movie) provides us with an excellent example of seeing how the various stories of our lives hang together to create a web of meaning, a whole cultural context. It also demonstrates how we can intervene in our cultures to practice transformation. But it is, in addition, a work of art that shows us the need for continuous transformation in all aspects of our life.

The struggle of the protagonist, Tita, against Mama Elena and the story of matriarchy was quite heroic and ultimately transformative. But it was Tita's relationship to Pedro and its final unfolding that demonstrates the failure to achieve transformation in another key aspect of her life. Pedro and Tita's relationship was permeated by the story of romantic love in alliance with the story of patriarchy. Romantic love in this historical and cultural setting is in collusion with patriarchy because both of these dramas, although they begin in the service of emanation, ultimately end by diminishing women and therefore are in the service of deformation. Specifically, romantic love turns the lovers into projected fantasies so that they might possess each other. Nobody is home in this drama because each seeks to lose who they are in the other. When the relationship breaks or is threatened, one partner or the other feels betrayed and/or suicidal: I cannot live without you, you are my only reason for living.

Because Mama Elena demanded that Tita as the youngest should dedicate her life to her care, Tita was not allowed to marry Pedro. Instead, he married her sister, Rosaura, in order to be close to Tita. In this way Pedro, and to some extent, Tita, use Rosaura for their end. There are several hidden liaisons between Tita and Pedro throughout the years. Finally, Rosaura dies, allowing Tita and Pedro to express their love openly. Following a dinner, Tita and Pedro find themselves alone and realize that for the first time in their lives they can make love freely. They proceed to make passionate love. But Tita checks her passion because she does not want to let it totally consume her: "She didn't want to die. She wanted to explore these emotions many more times. This was only the beginning."[18] Pedro did not succeed in this and dies in the midst of ecstasy, as he entered a luminous tunnel "that shows us the way that we forgot when we were born and calls us to recover our lost divine origin. The soul longs to return to the place it came from leaving the body lifeless."[19] Now the sacred story of romantic love takes over with its relentless deadly logic.

In the language of the theory of transformation, Tita had already success-fully emptied herself in Act II, Scene 2 of her mother, of the story of matriarchy, the other face of patriarchy, when she told her mother's spirit to get out and never return. Having experienced the triumph of being a person in Act III, Scenes 1 and 2 in relationship to her mother, Tita now fails in the struggle with romantic love. Tita no longer wants to live because Pedro is dead. She is traumatized, paralyzed, unable to feel, utterly devas-tated. She does not hesitate long; she must be with Pedro, because alone she is nothing.

With Pedro died the possibility of ever again lighting her inner fire, with him went all the candles. She knew that the natural heat that she was now feeling would cool little by little, consuming itself as rapidly as if it lacked fuel to maintain itself. Surely Pedro had died at the moment of ecstasy. . . . She regretted not having done the same. . . . She could no longer feel anything. . . . She would but wander . . . alone, all alone.[20]

Tita rushes to feel the strong emotion that would light all of the candles within her that she had earlier checked because she did not want to lose herself. Earlier in the novel we learned that Tita had been told by a friend that each of us has powerful passions, or candles, that we have to treat with respect so that they do not consume us. Thus Tita begins eating the matches and seeking to light her candles or passion in order to be together with Pedro in death: "There at its entrance was the luminous figure of Pedro waiting for her. Tita did not hesitate. She let herself go to the encounter . . . again experiencing an amorous climax, they left together for the lost Eden. Never again would they be apart."[21]

Caught by the story of romantic love allied to patriarchal loyalty, Tita committed suicide. In a terrifying, yet eerily fascinating scene, Tita and Pedro, together with the whole ranch, are burned in an orgy of flames in the service of deformation. Tita did not want to live; her life was now over because she was still living Pedro's story. And yet Tita had experienced transformation, as we have seen, in relationship to her mother. But in regard to her relationship to Pedro, Tita gave up her self, her own story, so the story of romantic love in alliance with the story of patriarchy totally consumed her in the flames.

This is very disturbing because the message for women is that they need a man to ultimately find themselves. If that man dies, the woman dies with him. In the fantasy of romantic love, this makes sense because you are nothing without your lover. You have not found yourself but given yourself to the other; if they die, or leave, you are devastated since you have no self apart from him or her. Tita was unable to deal with a new situation because this story says that our lives belong to others and that apart from our sources of emanation, we have no real meaning or existence. Due to this wounded-ness, the story of romantic love renders men and women permanent victims by diminishing their humanity and therefore enters into the service of deformation.

Yet there is a woman in the novel, Gertrudis, who clearly refused to surrender her own life and passion to a tradition. She is an example of women who refuse to sacrifice their lives to satisfy the needs of others. She is symbolic of the reality that in all historical periods there have been women willing to take the risk of transformation. In a marvelous scene in the novel, Gertrudis rebels against her repressive past as she rides away with her lover, nude and on horseback with her arms outstretched to embrace life.

It is hard to say if Esquivel approved of Tita's choice, but the novel ends with a sense of triumph in the belief that love conquers all. If this is the message, it is symptomatic of the failure of some of our current artists, philosophers, social scientists, theologians, and writers to provide us with alternative stories by which to guide us in transforming our lives. There is an alternative to romantic love, the story of mutual love, of transforming love that affirms the sacredness of men and women equally. In the story of transforming love, women and men love in order to find themselves and each other, not, as in the case of the story of romantic love, to lose themselves in one another. Thus when a relationship of transforming love ends, either due to death or to some other reason, the partner is deeply hurt but not devastated because she or he has an authentic self that was discov-ered in the relationship. In this story, each person must be able to discover his or her own story and to help each other to discover that uniqueness; then they can create a third story together.

CONCLUSION

It is up to us from within our classrooms to critique and analyze the stories of the many cultures that make up our nation with one criterion in mind: What is conducive to the story of democracy in the service of transforma-tion? We are free to discontinue those stories of the culture, such as tribalism, patriarchy, and the market society, that are destructive and to choose to create and nurture those stories, such as participatory democracy, mutual love, and our personal face as another face of God, that protect our humanity and affirm the political imperative of discerning what we can and need to do together.

A community and culture resting on this foundation will be strong because the individual members who constitute the body politic are each valued in their uniqueness. Such a community will be strong because each group respects the other without giving up the right to be critical of each other. We need each other in order to be fully who we are in our individuality and fully who we are in our common humanity. Unfortunately, we are often like Robinson Crusoe, who, after degrading Friday, came to realize that he owed his humanity to him.[22]

Once we have faced ourselves, vomited out the poison of living unconsciously the destructive stories inherited from our culture, we feel strong and free to discover and practice anew the story of democracy in the service of transformation. We need a multicultural and gender-fair consciousness practiced within a democratic culture. A democratic culture in the service of transformation is a persistent personal, political, historical, and sacred creation of the fundamentally more human and loving in all aspects of our lives.

In the final analysis, we all know as American citizens that there is no one American story or one American culture or community.[23] We cannot build an identity on race, class, gender, religious allegiance, or national origin. I can only know what kind of people we are and the quality of the culture and the stories that we are living by asking the decisive question: In the service of what way of life are we living the stories of our life? The most authentic women and men who are creating a new story and culture in this country are those who live and practice the archetypal story of democracy in the service of transformation by caring deeply about others; they look for ways to make life fundamentally more human and just now, here, and today. Such men and women ask the question: Since each person is sacred, what is it that we need to do together to establish food co-ops, daycare centers, unions that truly protect the workers, political parties, medical clinics, develop self-esteem in our youth, end the devastating drop-out rate in our schools, establish mentoring programs, tutoring, scholarships and on and on? There is no end to the work of transformation. We always have to take the next step in creating the fundamentally new and better.

In the service of transformation, we can together as Native American Indians, European Americans, African Americans, Latinas and Latinos, Asian Americans, and women help to bring about a transforming American democracy and culture firmly grounded on uniqueness and diversity. As we struggle to transform our cultural story and uniqueness, each of us enriches the American experiment, which held out the promise of a fuller humanity for all of us. Yes, we are members of a community, but of a particular kind of community, because we live and practice the story of democracy in the service of transformation that awakens us to the deepest humanity in all of us.

NOTES

1. Manfred Halpern, "Why Are Most of Us Partial Selves? Why Do Partial Selves Enter the Road into Deformation?" Paper delivered at the annual meeting of the American Political Science Association, Washington, D.C., August 29, 1991.

2. Juan Gomez-Quiñones, *On Culture* (Los Angeles: UCLA, Chicano Studies Center Publications, n.d.), p. 7. See Kwame Anthony Appiah for a fine study that demonstrates the presence of many cultures in what we often mistake for one culture, in *In My Father's House: Africa in the Philosophy of Culture* (New York: Oxford University Press, 1992).

3. Manfred Halpern, "Toward an Ecology of Human Institutions: The Transformation of Self, World, and Politics in Our Time." Paper delivered at a national symposium, "Beyond the Nation State: Transforming Visions of Human Society," College of William and Mary, September 24–27, 1993, pp. 7–8.

4. Ibid., p. 11.

5. Edward Said, *Culture and Imperialism* (New York: Alfred A. Knopf, 1993), Introduction, p. xx.

6. Henry Louis Gates, Jr., ed., *Bearing Witness, Selections from African-American Autobiography in the Twentieth Century* (New York: Pantheon Books, 1992), p. 7; see also in this regard Gates's *The Signifying Monkey, A Theory of Afro-American Criticism* (New York: Oxford University Press, 1988), pp. 146–69.

7. Humberto Solas, *Lucía*, produced in Havana, Cuba, 1968. For an analysis of this film from the perspective of the theory of transformation, see David T. Abalos, *The Latino Family and the Politics of Transformation* (New York: Praeger, 1993), Chapter 5, and "Latino Female/Male Relationships: Strategies for Creating New Archetypal Dramas," *Latino Studies Journal*: (1990), pp. 48–69.

8. Sandra Cisneros, *Woman Hollering Creek and Other Stories* (New York: Random House, 1991), pp. 43–56.

9. Gloria Anzaldúa, ed., *Making Faces, Making Soul, Haciendo Caras* (San Francisco: Aunt Lute Foundation Book, 1990), Introduction.

10. Leslie Marmon Silko, *Ceremony* (New York: Penguin Books, 1986).

11. Ibid., p. 191.

12. Oscar Hijuelos, *The Mambo Kings Play Songs of Love* (New York: Harper and Row, 1989).

13. René Marques, *La Carreta* (Rio Piedras, Puerto Rico: Editorial Cultural, 1971).

14. Iris M. Young, *Justice and the Politics of Difference* (Princeton, N.J.: Princeton University Press, 1990), pp. 39–65.

15. Marques, *La Carreta*, p. 171.

16. Ibid., p. 172 (translation by the author).

17. Laura Esquivel, *Like Water for Chocolate* (New York: Doubleday, 1992).

18. Ibid., p. 244.

19. Ibid., p. 245.

20. Ibid., p. 244.

21. Ibid., p. 245.

22. Carlos Fuentes, "Writing in Time," *Democracy* 2:1 (1982), pp. 61–74.

23. In an earlier work I attempted to develop a way to see how a community of people of color, Latinas and Latinos in the United States, struggle with the issue of their unique culture in a multicultural context. See "The Personal, Political, Historical and Sacred Grounding of Culture: Some Reflections on the Creation of Latino Culture in the United States from the Perspective of a Theory of Transformation," paper delivered at a national conference on Latinos and Religion in the United States," Princeton University, April 15–18, 1993, and published as a chapter in *Old Masks, New Faces: Religion and Latino Identities*, Vol. 3, Anthony Stevens Diaz Arroyo and Gilbert Cadena, eds. (New York: Bildner Center, CUNY, 1994).

CHAPTER 4

The Relationship between Multicultural Scholarship and the Feminine as the Principle of Liberation and Transformation

We are experiencing in these days an extraordinary awakening that we can truly call a worldwide revolution. South Africa is undergoing a rebirth, coming forth out of the belly of the living dead, the system of apartheid. The Soviet Union as a political entity and threat is gone, and the Cold War is over. Eastern Europe is dying in its old form but through leadership and struggle most of the nations may be able to avoid the pitfalls of a deformative nationalism as in the case of Yugoslavia. China has broken the placenta in the midst of the flow of blood and water but has been temporarily caught in the birth canal due to the fear and violence of octogenarians who no longer know how to midwife permanent revolution and continuous creation. For some time now, throughout Latin America the theology of liberation has rejected the domesticated god of the powerful and has turned our focus on the god of new beginnings, the birth of the new woman and man.

Since the 1960s in this country, there is a new America being born out of the struggles of the Civil Rights movement, the women's movement, the movement of students, the gay and lesbian struggle, the emergence of Black Power, Brown Power, and the Native American Indian revolutions. The personal anger of so many individuals took on a political, historical, and sacred face as well. Old identities—Negro, Spanish American, Oriental, Red Man—were all dying because these were forms of internalized oppression based on others defining and preserving the status quo on the backs of the dispossessed.

We are all aware that if an individual or a group represses aspects of itself, what has been veiled does not go away but returns in an unconscious and very dangerous way. For this reason we, as people of color and women, are entering into a decisive stage in these revolutionary times. We cannot afford to exhaust ourselves in angry paroxysms over which we have no control. To do this is to enter into a permanent rebellion, that is, to allow the consciousness of the oppressor to continue to control us without creating a liberating alternative. In this way, we become stillborn or remain in the womb of the status quo because we legitimize the structures of oppression by not creating alternatives.

It was James Baldwin who reminded us to resist such sterile rebellion when he wrote, "The object of one's hatred is never, alas, conveniently outside but is seated in one's lap, stirring in one's bowels and dictating the beat of one's heart. And if one does not know this, one risks becoming an imitation—and, therefore, a continuation—of principles one imagines one-self to despise."[1] Or as Pogo said in 1955, "We have met the enemy and he is ourselves."

Rebellion is necessary as an initial step to break the spell of those who have held us in a container arrested in Act I of the story of transformation characterized by loyalty and uncritical obedience. But to remain locked in perpetual polarization in the first scene of Act II allows the powerful others in our lives to continue to dominate our consciousness. We are angry and want to get back at people and prove the system wrong. What happens is that we wake up one day and realize that the system is still dominating our choices. Eventually this breeds a form of self-hatred and self-destruction that prevents the birth of the self and community. The worst forms of this rebellion that end in deformation are everyday occurrences in our communities: people killing themselves with drugs, AIDS, alcohol, and other forms of death.

There is no intent here to blame the victim; what I am doing is exposing a kind of false consciousness that is hatched by a culture of domination. That message is that some are not worthy of better health, education, employment, and housing. After generations of this kind of exclusion from the resources of the society, many began to believe that it was their fault and so they developed self-doubt and even self-hatred. To escape the double bind of non-acceptance into the society of power and the stigmatization of their culture, race, and/or gender, too many saw assimilation into the structures of power as the answer.

This strategy was and is doomed because it assumes our entry into the story of tribalism, that is, an acceptance of superiority over alleged inferiority. Once hooked by this intellectual drug, people of color and women wanted to belong to the world of the wolves. But assimilation carries a heavy price in this society. Assimilation means to become like the other, the white, masculine system. The opposite side of the dialectic is the price we have to pay: To be like the powerful is not to be like ourselves. Thus, we cannot be born except in the image and likeness of the dominator. All of us have known this in our bones.

Many of us as people of color and women were taught to reject our traditions and to become like European Americans or whites. But we could not succeed in such an endeavor of self-erasure. After a while we did not know what it meant to be Native American Indian, Latina or Latino, African American, or Asian American. There is no such thing as a psychological vacuum. Thus, into this tortuous confusion arose a deformational inspiration: You will fulfill the image that the white man has engraved on your soul, you will become just another outsider and end by killing others and eventually being killed by your own kind.[2]

Too many of us have internalized the story of oppression. We allow the powerful to co-opt our anger against whites by using it for their purposes to strengthen the very system that has also been oppressing European Americans. The mistake to which many of us as people of color are vulnerable is to try to get revenge by doing to others what was done to us.[3]

I reject the inevitability of deformation in the form of revenge, self-hatred, and self-murder and choose to take the journey through the core drama of life, the story of transformation. This is a story in which we are invited to consciously participate with the deepest depths of our being in creating and moving toward a more just and compassionate society.[4] I also refuse to accept assimilation into the power structures of U.S society as the answer for women and people of color. We cannot in addition return to some golden age of security and ultimate truths.

THE BIRTH AND DEATH OF SACRED STORIES

Let us return to the symbolism with which we began: the eruption, birth, and archetypal emergence of a new and revolutionary world. This is at one and the same time a personal/psychological, biological, intellectual, religious, historical, and political upheaval.[5] All of these phenomena are aspects of life that are subject to the archetypal process of creation, nourishment, and destruction so that we might create anew.

To give an example, we know that in the biological realm, the fetus must go through a period of gestation and nourishment. But the second stage of transition through the birth canal is always dangerous; the child could be strangled by the umbilical cord, come out feet first as a breech birth, or suffer other complications. This stage of birth or withdrawal from the womb is necessary for the child. In like manner there is a psychological growth that follows this process: The pre-ego stage comes to an end with the expulsion from the security of the container. The ego is now an isolated, alienated, polarized ego. The reality of a second birth is complete only with the establishment of the new self in community with others, which is accomplished by living the story of transformation in all aspects of our being.

Some natural scientists have also known, at least intuitively, the archetypal nature of their work. All scientists are socialized into a paradigm, a vision of the world and of what constitutes nature. This socialization allows them to take their place in the community of scientists. Doubts inevitably arise with the emergence of anomalies or novelty in the second scene of Act I that cannot be reduced to the officially established understanding of how nature works. These doubts persist until the dominant paradigm enters into a crisis and competing paradigms or alternative explanations of the workings of nature emerge in Act II, Scenes 1 and 2. When the alternative paradigm is accepted, *a* revolution, not *the* revolution in science is completed in Act III, Scenes 1 and 2.

It is only one revolution, only one birth, only one more aspect of our ego because this is a cosmos of continuous creation. Any new birth into a new matrix is also the beginning of a new gestation and nourishment, so that the process is always a dialectic between *solve et coagula*, dissolving and re-forming, death and rebirth. Science as a task of human creativity can be used and abused. This highlights the responsibility of scientists to help build a more just and compassionate society precisely by refusing to hide behind the veil of value-free science and making a political choice to do science in the service of transformation.

On a larger societal, global level, the same archetypal process is at work. Just as on the physical/natural level the movement of tectonic plates created the Himalayas some thirty-six million years ago, so too deep archetypal processes, which are underlying sacred, forming sources, are responsible for the utterly revolutionary upheavals of our times.

MULTICULTURAL AND GENDER SCHOLARSHIP

I would like to focus on the emergence of multicultural and gender scholarship from the perspective of this deeper, ontological, sacred matrix.

We are living and participating in a process of birth and death. The story of the white, masculine, Western consciousness is dying. This is why the efforts of scholars like Harold Bloom to reassert the dominance and importance of Western civilization is really an indication of the fragility of the culture based on this consciousness. Cultures that are alive and thriving do not enter into morbid forms of defensiveness.

Let us look at the story of masculine, white, patriarchal consciousness and what it accomplished. Before it became the story in crisis, it represented the emergence of a new vision. That vision several thousand years ago constituted the breakthrough of a new but wounded consciousness. It gave birth to the Western mind by pulling itself out of the creative recesses of the feminine unconscious in order to forge a patriarchal domination.[6] The rejection of the Great Mother, of nature in order to dominate the cosmos through rational thought and science meant a separation, a detachment, an alienation from these origins. Western culture was decisively wounded by this primordial separation which is made visible in our patriarchal religion and emphasis on the individual's ego and freedom. It gave rise to warriors and free enterprisers who sought above all to dominate. To accomplish this, the masculine, white male had to repress the feminine and the people of color who were seen as backward precisely because they were not seen as the same kind of warriors.

Just as the collapse of the ancient-medieval cosmic ecclesiastical womb represented modern humanity's birth into the world of the Renaissance and Reformation, so too today we are witnessing a massive and radical collapse of all of our structures—cultural, philosophical, scientific, religious, political, psychological, moral, ecological.[7] This points to a deconstruction prior to the birth of a paradigm, a new archetypal story that is forming in the depths.

Thus, I would argue that what we are experiencing today in regard to scholarship, curriculum, and education represents the crisis of the old patriarchal, white, male consciousness. The scholarly shifts we are seeing represent an archetypal process that points to the revolutionary process taking place within the underlying forming sacred sources and within our personal depths as people of color and women. It is our task, together with our European American colleagues, to share in the work of creating the concrete expression of the fundamentally new.[8] Our questions and emphases in scholarship are not changing because it is a fad, a merely intellectual or politically correct movement, but because these new questions represent a change in the inner gestalt. Looking at ourselves and at the world afresh means that we see configurations, connections, nuances, and contours that were not there before because we had not created them. Therefore, new evidence falls into place, pertinent writings from the past are suddenly rediscovered: "The collective psyche seems to be in the grip of a powerful archetypal dynamic in which the long alienated modern mind is breaking through, out of the contractions of its birth process, out of its mind forg'd manacles, to rediscover its intimate relationship with nature and the larger cosmos."[9]

This emergence and formation of a new archetypal story is moving toward the articulation of a holistic, inclusive, participatory world view. I see much of the multicultural scholarship of people of color and of women as especially dedicated to warning us and preparing us for the death of the old story of patriarchal, male, white consciousness and marking out the journey ahead for us.

However, it is important to stress here that we must not be naively optimistic. The story of patriarchy may indeed be dying, but this drama and its adherents will not go down without great cost. In fact, patriarchy can be said to be very much alive since we know that every eleven seconds a child or woman is abused in the home. The greatest violence in our society is taking place in the bedrooms of this country. Again it is important to remind ourselves that we are engaging a sacred story that is dying. Because it has lost much of its emanational mystery, the adherents of this story now turn to violence to preserve this story, and thereby they practice deformation. As we have said, men and women together must empty themselves twice over, by not only rejecting the concrete manifestation of this archetypal drama in Act II, Scene 1, of a man dominating a woman, but they must also empty themselves in Act II, Scene 2 of the archetypal story in the service of a deeper way of life that possesses the souls of both men and women, the story of patriarchy. I am optimistic that we can indeed do this but I am less hopeful when it means that we will pay the price necessary to reject this inherited story. Our entire society is permeated by this archetypal story. Having made these cautionary qualifications, I would like to continue to consider what the emerging liberation might be like.

I have been emphasizing feminine and maternal, nurturing language. This is very conscious since what I am about to argue is that the male, white patriarchal consciousness constitutes only a fragment of what it means to be human. It is bankrupt because it successfully repressed the feminine. Consequently we are left as partial selves. Thus, the crisis of modern "man" is essentially a masculine crisis that is moving toward a historic and momentous resolution in the phenomenal rise of the feminine in all cultures.[10] It is no accident that Taylor Branch's excellent study on the Martin Luther King, Jr. years is titled *Parting the Waters*.[11] This period was an epochal event initiating the birth of a people. *Men of Maize*, by Miguel

Angel Asturias, captures the sense of loss of the Mayan Indians as the market economy, permeated with the pursuit of self-interest and power in the name of "free" enterprise, penetrates their culture. It thereby denies the ecology relationship between nature and human beings and rejects the non-rational, mystery, and ambiguity, the imagination, emotions, instincts, the body, nature, women.[12]

Carol Gilligan has taught us that separation, individuation, and polarization alarm women and call forth a response of connectedness, intimacy, and interdependence.[13] The striving of upwardly mobile men to get to the top makes sense only in a paradigmatic archetypal world in the service of incoherence arrested in Act II, Scene 1, where intimacy is a hindrance to the pursuit of self-interest and power.

I have been deeply attracted to the works of Miguel Angel Asturias, René Marques, Michael Dorris, and Naguib Mahfouz—a Guatemalan, a Puerto Rican, a Native American Indian, and an Egyptian male—who all write with great sensitivity and insight about women and their lives. Each of these men has intuited as artists the archetypal process and the terrible cost of the masculine, autonomous, individualistic ego and its corresponding structures. These four writers speak of the dialectic of the struggle between the feudal and the modern, the masculine/feminine, the rural/urban, the machine/nature, the individual/community, the human and the sacred. In each of these works women and the feminine represent transformation and liberation.[14]

Why are we suddenly rediscovering William Attaway's *Blood on the Forge* or Zora Neale Hurston's *Their Eyes Were Watching God*[15] unless they strike a deep archetypal chord both within us and outside of us? These works remind us that when we tear ourselves from the land, the other, the feminine, nature, the instincts, the emotions, and the sacred, we repress our humanity and our wholeness. But this is not just a cyclical return of the repressed or a compensation for what was lost.[16] The story of transformation demands that we fulfill all three of its acts so that breaking away in Act I from the closed world of final truth, emptying ourselves in Act II, Scene 2, of the inherited, sacred stories that have crippled us and the partial ways of life in which we lived the stories of our life, and in Act III the experience of a new wholeness, ends in a rediscovery, a reuniting with the ground of our being as the rebirth of the self. In the matrix of this rebirth we rediscover, reclaim, reinvent, re-create the feminine, nature, the mystery of life, of soul. Now the embrace of the feminine and the reuniting of the masculine and the feminine as co-equal principles of our humanity is no longer fusion and immersion in an emanational, primitive, pre-ego, unconscious unity because "the long evolution of human consciousness has prepared it to be capable of embracing the ground of its own being freely and consciously."[17]

To reclaim the repressed feminine and excluded cultures, the Western mind must undergo an ego death.[18] This demands radically authentic men and women of all races and cultures who are heroic precisely in their letting go of the masculine world and its habits. Mutuality replaces domination. To allow ourselves to be penetrated by the feminine, to surrender to the feminine is to allow the spirit to dwell within us and to make of us temples or sacred vessels wherein the fundamentally new and better is being born afresh.

Again, I stress that the great marriage or *heirgamos* (divine marriage) that reunites the masculine and feminine is the great challenge of our time—the fulfillment of the archetypal process that was frozen for centuries by the domination of the white, masculine consciousness, which could not bring about the rebirth of the fundamentally more loving and compassionate. I see leadership in this rebirth and completion of the process as the work of people of color and women because at this point they are perhaps more sensitive to the effects of domination. To accomplish this task we have to choose consciously to reject the poison of self-hatred that led to assimilation and the resulting denial of our roots. Unless we take our authentic selfhood back, we will only be part of the dying patriarchal world.

To take ourselves back is a personal, political, historical, and sacred task. This we do by telling our stories, by returning to our sources, our instincts, our soul, our body, our intuitions, our feminine. Redefining ourselves is a personal affirmation and a political act because it empowers us from within to reject the scholarship and the society that made us invisible. Telling our stories is a historical act because it takes up the story of an interrupted archetypal process that did not allow us to be born again; in the process of self-discovery we become a new face of the sacred.

Anzia Yezierska, in *Bread Givers*, tells the story of Jewish women in the early part of the twentieth century.[19] Sara's rejection of her father's domination was more than a personal act; by resisting her father she was also passing judgment on the whole array of political, cultural, historical, and religious structures enacted within the drama of patriarchy that legitimized the domination of women. Sara's rebellion became a revolution, the creation of a fundamentally new and better life, because she validated and blessed her own life as a new manifestation of the sacred. In the act of writing such a novel, Yezierska posed the question of why women were controlled and voiceless for so long. Who benefited from this corruption of powerlessness, and why do women continue to participate in their own crippling as Sara's sisters did?

Not to resist this invisibility, this imposed silence, is to confirm the patriarchal wound in the culture. We must reject the history of the powerful, who lied by telling partial truths. Finally, we and the sacred are called upon to co-create the world. In this cooperation we become as gods, who cannot and must not live in fear of the white, masculine, grey-bearded, cultural god. We come to recognize that god, the sacred source of all sources, has an infinite number of faces and that our deepest source now has a black, yellow, red, brown, and feminine face because we provided it.

DENIAL OF THE FEMININE: A FORM OF SELF-WOUNDING

All of us in our society have been deeply affected by white, male consciousness. This means that as people of color and women, we did not escape being colonized by the consciousness of the oppressor. Indeed, I would contend that to the extent that white males accepted their perspective as the only truth, they were also crippled. I would like to address at this point the effect that male domination has had on male/female relationships among people of color.

The influence of the drama of patriarchy on people of color resulted in rejection of the feminine by both men and women. I am convinced that men of color have such a difficult time with women because the majority of us cannot accept women as equals. This domination is condoned in most, if not all, of our cultures. But the psychological and political results of assimilating into the white, male consciousness have been an even sadder drama for men of color. This is a tragic story because men of color are doubly wounded and made more incapable of achieving fulfillment. It is therefore not only patriarchal consciousness but also the Western European form of patriarchy that is the issue here.

A distinction must be made between the forms of patriarchy practiced by the West after the Industrial Revolution and the much older forms of patriarchy. What characterized the more ancient forms of patriarchy was the reduction of women to purely gender roles and a situation of male domination. Women were inferior to men but they were considered as necessary, in their proper place. The more recent strain of patriarchy developed within the Western nation state, especially under the influence of science and technology, was more destructive. As the drive to control nature became more pronounced, and as the market society led to an increased division between the public and the private realm of the home, women were increasingly considered a source of cheap labor or superfluous and unproductive. Eventually, in advanced industrialized societies, women were reduced to being consumers rather than semi-partners in the preparation of goods. If we push the logic of technology to its ultimate point, as David Noble has written, it leads to a world for which men have long fantasized, where life could be artificially and technologically reproduced: "In vitro fertilization and embryo transplant are, after all, only steps toward the artificial womb—a womb for men. After a thousand years, the obsessive scientific pursuit of a motherless child remains the telltale preoccupation of a womanless world."[20] This kind of development in the story of patriarchy leaves women extremely vulnerable. As men feel more threatened by the success of the women's movement, violence and attacks against women can be expected to continue to increase dramatically.

A Latino, African American, Asian American, or American Indian culture that is based on the story of patriarchy is stunted, destructive, and incomplete because it subordinates the feminine. This is certainly bad enough, but to then assimilate into and accept the more recent and deadlier forms of patriarchy of the Western, white male is not only to further diminish the feminine but to exclude it. To deny the feminine means that current female/male relationships legitimize the structural violence that gives power to men and permission to abuse and exclude women. If we are cut off from our deepest archetypal sources, we have no ground from which to counter the institutions of deformation. Therefore, women and men of color have to go home again to the sources within ourselves to rediscover the feminine within our own inner depths.

To be a whole person is to be both masculine and feminine for both men and women. By feminine or masculine I do not mean some human trait that we can arbitrarily designate as feminine or masculine. There has never been a single or monolithic way or even just a few ways to express the masculine or the feminine. As I understand these two terms, they represent two faces within each human being that have been radically deformed through the politics of gender roles that attribute to women certain social, personal, and political roles and others to men. Thus, the masculine and feminine that make sense only as opposites that coincide in wholeness are both crippled when separated into fragments. On a deeper level the words masculine and feminine represent underlying archetypal forming sources that shape the patterns of our lives. Thus, we are in a process of continuous creation as we seek to give new and creative concrete forms to the feminine and masculine in our daily lives. For this reason all of us, men and women, are said to be in the process of growing our feminine and masculine faces. As a result, the masculine and feminine will no doubt be expressed differently by actual women and men.

Historically, men have monopolized all connections to those masculine archetypal forces that are useful for their dominance and in the process have limited feminine and masculine archetypes that are not conducive to male domination.[21]   As a result of the dominance of impoverished concrete manifestations of the masculine, not only were men and women cut off from other creative manifestations of the masculine but we were all deprived of the experience of the feminine ground of our being. Not to be both masculine and feminine simultaneously is to have our personhood deeply wounded, fragmented as we become partial selves cut off from the dialectical opposite within us that creates the tension for us to be fully human— masculine and feminine.

I raise this critique from the perspective of transformation because transformation in our being cannot proceed without the full participation of both masculine and feminine archetypal forces in all human beings. . . . The liberation now being initiated above all by women to free the fullness of the masculine and feminine capacity of being thus inescapably challenges the legitimacy and power of all fragments that seek to arrest and contain people.[22]

This means that men cannot project onto women the lack of their feminine self; similarly, women must not seek their masculine self in men. In the archetypal drama of relationships based on mutuality, men and women awaken in one another the desire to be whole and to embrace our sexuality in all its fullness. Yet our society and culture militates against this mutual fulfillment. Therefore, our choice must be clear; to go home is to enter into our deepest sources within and to re-create wholeness.

The novels of Toni Morrison, Alice Walker, Leslie Marmon Silko, Naguib Mahfouz, and Miguel Angel Asturias can all be seen from the perspective of restoring the feminine and telling the story of people of color in our cultures. It is not just the feminine but everything related to the feminine that has been lost or jeopardized: nature, our emotions, the instinctual, the sacred, the intuitive, the soul and compassion. Without these human qualities, we are badly wounded.

AUTOBIOGRAPHICAL WITNESS: TELLING MY STORY

I would like to share aspects of my journey as a man of color, as a Chicano, a Mejicano, a Latino *mestizo* who has in his blood the heritage of the Jews, Muslims, and Christians. I am the result of this *mestizaje*, which was later enriched by our American Indian and African heritage and once again enhanced when our foremothers and forefathers came to the United States, with the European American cultures. I have lived between two worlds, wedged between two magics, and often caught in the shadows of the twin towers of hate, lack of self-esteem, and rejection by the wider society. *El choque de las culturas*, the clash of cultures, points out how I and others were caught in the birth canal between our inherited womb of culture and the individuating, isolating, fragmenting process of the world of the market economy and white, masculine consciousness.

Recently I have attempted to discover the source of my sadness and anger. Few things give me pleasure and I feel that I am in the desert. In re-envisioning my past, I have come to realize that I had repressed the libidinal, the instinctual, the emotional, the body, the sensual, the feminine. I had a goal to become a good man, a pure person, without taking into account the inherited archetypal stories of my own cultural past. I made a decision to dominate my body rationally in order to become a scholar. The cost of repression has proved to be too high.

It is not coincidental that this awakening has taken place while I have dedicated much time to reading feminist and multicultural literature. I consider this to be synchronistic and providential. This literature is telling my story as well as that of so many others like me. When I read this literature I often become emotional and I cry for myself and for my communities, which have been cut off from their creative spirit-filled feminine and sacred sources. At times my anger knows no bounds. This inner impoverishment, together with the assault from the wider society, tempts me toward revenge and thus the abyss. This is what our masters in this society want us to do so that we can fulfill their murderous stereotype and they can say the deadly phrase, "I told you so."

I decided with many others to participate in the current archetypal emergence of the feminine by emptying myself in Act II, Scene 2 of the story of patriarchy. Once I have broken away on this deeper archetypal level, it is necessary for me to wait patiently until I am filled by a new and better story. But this cannot be a blind discipleship. Each of us has to choose to participate in the core drama of life, the story of transformation. In this process we must be at one and the same time prophets, philosophers, and political participants. Prophets by their very calling remain open to being filled by the fundamentally new. But not even the sacred has the right to possess us. Therefore, we have to become philosophers who question, evaluate, and struggle with sacred forces until they reveal their intent and bless us with their hidden message. Finally, we are to be participants together with the sacred in co-creating the self, the world, and the sacred itself. This encounter with the sacred means that if we discover the inspiration to be false—if, for example, we are being inspired to cripple others based on an alleged sense of superiority—we have the right to reject such sacred voices as the destructive faces of the sacred.[23]

Lately I have had some dreams filled with transformational capacity. The dreams were like a burning bush in the desert. I dreamed that I was going home assisted by two young women, who to me represented the feminine, the instinctual, sensual, and sacred. All of these qualities I had left behind to follow the masculine archetype of overpowering myself with rationality and repression. To reconnect to the feminine is not to reject my manhood, my intelligence, or indeed my masculine consciousness but rather to fulfill these aspects of my life in a new relationship to the feminine. Thus when I and other men of color and all people of goodwill throw off the one-dimensional, masculine, non-dialectical, frozen consciousness of the patriarchal story, it is in favor of choosing a fundamentally new and more compassionate life in the service of transformation.

THE PEDAGOGY OF TRANSFORMATION

From a pedagogical perspective, it is a real joy when teaching multicultural and women's literature to assist the students not only to recognize the archetypal story of transformation and the process of death and rebirth in the novels and literature being discussed, but also to see these same archetypal processes in their own lives. In multicultural and women's stories we hear and see our own story. The excluded have always had a very incisive understanding of the cost of oppression for the whole society. For this reason, experiences, situations, dialogues, and scenes jump off the page at us, electrify us because we now understand our lives in a new light, from the perspective of transformation.

In *Fusus al Hikam*, or *The Wisdom of the Prophets*, Ibn Arabi tells us how important it is to set a jewel correctly so that the light will not overwhelm the stone, turn it opaque, or be refracted. The aim is to capture the light in such a way that it reflects all of the beauty within the stone.[24] For too long, people of color and women, including European American males, have had their own brilliance overwhelmed, refracted, and clouded over by those who set the stones of our lives to their own advantage. Currently, the setting of a new context is being accomplished by people of color and women telling their own stories and illuminating their lives, thereby also restoring the integrity of education, which, at its best, means to lead people out of themselves so that they can realize all of their capacity. Women and people of color have been away a long time, either asleep or enmeshed in a white, masculine tomb—a machine, a non-womb that cannot give birth to the fundamentally more just but can only reproduce in a repetitive, mechanistic manner. We are rejecting the scholarship of exclusion based on power, deformation, and blind loyalty to a system for the sake of taking our lives and destiny back into our own hands; that is, we are creating a new setting for the stone so that our inner light shows us the way.

CONCLUSION

There must not be any misunderstanding: Multicultural and gender scholarship is not grounded in anger or the desire to play power politics. Multicultural and gender scholarship committed to transformation is, however, anti-deformation and opposed to a non-dialectical, once-for-all establishment of the truth in an allegedly preordained, superior culture, gender, race, or class. The white, masculine world needs people of color and women because on the deeper level women and people of color speak for our European American brethren as well as for ourselves in reclaiming the fullness of our humanity and in restoring the integrity of our scholarship.

It was Friday in *Robinson Crusoe* and the protagonist of Ellison's *Invisible Man* who took upon themselves the responsibility of saving the humanity of Robinson Crusoe and of his white antagonists. We must be prepared to rediscover our European American brothers and sisters since we are all in trouble. If we lose sight of the principles upon which this country was founded, if we do not keep our eye on the prize, we will go down together. We are inextricably connected and the quality of our connectedness will determine the future of democracy in our nation.

All of us, in the final analysis, are like Amina, the heroine of Naguib Mahfouz's novel, *Palace Walk*. In telling the story of Amina, the author describes a woman who provided a domestic womb for her patriarchal man/child husband without leaving the house for twenty-five years. Finally, through the support of her children and her own inner voice (which she does not immediately recognize), she ventures into the dangerous world of the public realm, where it is necessary for her to create a new political, historical, and sacred face.

NOTES

1. James Baldwin, "Here Be Dragons," in *The Price of the Ticket: Collected Nonfiction 1948–1985* (New York: St. Martin's Press, 1985).

2. Leslie Marmon Silko, *Ceremony* (New York: Penguin Books, 1986).

3. William Attaway, *Blood on the Forge* (New York: Monthly Review Press, 1987).

4. For an excellent analysis of our revolutionary situation from the perspective of a theory of transformation, see Manfred Halpern, "Choosing Between Ways of Life and Death and Between Forms of Democracy: An Archetypal Analysis," *Alternatives*, 12:1 (January 1987), pp. 5–34.

5. In the writing of this chapter I have been very much influenced by Richard Tarnas's provocative article, "The Transfiguration of the Western Mind," in *Cross Currents* 39:3 (Fall 1989), pp. 259–80.

6. In this regard, see Erich Neumann, *The Origins and History of Consciousness* (Princeton, N.J.: Princeton University Press, Bollingen Series, XLII, 1971).

7. Tarnas, "Transfiguration," p. 277.

8. I am greatly indebted to my friend and colleague Manfred Halpern, who has taught me that all paradigm shifts are the result of the birth and death of archetypal sources, that is, the underlying forming, sacred sources that constitute the ground of our concrete everyday life. The role of the sacred is brilliantly explored in his Chapter 14, "Archetypes as Sacred Sources: A Cosmos of Creative Participation," in his forthcoming book, *Transformation: Its Theory and Practice in Personal, Political, Historical, and Sacred Being* (Princeton: Princeton University Press).

9. Tarnas, "Transfiguration," p. 277.

10. Ibid., p. 279.

11. Taylor Branch, *Parting the Waters, America in the King Years 1954–1963* (London: Simon and Schuster, 1988).

12. Miguel Angel Asturias, *Men of Maize* (London: Verso, 1988).

13. Carol Gilligan, *In a Different Voice* (Cambridge, Mass.: Harvard University Press, 1982).

14. In addition to Asturias's *Men of Maize* cited above, see René Marques, *La Carreta* (Rio Piedras, Puerto Rico: Editorial Cultural, 1971); Michael Dorris, *A Yellow Raft in Blue Water* (New York: Warner Books, 1988); and Naguib Mahfouz, *Palace Walk* (New York: Doubleday, 1990).

15. Attaway, *Blood on the Forge*; and Zora Neale Hurston, *Their Eyes Were Watching God* (New York: Harper and Row, 1990).

16. Tarnas, "Transfiguration," p. 280.

17. Ibid.

18. Ibid.

19. Anzia Yezierska, *Bread Givers* (New York: Persea Books, 1975).

20. David Noble, *A World Without Women* (New York: Alfred A. Knopf, 1992), p. 286.

21. Manfred Halpern, "Why are Most of Us Partial Selves? Why Do Partial Selves Enter the Road into Deformation?" Paper delivered at a panel on "Concepts of Self: Transformation and Politics," for the annual meeting of the American Political Science Association, Washington D.C., August 29, 1991, p. 12.

22. Ibid.

23. Halpern, *Transformation*, Chapter 5.

24. Ibn Arabi, *The Wisdom of the Prophets* (Aldsworth, Gloucestershire: Bashara Publications, 1975).

CHAPTER 5

Teaching and Practicing Multicultural and Gender-Fair Education from the Perspective of Transformational Politics

In this final chapter I am going to describe ways to teach and practice the archetypal story of transformation, which is the only way we can be fully ourselves and connected to our deepest sources and to other people. This story provides us with a normative approach that enables us to assess relationships and stories in the culture that fragment us as persons and therefore diminish our humanity. At times we might feel pressured not to criticize our culture or the cultures of others, as if we have no right to do this. But tribalism in the United States is just as destructive in Northern Ireland or Zaire. We must not in the name of a false multicultural forbearance overlook the destructive aspects that are present in all cultures. Our task is the enactment of transformation in all facets of our lives. In this regard there is only one universal story that does justice to our humanity, the journey of transformation. There is only one journey but an infinite number of different ways to concretely live this journey and story. Each of us is human and a brother and sister to each other because of the common call and experience of the core drama of transformation.

Contrary to what many critics are saying, multicultural and gender-fair education is not anti-European American, not anti-male or anti-Western. It is certainly not remedial education, not for women and students of color only, and not an attempt to solve all of our problems as a society. Multicultural education is opposed to any form of cultural elitism such as Eurocentricism or forms of rebellion against cultural imperialism, whether they are called Latinocentric or Afrocentric. Multicultural education is a new and emerging aspect of the archetypal story of democracy that seeks to restore the integrity of the curriculum by taking seriously the scholarship of all groups in our nation. The lie of history is not only what was written and said but also what was left out: the journey and archetypal stories of people of color and women. Indeed, many European American white groups, because they were assimilated into the dominant Anglo Saxon culture, have also lost touch with their own personal, political, historical, and sacred faces.

The determination of who is present and who is excluded means that the curriculum has always been political. That is, the exercise of political power has been in the service of incoherence, because a dominant group or groups determined what was best for the less powerful. It was assumed that what the "better people" chose was good for all of us and in some sense was neutrally superior. In this way, the subjective values of the dominant became the objective truth for all. "American" values were created and sustained in accordance with the desires of the powerful. We often hear examples of people in positions of authority, from the school board to municipal offices, admonishing people who have recently arrived in this country that "this is America." In other words, get with it, forget your background, assimilate, become a good citizen. What is so pernicious about this hostility is that "getting with it" involves a stripping process that is inflicted by both the wider society and the persons who participate in the assault upon themselves. In spite of all of our rhetoric, over the generations American society has been very intolerant of differences. This is the climate in which we live and in which we are attempting to create multicultural diversity as an aspect of the story of democracy in the service of transformation.

THE FOUR FACES OF TEACHING AND LEARNING: THE CRUCIBLE OF THE CLASSROOM

For the last twenty years I have been teaching strategies of transformation. For the last ten years all of my courses, whether in religious studies, politics, or sociology, have been taught from the perspective of transformation. In my courses I challenge myself and my students to participate in archetypal analysis. This kind of analysis entails asking ourselves questions: What act and scene am I now in as regards the core drama of transformation? What archetypal story am I living? In the service of what deeper, underlying way of life am I living this particular drama of my life?

Am I currently living several different stories in the service of two or more ways of life? Am I able to fully enact the four faces of my being or do I settle for less by repressing key aspects of who I am as a personal, political, historical, and sacred being?

Students are initially threatened by these kinds of questions. This is to be expected because they are hearing strange language and, above all, they sense that this will not be an ordinary course. They intuit early on that we are discussing the archetypal stories and the deeper ways of life in which their own deepest being is caught. It is made clear from the first class that the theory of transformation being presented is not an abstraction to be memorized for grades; they are invited to be fully present so that they can live and practice the story of transformation as the core drama of their lives. From the very beginning I assure them that this is a perspective that they will be able to carry with them the rest of their lives so that when they walk into an office, they will be able to see the underlying dramas that are being practiced and in the service of what way of life. They will have carried with them the ability to engage in the most profound kind of critical thinking by practicing archetypal analysis wherever they find themselves. As one of my students put it, they will be capable of answering the question: What is really going on here?

I have always found it to be pedagogically very powerful to begin with archetypal stories that touch the daily lives of students when explaining the drama of transformation. Once they see how these stories relate to their personal lives, they have much less difficulty understanding how they apply to the political, historical, and sacred aspects of their being and to the lives of others.

We begin by looking inside archetypal stories that most of us have experienced: the wounded self, the collusion between two stories, romantic love and the market society of capitalism, and finally, transforming love. I inform my students that I learned the story of the wounded self by reading papers in which students have shared the story of their life. Increasingly, students who walk into my classroom have already lived a lifetime. Almost all of them, regardless of race, class, gender, or religious background, have suffered a variety of stories that have left them wounded: sexual abuse, physical abuse, drug abuse, alcohol abuse, or the trauma of desertion due to the death of a parent, divorce, or abandonment. After presenting these stories I emphasize that so many of us have not been able to come forth as a person because we are deeply wounded. Because our personal face is either repressed or suppressed, we cannot initiate any new political effort since we believe that all that we can and need to do together is survive. Neither are we able to bring about new turning points that will free us from our wounded past because we are permanent victims fated to be the way we are; we have no sacred face of our own because the sacred is co-opted by a stern-faced lord sitting on a throne.

Other archetypal stories, like the story of capitalism, further disable us and prevent us from facing the anxiety of being a wounded self. As we have seen, to arrest life in the first scene of Act II is to turn our rebellion into a permanent and partial way of life, the way of life of incoherence. In this way of life we can enact no stories that allow us to deal with fundamentally new kinds of problems. Capitalism as an archetypal story turns all of our relationships into contests of competition for power. We see each other as potential rivals as we look over our shoulder. Therefore we cannot afford to be vulnerable by revealing our woundedness. As a result we repress and suppress the personal face of our being. Our political face is concerned above all with being left alone so that we are each free to pursue our own self-interest. Our historical face creates no new turning points but seeks to pursue power in order to become a more powerful fragment. The sacred face of our being reduces the sacred to lords who reward us with power in exchange for repressing our personal face in order to work harder and harder.

The story of capitalism, because it is so brutal, leads to a collusion with the story of romantic love, which is also enacted in the service of incoherence. Romantic love is a fantasy that says, "Since in the story of capitalism everybody is only out for themselves, I have to find somebody who will live only for me." Thus I project this need onto another person and choose him or her as my lover. If we are lucky, the other persons will reciprocate in projecting their needs upon me so that together we collaborate in this story. Both parties expect perfection and total loyalty from the other. This story always ends in deep disappointment because each of the two will inevitably fail to live up to the unreal expectations of the other's projected fantasy. The reason is that there is no one home; both are projecting and living out the expected behavior of the other. When the relationship breaks, either one or both are suicidal. Because they invested their total selves in the other and gave up their own lives, the one being abandoned or betrayed states that he or she cannot live without the other. They possessed each other and now that the fantasy is over, there is often violence: "If you don't belong to me, then nobody else can have you." Thus many will choose to stay together for fear that the other will harm himself or herself. As a result we have to once again hide the woundedness of the personal face of our being. Because our personal face is thus crippled, we cannot initiate any new political, historical, or sacred face. Our life is caught in the sacred story of capitalism in collusion with the story of romantic love, which makes it impossible for us to confront and redeem our wounded self.

In regard to the drama of transformation, we are caught within the way of life of incoherence. The story of capitalism in the service of incoherence takes us over and possesses us. Because we do not understand the power of these archetypal stories, they continue to possess us even as we become disillusioned with them. What we usually do is break up with a person in Act II, Scene 1 who previously held us in an emanational relationship. The problem is that since we have not emptied ourselves of the story of romantic love in Act II, Scene 2 or of the way of life of incoherence, we are doomed to repeat the same story with another lover.

The other problem is that we are still stuck with OHIM, or "Oh, hell, it's Monday!" When we live the intense private love affair of romantic love at most we get some relief on the weekend or for several days. But the rest of the time we have to return to the story of capitalism that created the need for this escape into fantasy. We end up conceding the brutality of the system, that is, the story of capitalism in the service of incoherence, because that story and way of life encourages us to conclude that there is nothing we can do about our situation, so work hard and play hard.

Fortunately, as I tell my students, there are stories of love that can be enacted in the service of transformation. One of these is the story of transforming love. Unlike romantic love, I fall in love with something in the other that I want to experience and develop within myself. The other reciprocates and is deeply attracted to some quality in me that she or he wants to develop in their own life. There are two people who are present to each other, each in a unique way, and not through projected fantasies. Both may indeed initially be swept off their feet by one another, but both begin to ask questions about this experience: What is happening to me? Where is this relationship taking me? Is this really a relationship in which I am willing to risk trust? And perhaps the most important question: Can I share who I really am at this time, which means my strengths and my wounded self? Both are seeking each other so that together they can guide one another through the drama of transformation. In this way they can come forth as real human beings and heal each other. If the relationship ends, they are hurt but not devastated, because through this relationship they discovered the four faces of their being; they were not lost, as in the case of romantic love. They can walk away from each other knowing that they met a real person and also that through one another they received the gift of being able to love not only the other but especially themselves. This kind of personal relationship allows us to enact the political, historical, and sacred face of our being in the service of transformation because we are fully present.

This is to enter Act III, Scenes 1 and 2. Once we have emptied ourselves of the previous stories and ways of life that held us, we can count on being filled anew. In the first scene of Act III, each person experiences and knows a sense of wholeness and fulfillment that has made his or her life fundamentally new and better. Perhaps for the first time they are able to hug themselves and to bless the personal and sacred face of their life. But in the second scene of Act III, we reach out to others by enacting the political and historical face of our being by testing and asking together whether this story, this relationship, this way of life is indeed more loving, just, and compassionate. In this way together we create new turning points, new stories in the present of our lives that help us redeem the past and anticipate the future with new hope.

The above represents the material that I cover in the first two weeks of class. During these presentations students are free to challenge, discuss, ask questions, and dissent. What I have found remarkable is that many of the students, both in class and in private, will reveal that they felt as if I were speaking to them personally. My response is that they have already begun to do the task of this course by testing the theory with their own lives. The teacher does not put anything into them, as if to deposit knowledge. Good teachers provide the students with good words to express what they are feeling and thinking. In this way education is truly *educo*, that is, guiding people so that they can participate in their own healing through transformative action. Together with others they can bring about fundamentally new and better forms of love and justice.

Having linked theory to practice in this way, that is, providing students with concrete examples of our underlying archetypal stories and ways of life and how this throws new light on the concrete stories of their lives, we go on to test the theory by reading novels. Our task is to see how various characters journey through the core drama of transformation. In what act and scene do we encounter the protagonist at various parts of the novel, the stories that they are living? In the service of what ways of life are they living these stories? And finally, how do these characters succeed or fail in living the core drama of transformation?

I begin with a literary work that emphasizes the emergence of the personal face of our being, because transformation must begin with this face of our being. Depending on the course I might use *Siddhartha*, *Blood on the Forge*, *The Grapes of Wrath*, *Invisible Man*, *Demian*, or *Ceremony*, to name but a few. For example, *Siddhartha* begins by describing the emanational container of the Brahmin world and the place of privilege that the protagonist held in this world arrested in Act I, Scene 1 in the way of life of emanation as a fragment of the drama of transformation. But by page 5 of the Bantam paperback edition, we are told, "but Siddhartha himself was not happy."[1] The students are given the assignment, after we have discussed the story of transformation and the novel, to "follow Siddhartha through the core drama of transformation. In what way does this novel help you to understand your own story and journey?" In writing on this topic and similar assignments, students are required to make explicit use of the theory of transformation as they apply theory to practice.

These kinds of papers are intended to accomplish several goals. First, they provide students with an opportunity to test the theory on their own as they interpret and analyze the book. Second, this kind of work allows them to recognize and analyze their own story so that they can realize where they might be caught and find some indications as to what they can do about freeing the four faces of their being from destructive archetypal stories and ways of life. And third, students develop the capacity to do radical analysis, that is, to get to the roots of issues and problems precisely by participating in archetypal analysis in all aspects of their lives. This kind of education prepares students for transformational politics because they are learning to dissent, to analyze, and above all to be creative. The politics of transformation requires that we actually create new and better alternatives.

I would like to address the issue of creative and critical education in a little more detail. Above all, what is presented to the students in my classes is an invitation to participate in doing theory, not memorizing a group of power terms. This means applying theory to practice by actually getting under, standing under the process in order to intuitively and conceptually grasp the reality that we are confronting. This is what we mean when we say: Now I *see it*; now I *get it*; now I really *under-stand*. Once students learn the concepts, they can creatively apply them in whatever situation they find themselves. Recently I heard a doctor speaking to a medical student and urging her never to memorize but to learn concepts so that when she was faced with a problem she could use a combination of conceptual material and her intuition to guide her to grasp the heart of the matter in an unfamiliar situation. He went on to say that the worst doctors are those who memorized everything and as a result never learned how to practice medicine. After all, to conceptualize is not repetition but participation in doing medicine or the art of healing based on one's insights that lead to the development of new and better concepts. In some cases this will lead to a fundamental disagreement with one's earlier education, which means that the education did its job well; new concepts have replaced ones that are now inadequate. This is what is meant when we test theory with practice. The conceptual, theoretical language must always be open to change when exploring the reality to which it points us. People who memorize cannot do this kind of creative work because they have been crippled and have wounded themselves by being restricted to becoming competent in the power language of the existing understanding of the dominant perspective.

It is important to note here that we as teachers need to respect the privacy of our students. Although I ask them to apply the story of transformation to their own experiences, they are free to write about the struggle of a friend, or of a protagonist in another literary work, or an issue of importance to them. But almost all of the students choose to write about themselves and often in a very personal and revealing way.

I would now like to give some examples of responses that I have received from assignments that connect the four faces of our being as the students learn the archetypal stories and ways of life within which the various protagonists, and they themselves as students, shape their lives. For example, one student chose to reveal her struggle to be an "American." She was a senior preparing to graduate who had often thought of her dilemma but had no context in which to resolve the issue. In the midst of her search for the personal face of her being, we were discussing in class the price of the story of capitalism rooted in the deeper story of incoherence and of how this story is often found together with the story of racism/tribalism in the service of deformation. This discussion took place as we read the novel *Ceremony*. Tayo cannot pull his life together. He has been taught to love his Native American heritage by his Uncle Josiah and yet to see it as an obstacle by the wider society, especially his teachers.[2] Tayo is deeply affected by the story of racism in the service of deformation because it denies his humanity as a Native American. This story colludes with the story of capitalism, which considers only the powerful, who are usually white, to be worthwhile, to prevent him from continuing his story of transformation.

As this student listened to the views of her colleagues and read the novel, she came to see that Tayo's dilemma was her own. Consequently, in her paper she wove the four faces of her being with those of Tayo as she analyzed the frightening cost of the stories of capitalism and racism. She wrote with much insight as to how these stories had prevented her from knowing who she was and who she really wanted to be. She revealed that for most of her schooling she was ashamed of her ethnic heritage. She looked like and passed for a white, European American woman, but her mother was Japanese. She was ashamed of her biracial background and even angrily denounced her father when she was younger for not marrying an "American" woman. She lived with the constant fear that her schoolmates would discover her secret. She felt guilty about this, but since her family moved to an exclusive community she felt that she had to fit into the power group at school and elsewhere. This meant that she harbored anger and hatred for herself and her mother. As she wrote her paper she spoke very clearly about how it was necessary to empty herself in Act II, Scene 2 of the stories that had prevented her from loving herself and her mother. Her final comments expressed a strong desire to learn about her Japanese heritage and to embrace those aspects of it that would help her to live a life of transformation. I was deeply touched by her paper because it demonstrated the power of archetypal stories and ways of life to take over our lives.

Another young woman wrote about how she was caught by the story of romantic love because she was involved in a possessive relationship with a man. She identified with Sara in *Bread Givers*, who was fighting to empty herself of two stories often found in collusion with each other, patriarchy and romantic love. She analyzed how these stories kept her arrested in fragments of the core drama, in the service of incoherence and emanation, and of how they often led to violence in the service of deformation as she threatened this man's crumbling container. She clearly saw that she had arrested her journey caught by two stories—in Act I, Scene 1, living the story of patriarchy, and in Act II, Scene 1, possessed by the story of romantic love. As to the four faces of her being, she wrote that she could not really speak about her desires because they threatened him. Because she could not discover her personal face, her political, historical, and sacred face were reduced to an uncritical loyalty to the men and the stories that she had seen almost all of the women of her history live and repeat. She could not discover her own sacred face; only the needs of a masculine, patriarchal lord were to be obeyed. But she concluded with a complaint: "What am I going to do? I need him. I know that I am caught but I don't have the strength to fight him."

This complaint was also a cry for help. When we as teachers choose to teach courses on transformation, we have to be ready to take "response-ability" for the doors that we open in the lives of our students. By the nature of what we are teaching, we make the four faces of our being a priority. It is only as persons fully connected to the political, historical, and sacred aspects of our being that we can practice transformation. Therefore, we need to do everything we can to be available to students by announcing extra office hours, meeting with them in small groups, having lunch with one or several students, and listening carefully to their concerns. I would also encourage anonymously written midterm course evaluations. In this way we can get a fairly accurate idea as to how the students feel about the course and where they are still confused. Several semesters ago, I asked my students to write down all of the aspects of the theory of transformation that were still obscure to them. I got back a wealth of insight that guided my teaching for the remainder of the semester. And because this is such a personal journey, we need to respect the inability or the refusal of the student to move beyond where they are caught in the core drama. Transformation cannot be commanded or lived for somebody else; it must be personally chosen. Thus it is important to say that a student is free to analyze where they are in regard to act and scene and what stories and ways of life they are living within. But it is up to them to choose to leave destructive stories and ways of life. Our job is to show examples of how this is done, not only through the help of literary works but also by sharing our own personal struggle with transformation and the study and analysis of historical examples such as the Civil Rights movement and the creation of a transformative union like the United Farm Workers.

It is good pedagogy to use books and give examples from daily life that show people caught sometimes for years, between acts and scenes of the core drama. For example, it took Celie in *The Color Purple* about fifteen years before she rebelled against Albert. She clearly knew, due to Sofia's help, that she could be a different kind of woman. But for years she remained caught between Act I, Scene 1 and Scene 2, possessed by the story of patriarchy because she continued to resist and repress her inner voice. Perhaps she felt that she wasn't strong enough but that she would be ready when the right moment came. That proper time came—as it did for many involved in the women's movement, the Civil Rights movement, and the gay and lesbian struggle—when a guide like Shug or César Chavez or Martin Luther King, Jr. came onto the scene to give concrete expression to what the people already knew in their bones: that they must risk everything for the sake of liberation and transformation.

THE TEACHER AS GUIDE THROUGH THE CORE DRAMA OF TRANSFORMATION

I hope that it is clear by now that I, as one who teaches multicultural and women's literature from the perspective of transformational politics, need to be a living concrete example that transformation is possible for all of us. Therefore, I have to begin by taking the gender, sexual preference, race, ethnicity, religious heritage, and cultural backgrounds of my students seriously. For this reason I begin my courses before the students arrive by making a personal decision to assign required readings and writings that will allow them to see, analyze, and assess their own personal faces. The books chosen represent their actual faces as representative authors from their backgrounds reveal the contours of their stories.

In all of my courses I require and/or recommend readings that represent women, different age groups, African Americans, Latinas and Latinos, Asian Americans, Native Americans, European Americans, and gays as they struggle with the stories of their lives and with the demands of transformation. As teachers, most of us are aware that students dislike textbooks, especially for introductory courses. Although at this point we are just beginning to do the necessary work, it is possible with a little imagination to teach all of the basic concepts in courses such as sociology, religion, politics, economics, philosophy, English, anthropology, history, the history of science, and many other subjects by making use of multicultural and women's literary works. The best scholarship and writing being done these days in many fields is gender- or culture-specific. This scholarship provides us with a unique opportunity to teach basic conceptual material in regard to different fields of study and to allow the student to see her and his cultural, racial, and sexual experience in the readings and assignments. There is, however, still a scarcity of teachers willing and able to use women's and multicultural literature and other scholarship so that we can vary the readings and change the emphasis depending on the cultural and racial composition of our class. Even if we are teaching a focused course, such as on Latino politics in the United States or the African American experience or feminist authors, it is crucial to permeate the course with a multicultural consciousness. This means, for example, relating the lives of Latinas to Irish women or Chinese women and the experiences of men in one culture to that of women and men in another. What allows us to do this is archetypal analysis, that is, the kind of analysis that cuts across all cultural, gender, class, and racial lines. Archetypal analysis tells us to look at the deeper underlying stories and the ways of life in which we practice these dramas. By the nature of our humanity, we share these stories in common. What varies and is unique are the particularities of the story, such as historical period or geography, or specific cultural details, such as wearing a veil in public. In this way students come to see their lives through the stories of others. For example, when we take up the story of patriarchy in the novel *Bread Givers*, it is obvious to the class that the forms of male control are almost identical in *The Color Purple* and *Like Water for Chocolate* or *Palace Walk*.[3] This multicultural and comparative approach is very powerful in its ability to break down the racist and ethnocentric stereotypes that we have all learned about one another. When students see Sara as a Jewish woman struggling to free herself from the story of patriarchy, they also recognize Celie as an African American woman, Tita as a Mejicana/Latina, and Amina as an Arab Muslim woman engaged in the same archetypal battle. But above all, this kind of literature helps them to see that this is their challenge as women and men from whatever background. The irony is that these kinds of novels give us a far more profound insight into the lives of people and the four faces of our being than does most current scholarship.

Multicultural education at its best creates a dialogue between cultures, between men and women, between religious communities and between different historical periods. Thus, advocates of multicultural education do not want to exclude Shakespeare, Hemingway, Blake, Tolstoy, Plato, Faulkner, Steinbeck, or other great authors. On the contrary, we want to see the deeper archetypal parallels, the shared stories, between Shakespeare and the author of *The Book of J*,[4] between William Attaway and John Steinbeck, between Sandra Cisneros and Emily Dickinson, between Mark Twain and Carlos Fuentes, between Oscar Handlin and René Marques, between Harriet Beecher Stowe and Toni Morrison, between Louisa May Alcott and Amy Tan.

Let us take for example John Steinbeck and William Attaway. Both authors wrote about one of the classic themes in literature, exile and displacement from the land. But most of us have only heard of John Steinbeck and his brilliant novel, *The Grapes of Wrath*,[5] which was popularized by a highly successful film of the same name. Because of the high profile of the author and of its commercial success, *The Grapes of Wrath* easily became part of the American curriculum, that list of books that was considered essential for understanding the American experience. On the other hand, William Attaway was a black man who wrote of the life of black sharecroppers in the South during the Jim Crow era of segregation in his novel *Blood on the Forge*. He also brilliantly told the story of exile, especially of black men who were forced to leave the soil that they loved because it was not possible, given the economics of racism, for them to support their families. This fact and the shortage of white manpower before, during, and after World War I was largely responsible for one of the largest internal migrations of people in American history. Millions of African Americans left the South to live and work in the North.

Both works are excellent examples of storytelling. Why do we know the one and not the other? Both exiles coincided with each other during the Great Depression. The Okie migration dramatically changed the lives of the people and of their new communities, especially in California. It can be argued that the migration of African Americans to the North changed our nation in a much more sweeping and dramatic way than did the migration of the Okies. Our ignorance, until quite recently, of the importance of the black migration highlights how history books, the authors published, what teachers teach, what is valuable to know, the subject matter of films, and the stories reported in the nation's newspapers all participate to make some groups real and others invisible.

In a good course on American literature, African American studies, American history, or the politics of the Depression, a sensitive teacher could easily assign both books. Comparisons could be made by asking questions: What was the system of landholding that so affected the lives of both whites and blacks? What was going on in the rest of American history during the upheaval of these two communities? What happened to the family under these conditions? How did conditions of exile affect male/female relationships? What was the reaction of the communities and cities to which the migrants came? What role did religion play in the lives of the people? Was there any attempt to form coalitions between displaced whites and blacks during this period? Did the government do anything on behalf of the exiled? What was the prevailing political ideology in Congress that led to action or inaction? Was belief in the American dream shaken by this experience of loss? Why have we heard of the Okies and John Steinbeck and not William Attaway? Why did it take years for Attaway to get his book published? Was his book reviewed? If so, where?

To broaden the historical and cultural perspective, it would be possible at this point to make a comparison with another historical example of displacement from the soil that took place in fourteenth-century England. In that period, the growing landholding aristocracy practiced the story of capitalism in the service of incoherence by undermining the peasantry, who lost their land and became agriculture laborers.[6] In the same semester or at another time the story of the displacement of Puerto Ricans from the rural areas of Puerto Rico can be compared with these other stories through a consideration of the work of René Marques, *La Carreta*.[7] This final example is so powerful because the Puerto Rican people responded to the American dream with great misgivings yet hope, only to be met with the stories of tribalism and capitalism that assaulted their humanity.

And then it is very important to let the literary creativity of the authors speak for them. It will soon be evident that based on merit alone, writers like Marques and Attaway deserved to be published and read. The fact that they were not successful can lead to a discussion of who gets published and why so that the students come to see that it is usually not ability that determines who is heard but that existing connections to the powerful more often than not guarantee success. This kind of analysis and discussion exposes the politics of the curriculum in the service of incoherence and deformation better than any lecture or reading in itself.

Transforming the existing curriculum with a multicultural and gender-fair perspective as described above is the best way to renew American education.

This means that the best strategy would not be to create special courses that are considered to be multicultural, except as an intervening step on the way to developing a fuller multicultural consciousness in the curriculum. Students and many teachers see a three-credit course or a special course for grade school and high school students as a way to fulfill just another requirement among many others. When the multicultural course has been taken, too many feel that it is enough. This trivializes the deeper meaning of what we are doing; multicultural consciousness and attitudes are not accomplished once for all by taking one or several course requirements. This is a consciousness that needs to infuse our lives as students and later as citizens of this nation and of the world. Students who are educated from a multicultural perspective receive a superior education. Who could argue against re-envisioning and re-creating American education as the confluence and contributions of the many cultures that constitute this nation? We have received a truncated version of American history, politics, literature, and culture from a very narrow viewpoint that distorted our heritage by filtering it through the lenses of the powerful and what served their interests.

Multicultural and gender-fair education at its best represents the politics of the curriculum in the service of transformation because it respects and enhances the inherent diversity of the four faces of a student's life. Each student is unique in her or his ethnic and racial background. Crucial aspects of who they are and of how they see themselves and of how others relate to them is inextricably tied to their being a Latina, a Jewish male, Asian American, Italian American, gay, or straight. This is part of the specificity of their personal and sacred face, of what makes them valuable and concretely who they are and must not deny. Yet as we have seen, individuals need to be critically aware of being a member of a specific group because not all aspects of their heritage are creative. For this reason, we and our students also have a political face that requires us to reach out to others outside our group so that together we can shape a new historical face by creating new turning points that lead to a more loving and just multicultural society.

A HUNGER FOR GOOD TALK AND GOOD THEORY

I have been deeply blessed in the opportunities that I have had to test the theoretical perspective of transformation described in this book. As mentioned earlier, I have been teaching transformational politics for the past twenty years. Many could say that this means that I have been working with a highly selective sample of the American public. In addition, students, no matter how open I may be as a teacher, may still feel constrained to voice their dissent. I respect this criticism even though I have had ample evidence over the years, especially from former students, that learning the drama of transformation decisively changed their lives.

But in addition to the classroom I have traveled throughout the nation, giving presentations to audiences that cannot be considered captive. For example, I gave a presentation to several thousand teachers in St. Louis on "The Personal and Sacred Face of Children and Youth: Education in the Service of Transformation." I presented many of the ideas found in this chapter. The response was overwhelming. Participants later shared with me their feelings. Above all, they said that I had succeeded in touching the child and youth in themselves that still needed to be rescued and loved. If we can heal the woundedness of our own childhood by loving ourselves with honesty and gentleness, we can reach out to the children who look to us for so much more than just information. At the School of Medicine of the University of California, Davis, I gave a keynote address on "The Four Faces of the Doctor/Patient Encounter." Once again, in a relatively different setting, the reaction was very positive. The medical students and doctors told me that I had articulated their feelings. They were looking for good talk, that is, the kind of talk that gives conceptual expression to what they had known and intuited but had never quite been able to put into words. At DeVry Institute of Technology in Chicago, I addressed the issue of "Male/Female Relationships in the Latino Community." During the question-and-answer period, a woman said that she now understood why her husband, to whom she was married for fourteen years, had never seen her face. This was a remarkable statement that she went on to explain. Based on my comments that relationships in the service of transformation mean that each of us is enabled to come forth as whole beings with our own personal, political, historical, and sacred face, she assessed her marriage as one in which she had lost her own personal and sacred face. This led her to realize that the politics of loyalty and power that were being practiced by her husband, with her collusion, meant that she could not change and thereby bring about a new historical turning point for her or her children. The conceptual framing of her experience was as if she had turned on a light.

In San Antonio, Texas, I gave a talk to a group of community college teachers on "Multicultural and Gender Scholarship from the Perspective of a Theory of Transformation." I stressed the need to permeate our existing courses with a multicultural and gender-fair approach. The teachers were challenged to see how they could apply theory to practice by re-envisioning the literature with which they were familiar and incorporating new readings into a theoretical structure. This would allow them to work with their students in theoretical, conceptual work, critical thinking, interpretive reading, comparative work, and interdisciplinary teaching, while allowing each student the freedom of creative writing by applying the core drama of transformation to their own stories. During an afternoon session we had quite a heated discussion over whether Tita, the protagonist in *Like Water for Chocolate*, had lived her life for others or whether this was an unfair question because we might be imposing our value judgments on another culture and another historical period. My response was that transformation has always been a possibility but that people had to be willing to pay the price. In Tita's case it meant a frightening realization that she would have to face her life alone.

At Princeton University I addressed a group of my peers, Latina and Latino social scientists and theologians, on "The Personal, Political, Historical and Sacred Grounding of Latino Culture in the United States." I shared with my colleagues a growing awareness on my part that we couldn't simply speak about religion, God, faith, or belief without asking the question: In the service of what sacred source do we practice our rituals and call ourselves Catholic, Muslim, Pentecostal, Jewish or a practitioner of santería? If we follow a particular religious doctrine, it is of utmost importance to know if that practice gives me permission to pursue my own self-interest and power or if the encounter with the sacred invites me to give preference to the poor.

Finally, I want to give an example of testing this theory of transformation in a community setting of Latino people primarily from a working-class background. I was invited to speak at the Centro de la Comunidad in New London, Connecticut, on "Transforming Latino Culture in the United States: Choosing Between Ways of Life and Death." In my comments I assessed both Latino culture and the dominant culture in U.S. society. The feedback that I received was very positive, but there was a concern that I had as a Latino been a little too harsh on "our culture." I had emphasized that as Latinos we cannot be caught by the stories of our culture if we choose to bring about real fundamental change. They heard me and were reluctant to go so far as to admit that transformation had to be so wrenching an experience. In this way they were no different from my students or my colleagues who are often deeply upset because they know, at least intuitively, that this theoretical perspective exposes the archetypal stories in which we are caught and the deeper way of life in which we have settled for less and therefore remain partial selves.

In addition to these more detailed examples of testing the theory, I have spoken to United Church of Christ ministers and laity in Chicago, students and faculty at Montclair High School in New Jersey, parents and community leaders in Chatham, New Jersey, to the academic community at Illinois State University in Normal, Illinois, and at The Third World Center at Princeton

University. These are but a few of the presentations, dialogues, discussions, and papers that I have given recently. The generosity of my audiences in providing me a forum to present these ideas has been for me a great opportunity. Their response has helped me to learn to apply the theory of transformation in ways that I had not even thought of. Above all, I have learned that people like you and me are looking for good talk, good theory that allows us not only to understand our lives but to move to transform the four faces of our being in the service of transformation.

MULTICULTURAL EDUCATION AS A NEW FACE OF THE STORY OF DEMOCRACY

During the last fifteen years I have taught at such diverse institutions as Seton Hall University, Kean College of New Jersey, Princeton University, Yale University, and the Irvington School District. I taught courses on contemporary moral values, principles of sociology, Latina and Latino politics in the United States, strategies of transformation, religion and social change, the politics of the Latino family, and multicultural and gender-fair education in the service of transformation (see Appendix for examples of course outlines). The theoretical perspective that I have used has been that of transformation. With this theory as the core around which I have organized my courses, I teach using multicultural and women's scholarship. I have learned a great deal about how to teach in this way from my students and my colleagues. Together we are involved in a common task of creating the scholarly content and the teaching methodologies that give a concrete reality to this emerging aspect of the archetypal story of democracy.

I would like now to present some of the characteristics of multicultural education that represent a new concrete dimension of the archetypal drama of democracy. I have learned that there is no such thing as multiculturalism because this noun sounds too much like a thing, an entity, a body of knowledge, all of which breeds specialists and consultants. Therefore I stress multicultural as an adjective because it is still being created by those who are working to make it a reality in our daily consciousness. In this sense multicultural education is a quest, not a finished product. There are no experts or elites here but people like you and me who are willing to participate in making concrete a new aspect of democracy in the service of transformation. For this reason I emphasize that this is not just another one of those passing fads that arise every few years in education. We are dealing with a new concrete manifestation of the story of democracy, a new expression of this story to which we can give direction and substance. In the service of transformation, democracy is an archetypal story that gives us the freedom and capacity to accomplish all that we can and need to do together. We are just beginning to be able to become multicultural and gender-fair, which is part of the content of a democratic society. At its best, multicultural and gender-fair education is radically democratic because each of us is free to discover her or his own voice, in its own uniqueness, in order to enrich the humanity of us all. It allows us and encourages us to ask new questions. For example, Walter Prescott Webb was one of the most eminent historians of the American West during the 1930s to the 1950s. In 1957 he despaired that there was nothing more for him to write about. He believed that this topic had been exhausted.[8] It never dawned on him in all of his research over the many years to ask who had been excluded.

Multicultural and women's scholarship asked questions that arose out of the lives of women and excluded groups: What was it like to be a woman traveling West? How did the communities that were conquered and displaced feel about manifest destiny? What happened to Americans as they confronted the West as a meeting of new peoples with different cultures and stories? What was it like to be a Chinese laborer on the railroad that opened up the West? Did Mexicans living in the Southwest since the sixteenth century consider themselves to be foreigners? Weren't there black cowboys who helped settle the West? The scholarship that arises out of attempts to answer these and similar questions exposes the nativistic, ethnocentric, and triumphalistic arrogance of so much of our scholarship. Western history seen from this new perspective is a process of cultural convergence, a constant political, economic, linguistic, cultural struggle among diverse people. It is a story of greed and heroism, the account of the contest over land, water, and resources in a very fragile ecosystem. In spite of the fact that no one region in the United States has had such a long and persistent record of racial intolerance, there remains a powerful legacy of multicultural diversity.[9]

Multicultural education rejects both assimilation and separatism in favor of a dialogue among differences so that we might find our common humanity. This is done by looking at archetypal themes and stories that all of us share, such as the family, authority, migration, oppression, the sacred, and culture. Within these broad themes we can rediscover ourselves and others through sharing the particular stories of each other. For example, I am very conscious of the fact that Toni Morrison is an African American woman. In her writings she has taught me in a very powerful way the enormous price that black people paid to assert their humanity in this country. But I am also aware of what she has taught me about my own humanity and my own experiences of suffering as a Latino man of color. This kind of personal identification with each other is one of the great advantages of literature. When we read a novel or short story, we are pulled out of ourselves and our own limited worlds by emotionally identifying with the characters. After a while we feel and see the world as Seth does in *Beloved* or as Amina in *Palace Walk* or as Casey in *The Grapes of Wrath* and we find ourselves comparing our own experiences to theirs. In this way Asian Americans, Native Americans, and Polish Americans are no longer abstractions or "those people" but take on human dimensions so that they are just like you and me.

Reading literary works that represent different ethnic and racial groups, identifying with the characters, and doing cross-cultural comparative work helps us to be at one and the same time cultural-specific and multicultural. We can go into depth regarding the literary merits, historical context, political message, and personal impact of a novel or play that tells the story of a particular group. We can then take the same kind of care to analyze a poem or other piece by an author from another group and feel free to compare how they are similar and how they differ in addressing the same archetypal issues. For example, a very rewarding comparison could be made between Nora, the heroine of Ibsen's *A Doll's House,* [10] and Cleofilas, in Cisneros's *Woman Hollering Creek.*[11] These are authors from different cultural, gender, and class backgrounds writing in different historical periods about the rights of women. These kinds of comparisons are tremendously helpful in assisting students to see the four faces of our being in different cultures and time periods and to realize that what matters is the story that is being lived in the service of a deeper way of life. It also helps them to place themselves and their struggle as women and men in a historical context and to understand that the stories they are living are the product of people not being able to or refusing to intervene against destructive stories.

This kind of archetypal analysis, a comparative and thematic approach that is related to one's own stories, allows us to move from mere tolerance for each other and our differences to real respect and affection. Within this context of mutual respect, we can honor a cultural heritage and still dissent from it insofar as it is destructive. We can do this because we are free, thanks to archetypal analysis, to assess fragmented and partial ways of life in whatever context we encounter them, including our own culture.

In summary, multicultural education as a face of democracy in the service of transformation is characterized by the following:

- Multicultural education rejects both assimilation and separatism in favor of a dialogue so that we can establish our common humanity.
- This concrete expression of the story of democracy moves us from the stinginess of tolerance to mutual respect.

- This is not a fad but the manifestation of a new concrete aspect of the underlying story of democracy.

- This is not about multiculturalism, an established something with experts to tell us about it. It is more of a quest, a process that is still unfolding and made concrete by people like you and me.

- What is asked of us is openness and risk in which we rediscover our stories through learning the stories of each other.

- This is a kind of education that provides us with both a window and a mirror so that we can see the four faces of our own specific being in the mirror of the curriculum but also look through it as a window to see the four faces of our neighbors' being.[12]

- A multicultural society is utterly democratic because each of us is urged to discover our own unique voice so that the whole community will be enriched.

- Multicultural education allows us to ask new questions: Who was left out? Why were they excluded? What have we learned about ourselves as a society as a result of the inclusion of these previously missing voices?

- Through the use of archetypal analysis, we can go beyond the concrete differences, without in any way disparaging them, to a comparative and thematic analysis. This is possible because we all share the underlying archetypal stories and ways of life that constitute the deepest ground of our common humanity, especially the core drama of transformation.

TRANSFORMING OURSELVES, OUR STUDENTS, OUR CLASSROOMS

Infusing our curricula with a gender and multicultural consciousness is also a political decision taken to ensure that our class will create an environment in which we will ask: What is it that you and I can and need to do together, in our concrete particularity as women, Asian Americans, African Americans, gays or lesbians, Latinas and Latinos, Native Americans, and European American males to create a more humane and just society? In this common enterprise in the classroom we prepare ourselves to create a new turning point not only in our encounters with each other in the class but also as we look forward to shaping a new and better story for the future of our nation. This is what the archetypal story of democracy is all about. By listening, learning, and struggling together, we come to see that although our goal unites us in the same quest, the story of transformation, each of our faces is valuable, and each person's journey in all its uniqueness is sacred. In this way the four faces of our being penetrate and connect with each other in the crucible of the classroom, which prepares us to participate in transformation in the wider society.

All teachers, whether consciously or not, guide students to the service of sacred sources in one of our four ways of life.[13] At the heart of all education is a relationship between the teacher and the student. This relationship is always an encounter with the sacred. Thus teachers as guides have at least implicitly chosen one of these deeper archetypal underlying ways of life in their own lives. Consequently, when they teach they can only lead students to the way of life that they know best. Beyond the obvious purpose of providing knowledge, a teacher living and doing transformational politics in the classroom is always a principal actor on a deeper level in the lives of her or his students.

This deeper level is the realm of sacred sources.[14] We experience this deepest source of our being in four fundamentally different ways. The first sacred source that I would like to describe is the lord that corresponds to the way of life of emanation that holds us and seduces us to remain totally loyal in the first scene of Act I. This is a lord of jealous possessiveness that gives us security in exchange for blind obedience; it is the lord of omniscience and omnipotence of fixed traditions in which all the truth has been found and all that remains is for us to more intensely bend ourselves to its will. Second, there is the lord that emerges from within the way of life of incoherence that gives us permission and the inspiration to pursue our own self-interest and power. This lord keeps us in Act II, Scene 1 and allows us to be either the dominator or the dominated. Relationships based on competition and mutual suspicion serve this lord. Our third lord is the source of deformation that leads us into the exit from the core drama into the abyss of eternal night and despair. This lord raises stories of revenge and violence that make life fundamentally worse. Finally, there is the source of transformation that invites us, never by command, as necessary actors to create fundamentally more loving and compassionate relationships and stories in Act III, Scenes 1 and 2. This sacred relationship always involves the continuous transformation of the four faces of our being.

The sacred source that we choose to concretely express will determine the ultimate meaning, that is, the deepest ground we can discover here and now for why we are who we are and why we are doing what we are doing. As we have seen and as will be further demonstrated, three of the four ways of life give us a biased and incomplete understanding of the ultimate ground of our being and action because they are only fragments of the core drama of transformation. These four ways of life, in the service of which we enact all the concrete relationships and stories of our life, means that there are four radically different kinds of teaching and learning that will prepare students for personal, political, historical, and sacred choices.

PRACTICING AND TEACHING TRANSFORMATIONAL POLITICS

To best explain the four different kinds of teaching and learning, guides, and education in the service of four distinct ways of life available to us, I would like to re-examine and recapture the root meaning of four Latin verbs: *seduco, reduco, deduco* and *educo*. The root word of all four verbs is *duco*, which means to lead or guide. *Seduco* is a kind of leadership that by mystique or charisma leads a student only to be enchanted by the brilliance of the teacher. This kind of education is really training students to accept possession by others, whereby students are made into permanent disciples because the teacher and all authority figures have all the answers. The verb *reduco* means that some teachers motivate their students along the path of reducing everything to the pursuit of personal power and profit. Instructors provide the power by giving skills of competency to be used eventually to dominate others. In the meantime students learn the story of domination by accepting the power of the teacher until it is their turn to exercise control. This teacher prepares rugged individualists for the "real world," usually without any explicit philosophical justification except to assert that getting ahead is what it is all about. In this choice of teaching the archetypal source of incoherence that is not acknowledged gives teacher and student alike the right to use each other to increase their marketability.

Then there is *deduco*, a frightening kind of education, a perverse kind of transformation because it is fundamentally new but worse; it is education in the service of deformation. It is another form of *duco*, literally to deduct, to take away, to strip away the personal, political, historical, and sacred meaning of those considered to be "those people." This kind of teaching leads the allegedly superior to take a fragment of life, such as one's anger, and give it a name—women, blacks, Latinos, gays, welfare people—and use this stereotyping to create scapegoats for the hurt that they do not understand because such education never leads them to confront the cause of the wound. This type of teaching preserves and enlarges forms of racism, sexism, and classism. It violates to the point that many feel nothing when they are hurt by others or when they hurt others. This nihilism has to be the deepest kind of wounding because when we feel nothing for others, we can also no longer feel our own personal face.

What does this kind of teaching look like? Adherents of this way of life and teaching are too smart to make overt statements or actions that could be immediately seen as prejudiced. Instead, they do it by turning students of color, women, or gays, or whoever may be the target, into invisible people in the class. There are no books or readings that represent their personal face. They are not called on; they are ignored. The teacher as authority figure is always turned away from them. Comments may be made indirectly, for example, "You live *there*?," meaning in a poor section of town. But even before they get to the school, many students are experiencing the five faces of the story of tribalism in the service of deformation. In this story the allegedly superior treat the outsiders in a way that leads toward increasing violence and death. The powerful treat the powerless as if they are invisible, inferior. "The better ones" deserve to be assimilated, exiled if disloyal, and exterminated if they rebel. A whole political environment is constructed in which the privileged are aware that they count and the outsiders clearly know that they do not belong. The presence of deformation throughout our society is ignored by some teachers who act as if there were no racism, poverty, or physical abuse to debilitate the energy and confidence of so many of our students. Instead, they just want to do math or English, ignoring the issues faced daily by their students.

Educo is a fundamentally different choice from the other three modes of education. It means to guide a student forth so that each can participate in personal, political, historical, and sacred transformation together with her or his neighbor. This is to guide students into a radically democratic process because it needs for its fulfillment the unique participation of each person. In this kind of education it is necessary for the individual student to come forth; otherwise, what is within them will die and their lost contribution will deprive us all. This kind of educational endeavor demands that students and teachers eventually become colleagues embarked on a common journey together.[15] I shall enlarge upon this kind of education later in this chapter.

Since we are speaking of choices and of underlying sacred sources as the deepest ways of structuring and organizing life, we cannot choose once for all the sacred source that we will listen to. It is a permanent struggle. There are times when we as teachers become afraid and tentative. We might lose our way, lecture too much, and feel threatened by dissent. This appeal to the lord of power or to the lord of loyalty and the temporary rejection of the source of transformation and risk is what students refer to when they say that the teacher is playing god. This is actually true, because when teachers respond to a student, they incarnate one of our four sacred ways of life.

The redeeming aspect of this conscious struggle is that teachers can come to know the choice they have been making so that they can, through humor, for example, acknowledge their own fears and choose again to risk themselves as they pursue issues with the students. This is what the politics of the classroom is all about—always taking the next step, choosing again and again to be honest and vulnerable, and refusing to stifle the emergence of the students. This kind of education, created by students and teachers alike, prepares students to see politics not only as cooperation but also as dissent, not only continuity but also change. The politics of the classroom sets the agenda for the politics of the wider community.

Knowing what we do about four fundamental choices allows us to ask new questions about authority. Our word "authority" comes from the Latin verb, *augeo, augere, aegi, auctus*, which means to help bring something into being, to assist others in becoming authors of their life. Any exercise of one's teaching that does not help students be the authors of their own life is illegitimate. Thus when we exercise authority in the classroom, we always have to ask the question: In the service of what way of life do I teach and guide? This means at times taking control. But students themselves have always known the difference between teachers who command them to be quiet so that they might reign supreme and those who insist that they sit down so that they can learn and grow. In its richest and deepest sense, this is what the professional teacher has always meant—a personal form of political commitment that served the need of others. It was Plato and Socrates who spoke of one's *daimonion*, that is, the presence and awareness of mystery as an integral part of the nature of a great teacher. The *daimonion* of the teacher protected education from becoming a merely rational pursuit by connecting it to an underlying mystery.[16] To fulfill one's own *daimonion* is a calling to serve others. But as we have seen earlier, we can serve the sacred in four fundamentally different ways. Whichever sacred source we respond to is the source to which we will lead our students. In this regard the four faces of our being are inextricably linked. The sacred forces that inspire us will determine whether we relate to students as disciples, as collaborators in the power game, as members of a group that make life worse, or as mutual friends on the journey of transformation.

EDUCATION IN THE SERVICE OF TRANSFORMATION AS SUBVERSION

Good teachers are always prepared to subvert so that loyalty to the teacher turns into a response to one's own inner voice. To subvert is literally to turn from below, to reorient, to turn a person's life around. Good teachers can touch others in a significant way beyond the sharing of facts. Through their personality they can attract others to themselves. Thus, when students come to see the four faces of their own being because they were initially drawn out of themselves by the teacher, they begin to realize that what drew them to the teacher is what the teacher awakened in them—the mystery of what it means to be who we are, a person, another incarnation of the sacred capable of creating new turning points in their life as we engage together with others to create a more humane society. What began as enchantment is transformed into an awareness of the student's own unrealized potential. *Seduco* in the service of emanation is thus subverted, turning students from discipleship to the acceptance of their own mystery. In this instance, the teacher as guide leads students away from false sacred sources in order to initiate the journey to become themselves practitioners of transformation.

Similarly, *reduco* can be redefined to mean taking students back to the heart of the matter, releading them anew to their original roots, their sacred sources. We have all repressed our sacred face because of an alleged secularism and institutionalized religion. Thus, we are all reduced to attaching ourselves to powerful others as our protectors. But once good teaching and education have taken us back to our origins, we can recognize the choices available to us. What ultimately lies behind any construction of the world and the stories by which we live is human beings responding to underlying forming sacred sources. Any new re-creation of the world can come only from people emptying themselves on the deeper levels of those sacred sources that preserve inherited stories of loyalty or power or destructive death and choosing to ask new questions, so that *reduco* becomes *educo*.

CHARACTERISTICS OF THE TEACHER AS AUTHENTIC GUIDE

In the encounter of teaching, the most detailed and structured course cannot avoid the eruption of underlying forces. We can explain the process of transformation and the four faces of our being, but there are always the deepest depths that demand that we let go, that we take risks ourselves and allow the process once again to take place in us. Even though the teacher as guide alerts students to this process, they will not be truly aware until they feel in their deepest selves the urge to depart from rote learning and memorization as safeguards from risking faith. But even the teachers—especially the teachers—although they have taken the journey with many classes before, are asked to take the journey through the core drama of transformation once again. They know the process, but not in relationship to this class—the reality of new students sitting in front of them.

Only this willingness to re-experience the call into the depths of creativity to participate in new birthing and transforming is what allows the teacher to be the authentic guide and prevents the process from becoming a repetitive story. This is not a power relationship—authority, yes, but not power. To use power is to exercise control over the process and the students, to manipulate their lives while teachers become tyrannical lords who want to make students into clones. The power that comes from mutual doubt and discovery is capacity, or linked power. The students and teacher in the crucible of transformation often entered as disciples or as other kinds of fragmented individuals. The alchemy of the classroom practicing transformational politics has metamorphosed them into colleagues, a learning community of equals.

Since time immemorial we have known about guides, but too often we gave ourselves over to the guide because we despaired of our own value. Hesse, in his archetypal novel, *Demian*, tells the story of the false guide and the true guide.[17] The title, *Demian*, contains two opposing sacred sources, the demon that seeks to possess us and the daimonion, our own destiny, that calls us from within to recreate the four faces of our being by intervening against the blind fate of simply accepting inherited stories and ways of life that disable us.

EDUCATION AS GUIDING AND BEING GUIDED INTO THE CREATIVE DEPTHS

Is it possible for teachers of all subject matter to be guides of transformation? The roots of all disciplines, whether math, literature, biology, politics, art, or chemistry, are to be found in underlying sacred sources. The sciences developed out of our desire to know and to cooperate with the source of all sources in the ongoing creation of the universe. All teaching is an invitation not only to the knowledge of a particular science but to return to the sacred origins of that science. Furthermore, this invitation to participate in a particular universe of discourse is a call to return to the creativity and imagination that produced all fields of human knowing. To return to these origins is to return to sacred sources in the depths that reveal to us the world of archetypes that creative people know how to embody. For example, Poincaré, the famous French mathematician, knew that his breakthrough in math was not due merely to willpower and rational thought. At certain points he lost his way and had to admit that he did not know how to go on.[18] He realized that he had to stop thinking about it; none of the patterns that he knew worked. And so, returning to the language of the story of transformation, he had to empty himself in Act II, Scene 2 of the story that he had learned and that threatened to continue to dominate his consciousness. Because he risked faith in the process of creativity, that is, waiting until the sacred sources spoke to him, he was filled anew in Act III, Scene 1 while he was, of all things, waiting for the bus. Honest teachers, just as honest scientists, must acknowledge when they have lost their way.[19]

When students confront math, philosophy, history, art, or physics, they can be led by the teacher as guide not only into the rational result of diagnosing the world, but to the deeper sources, the sacred roots of the creativity that led persons to be in awe of the world and from that awe-ful experience, to differentiate a language of concepts and methods by which to grasp the world. Unfortunately, too many of us have lost the awareness that our teaching points to deeper sources so that we no longer know about the underlying meaning of things. This is the deeper meaning of teaching to which together we can and need to return. Again, it is grounded in *educo*, leading students so that they can step outside of their skepticism to be touched by the sacred sources of the subject matter that they are exploring.

Granted, in some subjects, the language of sacred sources is more acceptable. But what is called for here are teachers who realize that they teach not only numbers and facts but the creative process by which they do education. Through attitudes of wonder and reverence, they allow the student to see the non-rational dimension of all true learning. Teachers should never lose the utter sense of amazement and humility when they recognize a student who sees and understands what algebra, philosophy, or biology is all about. At such moments we know that we are not in control. This is the creative process to which the rough hands of lecturing or rote learning cannot give birth. Too often, we teach students how to learn and how to be critical, but we usually fail to guide them to be creative.

Teachers who are aware of this creative process do not have to preach it but must live it and, even more so, *be* this process so that they teach the very process that sustains them. So as not to be overwhelmed by this process, they share it with others by guiding them into a still emerging field of human knowing. Teachers as persons and in their service as teachers are asked to participate persistently in transformation.

Some of us as teachers refuse the new call to depart again into the re-experiencing of the core drama of transformation. To remain rooted in the previous insight is to resort to what we spoke of above—exercising power through demanding rote learning or mystification by overwhelming the students with our brilliance. Burnt-out teachers turn to producing competent students who consume the subject matter because it will give them power over facts and skills and therefore over others. Often, teachers do not discover their own voices due to their teacher training, which does not provide them with "guide-ance" but with formulae of power and mystification. They have not departed from the emanational container of being mere extensions of their own trainers. Only those guides who have taken the journey of transformation in at least one aspect of their life know how to guide others. To break with the world of fixed truths arrested in Act I, Scene 1 is to descend into doubt, confusion, and searching. But this period of doubt is crucial because it is the time of a new gestation, a pregnancy that can be fruitful only if brought to its goal in transformation. We have to empty ourselves of old methods, old truths, and let the new emerge. This is the mystery of re-experiencing our creative sources and those peculiar to our subject matter. Ultimately, all archetypal stories are connected to each other and to the deepest source of being, which is the source of transformation as a way of life. To know again this co-mingling of the sources within us prepares us to return to the classroom ready to lead students through the creative process. We teach who we are.

Guiding students to touch the archetypal source of a particular science or field of study does not mean expecting all students to become another biologist or anthropologist. But it does allow the student to make a choice of a particular area of study that corresponds to her or his inner gifts or inclinations. This is radical education at its most profound because it leads us to the sources from which all knowledge derives its inspiration. In this way career choices would be subordinate to students' inner daimonion or destiny, which would enable them to enact best the political and historical faces of their being as members of the community. In this kind of human economy, each person is worthy of hire. Whatever they contribute to the community is also in keeping with their own inner being. Work performed in this context is not done to preserve a status quo or in the spirit of self-interest; it is labor that has a sacred meaning—to create a new and better world.

CONCLUSION

The above understanding of multicultural education sees schooling as an invitation to participate in the core drama of transformation. This kind of education carries with it certain implications for styles of teaching, for sharing and communicating. When a teacher invites students to join a process, they cannot give prefabricated truths or experiences. It is an invitation to participate on a common journey that needs all of our personal and collective energies. In this sense, nobody has a fixed truth. The teacher as guide has earned this right because she has traveled the road before. Guides can provide structure to keep us on the right path, but the risk to enter into the deepest depths of creativity can only be made by the person alone. Thus teaching pedagogy that emphasizes dialogue, discussion, and dissent is preferable because this style of teaching provides a legitimacy to each person's ideas and insights.

Teachers have more than knowledge to impart; they offer a depth of experience beyond the facts of the discipline. Teachers in the service of transformation lead students to the imaginative and creative sources where they encountered the meaning of history, art, or physics. Teachers relive the story of chemistry or music by telling their story, their discovery of how the underlying reality of their area touched them. Students are invited to weave their understanding with both a rational content and one that is grounded in the sources of what all human knowledge is pointing us toward. This ability to weave the sacred and concrete stories of the disciplines is what makes room for the revolutions in human knowing. In living the stories, students are not only repeating but bring to the enterprise their own creativity. They thereby enlarge and deepen the story based on what they have learned from their own insights. Contrary to the usual history of science, science is always renewed not through linear expansion but by a person who, although trained in the old story, rejects the old story in order to weave a new vision.

This is not an elitist adventure. All of us as students and teachers can participate in transformation. Part and parcel of the relationship between teacher and student is to encourage students to move toward their own insights and articulation. To do so is to rediscover students as colleagues. Practicing and teaching transformational politics educates students for a particular kind of task: archetypal participation with all of its concrete faces wherever they find themselves. Education is always a personal, political, historical, and sacred task in the service of an underlying way of life. Either we will prepare students for a life of accepting domination or we guide them toward their own liberation and that of others. To question and dissent in the classroom prepares students to confront authority and to call it to authenticity. Teaching students by exercising power relationships, not allowing them to create conflict or change, prepares them for a life of authoritarian liberalism wherein they can pursue their own interests if they are loyal to the powerful. Power relations that stress contracts and existing boundaries train students to compete with others in the larger society. Building a questioning community of learners in a classroom where each person's views are taken seriously is a beginning for true democratic citizenship in which each sees the other as being sacred.

Thus, how we seduce, reduce, deduct, or educate students will have enormous implications for the kind of society and politics they will create. The heart of schooling is discovering, evaluating, and creating archetypal stories in the service of the four deeper ways of life that give to our stories their ultimate meaning and purpose. Students are learning to reproduce in the larger world the reality of being docile followers, dominators, violators of others, or mutual friends. These distinct options will mean different kinds of democracy: authoritarian, liberal, or participatory democracy. All are called democracy but we know that there are four sacred sources that underlie the concept of democracy. Our choice is clear: to lead students to create a fundamentally new and loving society.

NOTES

1. Herman Hesse, *Siddhartha* (New York: Bantam Books, 1971).

2. Leslie Marmon Silko, *Ceremony* (New York: Penguin Books, 1986), pp. 19, 45, 68–69.

3. Naguib Mahfouz, *Palace Walk* (New York: Doubleday, 1990).

4. Harold Bloom, interpreter, *The Book of J*, translated from the Hebrew by David Rosenberg (New York: Grove Weidenfeld, 1990).

5. John Steinbeck, *The Grapes of Wrath* (New York: Penguin, 1989).

6. Frances Fox Piven and Richard A. Cloward, *The New Class War* (New York: Pantheon Books, 1982).

7. René Marques, *La Carreta* (Rio Piedras, Puerto Rico: Editorial Cultural, 1971).

8. Alan Brinkley, "The Western Historians," *New York Times Book Review*, September 20, 1992.

9. Ibid.

10. Henrik Ibsen, *A Doll's House, The Wild Duck, The Lady from the Sea* (New York: Dutton, 1910).

11. Sandra Cisneros, *Woman Hollering Creek and Other Stories* (New York: Random House, 1991).

12. I owe this symbol of window and mirror to my colleague and friend, Emily Jane Style, the co-director of the National S.E.E.D. Project, Seeking Educational Equity and Diversity.

13. Manfred Halpern, *Transformation: Its Theory and Practice in Personal, Political, Historical and Sacred Being.* Unpublished manuscript, 1994. Chapter 14, "Archetypes as Sacred Sources."

14. For another look into the world of archetypes, see the works of C. G. Jung and Jolande Jacobi, *Complex, Archetype, Symbol in the Psychology of C. G. Jung*, trans. Ralph Manheim (Princeton, N.J.: Princeton University Press, Bollingen Series LVII, 1959). For a practical application, see Jung's *Man and His Symbols* (New York: Dell Press, 1966).

15. For a similar view of education, see Paulo Freire, *The Pedagogy of the Oppressed* (New York: Herder and Herder, 1970).

16. Paul Friedlander, *Plato, An Introduction* (Princeton, N.J.: Princeton University Press, Bollingen Series LIX, 1973), pp. 32–58.

17. Herman Hesse, *Demian* (New York: Bantam Books, 1981).

18. Brewster Ghiselin, *The Creative Process* (New York: Mentor Books, 1963), pp. 33–42.

19. In this regard see Werner Heisenberg, *Physics and Beyond* (New York: Harper and Row, 1971); and Thomas Kuhn, *The Structure of Scientific Revolutions* (Chicago: University of Chicago Press, 1970).

Appendix: Reading and Film List and Course Outlines

Recommended Reading and Film List for Multicultural and Gender-Fair Courses

READING MATERIAL

David T. Abalos, *The Latino Family and the Politics of Transformation* (New York: Praeger Press, 1993).

———. *Latinos in the United States: The Sacred and the Political* (Notre Dame, Ind.: University of Notre Dame Press, 1986).

Paula Gunn Allen, ed., *Grandmothers of the Light: A Medicine Woman's Source-book* (Boston: Beacon Press, 1991).

———. *Spider Woman's Granddaughters: Traditional Tales and Contemporary Writing by Native American Women* (New York: Fawcett Colombine, 1989).

Julia Alvarez, *How the García Girls Lost Their Accent* (New York: Algonquin Press, 1992).

Rudolfo A. Anaya, *Bless Me Ultima* (Berkeley, Calif.: Tonatiuh-Quinto Sol International Publishers, 1988).

Gloria Anzaldúa, ed., *Making Faces, Making Soul: Haciendo Caras, Creative and Critical Perspectives by Women of Color* (San Francisco: Aunt Lute Foundation Book, 1990).

Kwame Anthony Appiah, *In My Father's House* (New York: Oxford University Press, 1992).

Asian Women United of California, eds., *Making Waves: An Anthology of Writings by and about Asian American Women* (Boston: Beacon Press, 1989).

Miguel Angel Asturias, *Men of Maize* (New York: Verso, 1988).

William Attaway, *Blood on the Forge* (New York: Monthly Review Press, 1987).

Mary Catherine Bateson, *Composing a Life* (New York: Atlantic Monthly Press, 1989).

Derrick Bell, *Faces at the Bottom of the Well* (New York: Basic Books, 1992).

Robert Bellah et al., *Habits of the Heart* (Berkeley: University of California Press, 1985).

Marshall Berman, *The Politics of Authenticity, Radical Individualism and the Rise of Modern Society* (New York: Atheneum Press, 1972).

Harold Bloom, *The Book of J* (New York: Grove Weidenfeld, 1990).

Thomas D. Boswell, *The Cuban American Experience: Culture, Images, and Perspectives* (Totowa, N.J.: Rowman and Allanhold, 1984).

Taylor Branch, *Parting the Waters: America in the King Years 1954–63* (New York: Simon and Schuster, 1988).

Joseph Epes Brown, *The Sacred Pipe* (Baltimore: Penguin Books, 1972).

Joseph Campbell, *The Hero With a Thousand Faces* (Princeton, N.J.: Princeton University Press, 1973).

Americo Castro, *The Spaniards*, trans. Willard King and Selma Margarettem (Berkeley: University of California Press, 1971).

Jeffrey Paul Chan et al., *The Big Aiiiieeeee! An Anthology of Chinese American and Japanese American Literature* (New York: Penguin Books 1991).

Sandra Cisneros, *The House on Mango Street* (Houston: Arte Publico Press, 1987).

_____. *Woman Hollering Creek and Other Stories* (New York: Random House, 1991).

Michael Cooke, *Afro-American Literature in the Twentieth Century: The Achievement of Intimacy* (New Haven, Conn.: Yale University Press, 1984).

Henri Corbin, *Creative Imagination in the Sufism of Ibn Arabi* (Princeton, N.J.: Princeton University Press, 1969).

Margaret Craven, *I Heard the Owl Call My Name* (New York: Dell Paperback Books, 1962).

Michael Dorris, *Yellow Raft on Blue Water* (New York: Warner Books, 1988).

W.E.B. Dubois, *The Souls of Black Folk* (New York: Signet Books, 1969).

Ralph Ellison, *Invisible Man* (New York: Vintage Books, 1972).

Erik Erikson, *Gandhi's Truth: On the Origins of Militant Non-Violence* (New York: W. W. Norton, 1968).

Laura Esquivel, *Like Water for Chocolate* (New York: Doubleday, 1992).

Samuel G. Freedman, *Small Victories: The Real World of a Teacher, Her Students and Their High School* (New York: Harper and Row, 1990).

Paulo Freire, *Pedagogy of the Oppressed* (New York: Continuum Books, 1970).

Cristina García, *Dreaming in Cuban* (New York: Alfred A. Knopf, 1992).

Henry Louis Gates, Jr., *Loose Canons: Notes on the Culture Wars* (New York: Oxford University Press, 1992).

_____. *The Signifying Monkey: A Theory of Afro-American Literary Criticism* (New York: Oxford University Press, 1988).

Paula Giddings, *Where and When I Enter: The Impact of Black Women on Race and Sex in America* (New York: Bantam Books, 1988).

Carol Gilligan, *In a Different Voice* (Cambridge, Mass.: Harvard University Press, 1982).

Francine DuPlessix Gray, *Soviet Women, Walking the Tightrope* (New York: Doubleday, 1989).

Richard Griswold del Castillo, *The Treaty of Guadalupe Hidalgo: A Legacy of Conflict* (Norman, Okla.: University of Oklahoma Press, 1990).

Gustavo Gutiérrez, *We Drink from Our Own Wells* (Maryknoll, N.Y.: Orbis Press, 1984).

Andrew Hacker, *Two Nations, Black and White, Separate, Hostile, Unequal* (New York: Charles Scribner's Sons, 1992).

Manfred Halpern, "Choosing Between Ways of Life and Death and Between Forms of Democracy," *Alternatives* (January 1987), pp. 5–34.

_____. *Transformation: Its Theory and Practice in Personal, Political, Historical, and Sacred Being* (unpublished manuscript, 1994).

Hermann Hesse, *Demian* (New York: Bantam Books, 1966).

———. *Siddhartha* (New York: Bantam Books, 1971).

Oscar Hijuelos, *The Mambo Kings Play Songs of Love* (New York: Harper and Row, 1990).

Asunción Horno-Delgado et al., *Breaking Boundaries, Latina Writings and Critical Readings* (Amherst, Mass.: University of Massachusetts Press, 1988).

Zora Neale Hurston, *Their Eyes Were Watching God* (New York: Harper and Row, 1989).

Ken Kesey, *One Flew Over the Cuckoo's Nest* (New York: Signet Books, 1962).

Martin Luther King, Jr., *Why We Can't Wait* (New York: Signet Books, 1964).

Maxine Hong Kingston, *The Woman Warrior* (New York: Vintage International Edition, 1989).

Jonathan Kozol, *Savage Inequalities: Children in America's Schools* (New York: Crown Publishers, 1991).

Penny Lernoux, *Cry of the People* (Baltimore: Penguin, 1979).

Oscar Lewis, *Five Families* (New York: New American Library, 1959).

Sara Lawrence Lightfoot, *Balm in Gilead* (New York: Addison-Wesley Publishing Co., 1988).

C. Eric Lincoln and Lawrence H. Mamiya. *The Black Church in the African American Experience* (Durham, N.C.: Duke University Press, 1991).

Lyn MacCorkle, *Cubans in the U.S.: A Bibliography for Research in the Social and Behavioral Sciences, 1960–1983* (Westport, Conn.: Greenwood Press, 1984).

Naguib Mahfouz, *Palace Walk* (New York: Doubleday, 1990).

Malcolm X, *The Autobiography of Malcolm X* (New York: Grove Press, 1966).

René Marques, *La Carreta* (Rio Piedras, Puerto Rico: Editorial Cultural, 1971).

Minnesota Humanities Council, *Braided Lives: An Anthology of Multicultural American Writings* (St. Paul, Minn.: Minnesota Humanities Council, 1991).

Alejandro Morales, *The Brick People* (Houston: Arte Publico Press, 1988).

Walter F. Morris, *Living Maya*, photography by Jeffrey Jay Foxx (New York: Harry N. Abrams, 1988).

Toni Morrison, *Beloved* (New York: New American Library, 1987).

———. *Playing in the Dark* (Cambridge, Mass.: Harvard University Press, 1992).

John G. Neihardt, *Black Elk Speaks* (Lincoln: University of Nebraska Press, 1961).

Elena Padilla, *Up from Puerto Rico* (New York: Columbia University Press, 1969).

Alan Paton, *Too Late the Phalarope* (New York: Scribner, 1953).

Octavio Paz, "Reflections: Mexico and the United States," *The New Yorker*, September 7, 1979.

———. *Sor Juana Ines* (Cambridge, Mass.: Harvard University Press, 1988).

Howell Raines, *My Soul is Rested: The Story of the Civil Rights Movement in the Deep South* (New York: Bantam Books, 1978).

Adrienne Rich, *On Lies, Secrets, and Silence: Selected Prose 1966–1978* (New York: W. W. Norton, 1978).

Edward Rivera, *Family Installments: Memories of Growing Up Hispanic* (New York: Penguin Books, 1983).

Tomas Rivera, . . . *Y No Se Lo Trago La Tierra* (and the Earth Did Not Devour Him) (Houston: Arte Publico Press, 1987).

Tom Robbins, *Even Cowgirls Get the Blues* (New York: Bantam Books, 1976).

Edward Said, *Culture and Imperialism* (New York: Alfred A. Knopf, 1993).

John Shockley, *Chicano Revolt in a Texas Town* (Notre Dame: University of Notre Dame Press, 1974).

Leslie Marmon Silko, *Almanac of the Dead* (New York: Simon and Schuster, 1991).

_____ . *Ceremony* (New York: Penguin Books, 1986).

Rick Simonson and Scott Walker, eds., *Multicultural Literacy* (St. Paul, Minn.: Graywolf Press, 1988).

Janet Madden Simpson and Sara Blake, *Emerging Voices: A Cross-Cultural Reader* (Fort Worth, Tex.: Holt, Rinehart and Winston, 1990).

Ronald Takaki, *A Different Mirror: A History of Multicultural America* (Boston: Little, Brown and Co., 1993).

_____ . *Strangers From a Different Shore* (Boston: Little, Brown and Co., 1989).

Amy Tan, *The Joy Luck Club* (New York: Vintage, 1991).

Piri Thomas, *Down These Mean Streets* (New York: Alfred A. Knopf, 1970).

Roberto E. Villarreal and Norma G. Hernandez, eds., *Latinos and Political Coalitions* (New York: Praeger Press, 1991).

Victor Villaseñor, *Rain of Gold* (Houston: Arte Publico Press, 1992).

Alice Walker, *The Color Purple* (New York: Pocket Books, 1982).

_____ . *Meridian* (New York: Pocket Books, 1986).

Cornel West, *Race Matters* (Boston: Beacon Press, 1993).

Anzia Yezierska, *Bread Givers* (New York: Persea Books, 1975).

Iris M. Young, *Justice and the Politics of Difference* (Princeton, N.J.: Princeton University Press, 1990).

FILMS

The Ballad of Gregorio Cortez, directed by Robert Young, PBS American Playhouse, 1982.

The Blood of the Condor, directed by Jorge Sanjines, Bolivia, 1969.

Camila, directed by Maria Luisa Bemberg, Argentina, 1984.

Hopi Songs of the Fourth World, directed by Pat Ferrero, New Day Films, 1985.

Like Water For Chocolate, directed by Alfonso Arau, Mexico, 1992.

Lucía, directed by Humberto Solas, Cuba, 1968.

El Norte, directed by Gregory Nava, Independent Productions, 1983.

Nothing But a Man, directed by Michael Roemer, Du/Art Cinema Video, 1964.

La Operación, directed by Ana M. Garcia, Cinema Guild, 1982.

Operation Bootstrap, directed by Carl Dudley, Universal Education and Visual Arts, 1964.

A Portrait of Teresa, directed by Pastor Vega, Cuba, 1979.

Raisin in the Sun, directed by Daniel Petrie, Columbia Pictures, 1961.

The Salt of the Earth, directed by Herbert Biberman, Independent Productions Corporation, 1954.

The Sewing Woman, Anti-Defamation League of B'Nai Brith, 1986.

La Strada, directed by Federico Fellini, Italy, 1954.

Yentl, directed by Barbra Streisand, MGM, 1983.

Politics Course: Latina/o Politics in the United States

Princeton University
Politics 342
Spring 1993

COURSE DESCRIPTION

In this course, we examine the political awakening and participation of Chicanos, Puerto Ricans and other Latinos from the perspective of a theory of transformation. Particular attention is given to the relationship between the personal, political, historical and sacred aspects of Latino life and culture in the United States. The course is intended to provide Latinos and other students the opportunity to witness a people becoming political. Strategies of transformation for Latinas/os will be examined.

Latinos have not had the opportunity to confront their problems on a plane of equality with others. The very fact that only a lecture here and there is devoted to Latinos in courses on the family, politics and economics attests to the invisibility of this group of people. We know from census statistics that Latinos are the youngest population in the United States and that their rate of increase through birth and migration is the largest in the nation. Their growing presence is having a significant impact on politics in the West, the Southwest, and increasingly in the eastern United States. Yet, Latinos as a group suffer from low employment rates and underemployment, poor education, substandard housing, inadequate social services, and under-representation in political spheres. This course seeks to explore the reasons for such powerlessness.

In this course, we will discuss important questions for Latinas/os: How shall we define ourselves? Why or why not assimilate? How do we gain participation? Should we form political parties? and, What are our ultimate choices?

COURSE OUTLINE

1. Introduction to the various Latino populations in the United States. Latinos do not constitute a monolith but are composed of diverse social, economic, racial and religious groups.

   Theme: What is a Latino?—The present Latino story.

Readings:

David T. Abalos, *Latinos in the United States*, Chapter 2: "Going Home: A Return to the Sources, the Search for Latino Identity"

Mary Ann Beck et al., eds., *The Analysis of Hispanic Texts*

Thomas D. Boswell and James R. Curtis, *The Cuban American Experience*

Americo Castro, *The Spaniards*

Francesco Cordasco and Eugene Bucchioni, *The Puerto Rican Experience*

Johan Huizinga, *Homo Ludens*

D. H. Lawrence, *The Plumed Serpent*

Richard Rodriguez, *Hunger of Memory*

Leslie Marmon Silko, *Ceremony*, pp. 1–63

Charles Wagley, *Latin American Tradition: Essays on the Unity and the Diversity of Latin American Culture*

2. Cultural comparison between Latino culture and Anglo-Saxon ethos.

   Theme: The tragedy of people speaking past one another—stories that seem to be at odds with one another but are not necessarily so.

   Readings:

   Norman O. Brown, *Life Against Death*

   Margaret Craven, *I Heard the Owl Call My Name*

   Virgilio Elizondo, *Galilean Journey: The Mexican-American Promise*

   Ralph Ellison, *Invisible Man*

   Juan Flores et. al., "La Carreta Made a U-Turn: Puerto Rican Culture and Language in the United States"

   René Marques, *La Carreta*

   Gabriel García Márquez, *One Hundred Years of Solitude*

   Octavio Paz, "Reflections, Mexico and the United States"

   Alan Riding, *Distant Neighbors: A Portrait of the Mexicans*

   Leslie Marmon Silko, *Ceremony*, pp. 64–100

   Frederick Turner, *Beyond Geography: The Western Spirit Against the Wilderness*

   Sheldon Wolin, "The People's Two Bodies"

3. Political participation. The social and historical experiences that underlie the current relationships of the Latino people to the social and political systems of the United States, viewed from the perspective of a theory of transformation.

   Theme: Ways of thinking about Latino politics.

Readings:

David T. Abalos, *Latinos in the United States*, "Foreword," "Introduction," Chapter 1: "A Theory of Transformation"

Robert N. Bellah et al., *Habits of the Heart: Individualism and Commitment in American Life*

Marshall Berman, *The Politics of Authenticity*, "Preface" and "Introduction: The Personal is Political"

Carlos E. Cortes, ed., *Cuban Exiles in the United States*

Takeo Doi, *The Anatomy of Dependency*

Richard R. Fagan, *Cubans in Exile*

F. Chris García, ed., *La Causa Politica: A Chicano Politics Reader*, pp. 19–85

Manfred Halpern, *Transformation: Its Theory and Practice in Personal, Political, Historical and Sacred Being*, Chapter 6: "The Archetypal Drama of Transformation"

Herbert Marcuse, *Eros and Civilization*

Alan Paton, *Too Late the Phalarope*

Frances F. Piven and Richard Cloward, *The New Class War*, pp. 1–39

Michael Polanyi, *The Tacit Dimension*

J. J. Rousseau, *The Social Contract*

Sheldon Wolin, "Political Theory as a Vocation"

4. Economic impediments to political participation.

Readings:

Mario Barrera, *Race and Class in the Southwest*, pp. 34–57

Frank Bonilla and Ricardo Campos, "Puerto Ricans in the New Economic Order"

Frances F. Piven and Richard Cloward, *The New Class War*, pp. 40–99

Thomas Sowell, *Race and Economics*

U.S. Commission on Civil Rights, *Puerto Ricans in the Continental United States*, Chapter 2

5. Race and ethnicity as political issues.

Theme: Latinas/os challenge traditional upward mobility and assimilation.

Readings:

David T. Abalos, *Latinos in the United States*, Chapter 6: "The Politics of Liberation versus the Politics of Assimilation," and Chapter 7: "Latino Professionals: A Transforming Middle Class"

Mario Barrera, *Race and Class in the Southwest*, pp. 174–219

Marshall Berman, *The Politics of Authenticity*, pp. 87–144

Edward Franklin Frazier, *Race and Culture Contacts in the Modern World*

Manuel Maldonado-Denis, *Puerto Rico: A Socio-Historic Interpretation*, pp. 130–147

Albert Memmi, *The Colonizer and the Colonized*

Joan Moore and Harry Pachón, "Colonialism: The Case of the Mexican American"

Clara Rodriguez, *The Puerto Rican Struggle*, pp. 31–46

Eleanor Meyer Rogg, *The Assimilation of Cuban Exiles*

Leslie Marmon Silko, *Ceremony*, pp. 100–152

Thomas Sowell, *Ethnic America*

6. The politics of bilingual/bicultural and multicultural education.

Theme: The United States public school system was established in the nineteenth century to socialize and nationalize immigrants; why did Congress support bilingualism and biculturalism in 1968? What is multiculturalism and how does it relate to specific ethnic and racial groups?

Readings:

David T. Abalos, *Latinos in the United States*, Chapter 4: "The Politics of Transformation in the Latino Community"

American Council on Education and Education Commission of the States, *One Third of a Nation*

Francesco Cordasco and Eugene Bucchioni, *The Puerto Rican Community and its Children on the Mainland*

June Macklin and Stanley A. West, *The Chicano Experience*

Earl J. Ogletree, *Education of the Spanish-Speaking Urban Child*

Alan Pifer, *Bilingual Education and the Hispanic Challenge*

Richard Rodriguez, *Hunger of Memory*

George Sánchez, "Bilingualism and Mental Measures: A Word of Caution"

Leslie Marmon Silko, *Ceremony*, pp. 153–78

U.S. Commission on Civil Rights, *Puerto Ricans in the Continental United States*, Chapter 3

7. Latina women and the family: an internal liberation movement.

Theme: Intra-group conflicts: the politics of male/female relations.

Readings:

David T. Abalos, *Latinos in the United States*, Chapter 3: "The Politics of the Latino Family"

Edna Acosta-Belen, *The Puerto Rican Woman*, pp. 51–63; 124–141

Maria Linda Apodaca, "The Chicana Woman: A Materialist Historical Perspective"

Marshall Berman, *The Politics of Authenticity*, pp. 3–53

Betty García-Bahne, "La Chicana and the Chicano Family"

Richard Griswold del Castillo, *La Familia: Chicano Families in the United States, 1848 to the Present*

Magdalena Mora and Adelaide R. del Castillo, *Mexican Women in the United States*, pp. 29–61

Toni Morrison, *Beloved*

Elaine Pagels, *The Gnostic Gospels*

Octavio Paz, *Sor Juana Inez*

Clara Rodriguez, *The Puerto Rican Struggle*, pp. 58–73

J. Rogler, "Intergenerational Change in Ethnic Identity in the Puerto Rican Family"

Alice Walker, *The Color Purple*

Eli Zaretsky, *Capitalism, The Family and Personal Life*, Chapters 1–3, 5

8. Latino politicization.

Theme: Grass roots politics and party politics.

Readings:

Paulo Freire, *Pedagogy of the Oppressed*

Armando Gutiérrez and Herbert Hirsch, "The Militant Challenge to the American Ethos: Chicanos and Mexican Americans"

Mark Levy and Michael Kramer, *The Ethnic Factor: How America's Minorities Decide Elections*

Joan W. Moore, "Minorities in the American Class System"

Felix Padilla, *Puerto Rican Chicago*

Frances F. Piven and Richard Cloward, *The New Class War*, pp. 100–124

Clara Rodriguez, *The Puerto Rican Struggle*, pp. 74–89; 90–128

John Shockley, *Chicano Revolt in a Texas Town*, Preface; pp. 1–41, 111–149

9. Nationalism, separatism and violence.

Theme: Rejection of politics of accommodation and turning toward deformation.

Readings:

Rudolfo Acuña, *Occupied America*, Chapters 9 and 10

Mario Barrera, Carlos Muñoz and Charles Ornelas, "The Barrio as an Internal Colony"

Marshall Berman, *The Politics of Authenticity*, pp. 231–310: "The Life and Death of Julie," and "More Escapes from Freedom"

R. Blauner, "Internal Colonialism and Ghetto Revolt"

Kenneth B. Clark, *Dark Ghetto: Dilemmas of Social Power*, Chapter 5

Frantz Fanon, *The Wretched of the Earth*

Alberto Juarez, "The Emergence of El Partido de la Raza Unida: California's New Chicano Party"

Alfredo Mirandé, *Gringo Justice*

Armando Morales, "The 1970–1971 East Los Angeles Chicano-Police Riots"

Leslie Marmon Silko, *Ceremony*, pp. 180–213

Jerome Skolnick, *The Politics of Protest*

10. Radical politics

Theme: Alternatives to violence.

Readings:

Marshall Berman, *The Politics of Authenticity*, pp. 163–199: "A New Morality: The Authentic Woman and Man," and pp. 200–228: "A New Politics: The Authentic Citizen"

Ralph Waldo Emerson, *Collected Essays*, "Politics"

Robert Fitch, "Tilting with the System"

Karl Marx, *Economic and Philosophic Manuscripts of 1844*

Peter Mattheisson, *Sal Si Puedes*

Hanna F. Pitkin and Sara Shumer, "On Participation"

Frances F. Piven and Richard Cloward, *The New Class War*, pp. 125–150

Sheldon Wolin, "What Revolutionary Action Means Today"

11. Latino politics and the sacred.

Theme: The role of religion in assimilation and liberation.

Readings:

David T. Abalos, *Latinos in the United States* and "Latinos and the Sacred"

Virgilio Elizondo, *Galilean Journey: The Mexican-American Promise*, Chapters 8 and 9

Manfred Halpern, *Transformation: Its Theory and Practice*, "The Human Being in the Image of God: A Cosmos of Creative Participation"

Penny Lernoux, *Cry of the People*, Chapters 9–12

Jorge V. Pixley, *On Exodus: A Liberation Perspective*

Leslie Marmon Silko, *Ceremony*, pp. 248–262

Ann Belford Ulanov, *The Feminine in Jungian Psychology and in Christian Theology*, pp. 277–285

U.S. Catholic Bishops, *The Hispanic Presence, Challenge and Commitment*, Pastoral Letter

12. Latinos look to the future.

Theme: Strategies for liberation—goals of Latino politics.

Readings:

David T. Abalos, *Latinos in the United States*, Chapter 8: "Choices for Latinos: Creating the Present and the Future"

Marshall Berman, *The Politics of Authenticity*, "Conclusion"

Frank Bonilla and Robert Girling, *Structures of Dependency*

Vernon J. Dixon and Badi Foster, *Beyond Black and White: An Alternative America*

Sara Evans and Harry Boyte, "Schools for Action: Radical Uses of Social Space"

Ralph Guzmán, "Mexican Americans in the Urban Area: Will they Riot?"

Frances F. Piven and Richard Cloward, *Poor People's Movement*, pp. 354–350

Nicos Poulantzas, *Political Power and Social Class*

John Shockley, *Chicano Revolt in a Texas Town*, pp. 196–226

Leslie Marmon Silko, *Ceremony*, pp. 248–262

William J. Wilson, *The Declining Significance of Race*, Chapters 1, 6, 7 and 8

ASSIGNMENT

Ask yourself one, two, or three questions and answer them.

Each question must allow you to make both creative and critical use of aspects of the theory of transformation as it relates to yourself and to Latinas/os in the United States. Take those aspects of the theory and of Latino/a life which have profoundly affected and personally touched you.

Pose questions that allow you to reflect on the work we did both before and after midterm.

Each question must allow you to link the personal, political, historical, and the sacred in the lives of Latinas/os. If you are not a Latino/a, consider how *your* experience in regard to the four faces of your being parallels the struggles of Latinos/as. Ask what stories or values or ideas or links you share with Latinas/os. Also ask on what grounds—that is, in the service of what way of life—you share or do not share these connections with la communidad Latina.

Here are some examples of the questions you might ask:

- What are the stories that have shaped Latina/o life in the United States? What is your own personal response or involvement with these stories?

- What is it that drives Latinas/os and members of your ethnic group to want to assimilate to the dominant culture? What does this do to the four faces of our being? What stories are involved? Where does this leave us in the core drama? Give examples.

- Why will incremental change as practiced in the service of incoherence in the story of the market society ultimately fail not only to meet the needs of Latinos and communities of color but also the needs of the dominant? Give examples of problems in which incremental change is not sufficient.

- In regard to male/female relationships, from your personal background, why do we have to see these relationships as political and historical as well as personal and sacred?

- How are the stories of either patriarchy or romantic love reinforced by the story of uncritical loyalty? Where does this place us in regard to the core drama, and what damage does this do to the four faces of our being? In the service of what way of life do these stories leave us?

- Analyze why Latinas/os are turning increasingly to forms of self wounding. Give examples of this in the Latino community. What does this tell us about the stories of the market society and the tribalism that are practiced in the wider society?

- Given what you have learned in this course, how would you go about creating the alternative story of transformation for Latinas/os in the United States? If politics is what we can and need to do together, what can we do here and now to make a difference for the better?

- Latinas/os are said to be very religious. Is this enough? What does this mean in relationship to seeing our life as sacred? In other words, will we have to rethink the role that religion has played in the Latino story? What does the idea of religion as a truth given once for all do to the other faces of our being? Give examples of how religion has helped and/or hindered la communidad Latina in relationship to transformation.

- To be simultaneously an insider and an outsider, to be in the world but not of the world, to become involved in the world but not dissolved in the world—how are these good strategies of transformation for Latinas/os and those people of goodwill who care deeply about their own communities?

Enter as deeply into the underlying patterning sources as you feel able. See what archetypal stories are at stake. Clarify the way of life within which the problem you are analyzing moves and the way of life within which your analysis of this problem is rooted.

Religious Studies Course:
Contemporary Moral Values

Seton Hall University
Religious Studies 1502
Spring 1994

COURSE DESCRIPTION

Perhaps the most pressing contemporary moral issue of our time is the story of the authentic self as we journey through the core drama of transformation. The struggle to be a self, to speak from a central core deep within one's own sources, to discover one's own story and relationship to others, is the central characteristic of being authentic and moral. Unlike the rugged individualists, competing with one another for power in the service of incoherence and/or deformation, to be an authentic self involves our intimate participation with others in building more human societies. We need others in order to be human. We are more than personal and social selves; we are all sacred, or religious persons. Our religious authenticity will ultimately depend upon a deeper realm, archetypal, sacred ways of life in the service of which we practice the four faces of our being: the personal, political, historical, and sacred.

As we consider the story of our quest for an authentic morality in the service of different archetypal ways of life, the course will address the moral implications of some of the most important stories that you and I have inherited and lived but of which we are seldom conscious: romantic love, the market society, tribalism, self-veiling, transforming love, the wounded self, mutuality and equality, the conquering hero, competence, patriarchy and matriarchy, and the story of transformation. In analyzing these stories, we shall see how they necessarily hang together in creating a world of meaning for us. In the course of the semester, we will discover how these stories either free us or wound us in the creation of moral decisions. Most important, we shall be answering a question that is seldom addressed: How does one practice and participate in transformation? Consequently, the most important symbol and story of the course will be the core drama of transformation.

In achieving the aim of the course, we shall make use of the combined insights of religious thinkers, literature, history, and depth psychology from a multicultural and feminist perspective. All of these branches of human learning have something to teach us regarding what it means to be human.

COURSE OUTLINE

1. The archetypal drama of the journey: the core drama of transformation and the dying way of life of emanation.

    Theme: The person as center of moral decision-making. Moral persons make moral decisions—the meaning of "person."

    Required Reading:

    Hermann Hesse, *Siddhartha*

    Recommended Reading:

    Marshall Berman, *The Politics of Authenticity*

    Martin Buber, *I and Thou*

    Joseph Campbell, *Myths to Live By*

    Erik Erikson, *Gandhi's Truth*

    Hermann Hesse, *Narcissus and Goldmund*; *Steppenwolf*

    Nikos Kazantzakis, *The Last Temptation of Christ* and *Zorba the Greek*

    Ken Kesey, *One Flew over the Cuckoo's Nest*

    Malcolm X, *The Autobiography of Malcolm X*

    Erich Neumann, *The Origins and History of Consciousness*

    Anne B. Ulanov, *The Feminine in Jungian Psychology and in Christian Theology*

    Marguerite Yourcenar, *The Abyss*

2. A theory of human relations: it allows us to see self, other, world, and our sacred sources in qualitatively new ways.

    Theme: The ability and conscious choice to participate with our neighbor and our sacred sources, in the dialectic to create, nourish, and destroy as the most fundamental transformation process in life.

    Required Reading:

    Manfred Halpern, "Notes on How to Analyze a Situation"

    Recommended Reading:

    David T. Abalos, *Latinos in the United States: The Sacred and the Political*, Chapter 1

    Norman Birnbaum, "Critical Theory and Psychohistory," *Explorations in Psychohistory*, R. J. Lifton, ed., pp. 182–213

    Norman O. Brown, *Life Against Death*

    Martin Buber, *I and Thou*

Titus Burckhardt, *Alchemy*

Carl G. Jung, *Memories, Dreams, Reflections*

Sheldon Wolin, "Political Theory as a Vocation

3. The archetypal drama/story of patriarchy/romantic love.

    Theme: Our journey of transformation is endangered by the stories enacted in the service of emanation, incoherence, and deformation that are legitimized by different faces of the sacred.

    Required Reading:

    Anzia Yezierska, *Bread Givers*

    Recommended Reading:

    Paula Gunn Allen, ed., *Spider Woman's Granddaughters*

    Gloria Anzaldúa, ed., *Making Face, Making Soul, Haciendo Caras*

    Mary Catherine Bateson, *Composing a Life*

    Sandra Cisneros, *Woman Hollering Creek*

    Paula Giddings, *Where and When I Enter*

    Carol Gilligan, *In a Different Voice*

    Zora Neale Hurston, *Their Eyes Were Watching God*

    Gerda Lerner, *The Creation of Patriarchy*

    Doris Lessing, *The Summer Before the Dark*

    Naguib Mahfouz, *Palace Walk*

    Octavio Paz, *Sor Juana Ines*

    Amy Tan, *The Joy Luck Club*

    Anne B. Ulanov, *The Feminine*

4. The archetypal drama of tribalism and racism: the threat of structural violence to personal, political, historical, and religious authenticity.

    Theme: The deformation that threatens the social and moral linkages of our contemporary situation.

    Required Reading:

    Alan Paton, *Too Late the Phalarope*

    Recommended Reading:

    Shlomo Avineri, *The Social and Political Thought of Karl Marx*

    W. McAfee Brown, *Religion and Violence*

    Ralph Ellison, *Invisible Man*

Franz Fanon, *The Wretched of the Earth*

Paulo Freire, *Pedagogy of the Oppressed*

Gustavo Gutiérrez, *A Theology of Liberation*

Jonathan Kozol, *Savage Inequalities*

Ursula LeGuin, *The Dispossessed*

Penny Lernoux, *Cry of the People*

Gary MacEoin, *Revolution Next Door*

Toni Morrison, *Beloved*

Frances Fox Piven and Richard A. Cloward, *The New Class War*

Edward Said, *Culture and Imperialism*

Philip Slater, *The Pursuit of Loneliness*; *Earthwalk*

U.S. Catholic Bishops' Pastoral Letter on Nuclear War, *The Challenge of Peace: God's Promise and Our Response*

5.   The archetypal drama of mutuality: rejecting the story of self veiling and tribalism and choosing authenticity as transformation.

Theme: By struggling with our antagonist we refuse to collude in inherited stories that cripple the whole society; the decision to move toward the creation of a fundamentally more just and loving society.

Required reading:

Howell Raines, *My Soul is Rested*

Recommended reading:

Peter Berger, *A Rumor of Angels*

Joseph E. Brown, *The Sacred Pipe*

Margaret Craven, *I Heard the Owl Call My Name*

K. Marx and F. Engels, *On Religion*

S. Freud, *The Future of an Illusion*

Gustavo Gutiérrez, *We Drink from Our Own Wells*

Werner Heisenberg, *Physics and Beyond*

Carl Gustav Jung, *Answer to Job*

P. W. Martin, *Experiment in Depth*

John Neihardt, *Black Elk Speaks*

Rudolf Otto, *The Idea of the Holy*

Elaine Pagels, *The Gnostic Gospels*

Theodore Roszak, *The Unfinished Animal*

Leslie Marmon Silko, *Ceremony*

Bishop John Spong, *Into the Whirlwind*

Alice Walker, *The Color Purple*

E. C. Whitmont, *The Symbolic Quest*

ASSIGNMENT

Spend several pages writing about what you have learned in this course that will help you to make moral decisions with real insight into what it is that you are truly doing. What is it that deeply touched you in this course? Be specific.

What story/stories were you socialized into by our society? What was the dominant story in your experience and how did this affect the four faces of your being? Where did this place you in the core drama of transformation? Give examples of daily encounters that demonstrate the presence of this story. What in your opinion are the most serious stories being faced by American society and why? The archetypal drama/story that characters like Reb, Malcolm, Siddhartha, Betsy, Sara, Elijah Muhammad, Buddha, Govinda were living—was it patriarchy, tribalism, the market society, romantic love, the guide, the wounded child, mutuality, transforming love? In the service of what ultimate way of life were the above relationships and archetypal dramas enacted?

For the characters in our readings, the way of life of emanation was no longer an option because they no longer lived in a society or culture in which the whole of life hangs together, in which everybody accepts the same values, and in which all feel secure because the final truth has been given to them to be lived once for all. However, there are emanational relationships to parents, and other key people in their lives. Some parents preserve fragments of the way of life of emanation that they brought with them from the previous culture or inherited from their parents. All of us begin, at the very least, in the relationship of emanation; all must have this relationship in order to begin life and to survive. The problem is that some were forced to leave the container or emanational relationship before they were ready. Others remained enchained and enchanted as extensions of mysterious others for too long in the relationship of emanation. Some also were caught within several ways of life. Increasingly, in the modern age people are enacting different aspects of their lives in different archetypal dramas, in the service of different ultimate ways of life.

The core drama of transformation: In what act of the core drama were any of the characters that we read about this semester resolving or not resolving a particular issue with a particular person? For example, deformation surrounds our daily life. Too often in the modern age, children are cast out of the container before they are prepared to live on an independent basis. In fact, far too many children are born in emanation in the service of deformation because they are raised in situations filled with violence, both in the home and in the wider society. This leaves many vulnerable and angry; they seek to build relationships in the service of incoherence or deformation so that with their power they can gain revenge or build a fortress wherein they and their children will not be hurt again. The problem with this strategy is that we remain partial selves who have not resolved the deformational issues within ourselves or in the society, and so we will be tempted toward the abyss, or deformation, because we have not emptied ourselves in Act II, Scene 2, of the underlying sacred source, the stories of deformation.

It is important to try to pick out one or two pivotal experiences in the lives of characters such as Siddhartha, Malcolm, Sara, or Masha. This is always a period of awakening. We are disillusioned and feel betrayed because our emanational source has failed us in Act I, Scene 2. Give examples of what happened that led to Act II, Scene 1. Often they tried to act as if nothing had changed to avoid facing the incoherence. Following this breaking away in Act II, Scene 1, what archetypal stories did our protagonists empty themselves of? What alternative stories did they create and in the service of what way of life were they enacted? For example, if they become a rebel, controlled by the story of the oppressor, looking for revenge in order to get back at persons or groups, this indicates a failure to empty ourselves in Act II, Scene 2 of the story that caught our antagonist and to repeat the same story in the service of deformation. Fania, who seeks to get away from her father by getting married, enters Act II, Scene 1 by leaving home. But because she has not emptied herself of the story of patriarchy, she finds herself in Act I, Scene 1 once again in an emanational relationship in the story of patriarchy but this time with a new man.

In the example of Malcolm X, there is great hope in the fact that after living in the service of deformation for so long, he could enter into incoherence with his hero, break with him, and then empty himself in Act II, Scene 2 of the story of tribalism and be filled anew in Act III, Scene 1 with a vision of a humanity in which each person is valuable. He then reached out to others in Act III, Scene 2 with the historical and political faces of his being to make relations between different races fundamentally new and better. This is what the essence of transformation is all about in Act III, Scenes 1 and 2: Malcolm, Sara, and Siddhartha were free to use all eight relationships in the service of transformation, to enter into incoherence again and again in order to respond openly to fundamentally new kinds of problems. They could create conflict and change as well as cooperate in continuing the best in the values of American society. The four faces of their being were constantly responding to the needs of others because they cared deeply about others.

The four faces of our being: You and I are suppressing very important personal aspects of our being if we enact life in the story of the market society in the service of incoherence because we are forced to be cagey, to hide our hurt so that others cannot use this information against us. We constantly look for people who can help us attain power, and we avoid issues that will not advance our self-interest. Thus we practice the politics of power: Who can hurt me and who can help me? We shape history by becoming a more powerful fragment. The strong survive and only the powerful are allowed to determine the quality of life; a sacred source inspires us to search out the avenues of self aggrandizement. However, if we are living in the service of transformation, the four faces of our being change dramatically. We come forth as whole persons who know that we need others in order to be fully human. Our politics—that is, what we can and need to do together, how we shape our environment together with others—becomes a politics of compassion and inclusion so that we look for ways to protect the humanity of all groups and of each individual. We are now prepared to create a new history that entails breaking with inherited or created stories to create a new turning point again and again so that life becomes fundamentally new and better. Our sacred face becomes that of a co-creator with the source of all sources so that we no longer live in guilt, fear, or denial of the sacred.

Your best guides: Do not be afraid to let your own voice be heard. Consult your notes and each other; make direct use of the readings and "How to Analyze a Situation."

Sociology Course: Principles of Sociology

Seton Hall University
Sociology 1101EF
Fall 1994

COURSE DESCRIPTION

Sociology is a course of study that invites us to participate in a threefold manner: in the analysis of the inherited archetypal stories that constitute our society and culture; in bringing to light through criticism those aspects of the culture that are destructive; and, finally, in providing us with the necessary theoretical perspective that enables us to create fundamentally new and better stories. Our participation includes intervening in the stories so that we can help transform our society, rather than unconsciously repeating the past.

Our theoretical task will consist of participating in and answering the following questions: What archetypal relationships, stories, and ways of life hold us? In what act and scene am I together with others living the stories of my life? How does the story in the service of a particular way of life affect the four faces of my being? And, last, how does a person like us actually live the story of transformation?

Transformation is the creation of a fundamentally more just and compassionate alternative. This is the choice that can be made by individuals like you and I who have broken with destructive relationships, disabling stories, and fragmented ways of life.

Throughout the semester, the main symbol for the course will be the archetypal story of the journey of transformation. Participation in this journey is what critical and creative sociology is all about.

COURSE OUTLINE

1. Analyzing, critiquing, and transforming the inherited stories of our lives.

    Theme: The emergence of the four faces of our being.

    Required reading:

    Ken Kesey, *One Flew Over the Cuckoo's Nest*

    Recommended reading:

    Peter Berger and Thomas Luckmann, *The Social Construction of Reality*

Marshall Berman, *The Politics of Authenticity*

Sandra Cisneros, *Woman Hollering Creek*

Takeo Doi, *The Anatomy of Dependence*

Hermann Hesse, *Demian*

Malcolm X, *The Autobiography of Malcolm X*

C. W. Mills, *The Power Elite*

2. A theory of transformation as our guide.

   Theme: Theory as participation in the life, death, and resurrection of sacred stories; the core drama of transformation.

   Required reading:

   David T. Abalos, "The Four Faces of Multicultural and Gender Scholarship from the Perspective of a Theory of Transformation"

   Manfred Halpern, "Notes on How to Analyze a Situation"

   Recommended reading:

   David T. Abalos, *The Latino Family and the Politics of Transformation*

   Manfred Halpern, *Transformation: Its Theory and Practice in Personal, Political, Historical and Sacred Being* and "Why Are Most of Us Partial Selves? Why Do Partial Selves Enter the Road to Deformation?"

   Werner Heisenberg, *Physics and Beyond*

   Thomas S. Kuhn, *The Structure of Scientific Revolutions*

   George Ritzer, *Sociology: A Multiple Paradigm Science*

   Albert Szymanski, "Toward a Radical Sociology," in George Ritzer, ed., *Issues, Debates, and Controversies*

3. Arresting and reentering the journey of transformation.

   Theme: Confronting and transforming unfinished aspects of the American experiment: the politics of male/female relationships and the archetypal stories of patriarchy and romantic love.

   Required reading:

   Laura Esquivel, *Like Water for Chocolate*

   Amy Tan, *The Joy Luck Club*

   Recommended reading:

   Paula Gunn Allen, ed., *Spider Woman's Granddaughters, Traditional Tales and Contemporary Writing by Native American Women*

Gloria Anzaldúa, ed., *Making Faces, Making Soul: Haciendo Caras, Creative and Critical Perspectives by Women of Color*

Asian Women United of California, eds., *Making Waves: An Anthology of Writings By and About Asian American Women*

Mary Catherine Bateson, *Composing a Life*

Paula Giddings, *Where and When I Enter, The Impact of Black Women on Race and Sex in America*

Carol Gilligan, *In a Different Voice*

Asunción Horno-Delgado, et al., *Breaking Boundaries, Latina Writings and Critical Readings*

Zora Neale Hurston, *Their Eyes Were Watching God*

Maxine Hong Kingston, *The Woman Warrior*

Sara Lawrence Lightfoot, *Balm in Gilead*

Naguib Mahfouz, *Palace Walk*

Octavio Paz, *Sor Juana Ines*

Adrienne Rich, *On Lies, Secrets, and Silence*

Ann Belford Ulanov, *The Feminine in Jungian Psychology and Christian Theology*

Anzia Yezierska, *Bread Givers*

Iris M. Young, *Justice and the Politics of Difference*

4.   American society in crisis: confronting the stories of tribalism, capitalism, and self-veiling in the service of deformation.,

Theme: The failure of transformation and the exit into the abyss.

Required reading:

William Attaway, *Blood on the Forge*

Recommended reading:

Derrick Bell, *Faces at the Bottom of the Well*

W. McAfee Brown, *Religion and Violence*

Ralph Ellison, *Invisible Man*

Richard Griswold del Castillo, *The Treaty of Guadalupe Hidalgo, A Legacy of Conflict*

Andrew Hacker, *Two Nations, Black and White, Separate, Hostile, Unequal*

Penny Lernoux, *Cry of the People*

Toni Morrison, *Beloved*

Alan Paton, *Too Late the Phalarope*

Edward Said, *Culture and Imperialism*

John Steinbeck, *The Grapes of Wrath*

Piri Thomas, *Down These Mean Streets*

Cornell West, *Race Matters*

5. Building an alternative culture in the service of transformation.

Theme: Toward the creation of new and better stories of transformation; transforming love, the role of the guide and democracy.

Required reading:

Martin Luther King, Jr., *Why We Can't Wait*

Alice Walker, *The Color Purple*

Recommended reading:

David T. Abalos, *Latinos in the United States: The Sacred and the Political*

Robert Bellah et al., *Habits of the Heart*

Taylor Branch, *Parting the Waters, America in the King Years 1954–1963*

Joseph Epes Brown, *The Sacred Pipe*

Michael Cooke, *Afro-American Literature in the Twentieth Century, The Achievement of Intimacy*

Henri Corbin, *Creative Imagination in the Sufism of Ibn Arabi*

Margaret Craven, *I Heard the Owl Call My Name*

Erik Erikson, *Gandhi's Truth*

Brewster Ghiselin, *The Creative Process*

Gustavo Gutiérrez, *We Drink from Our Own Wells*

Manfred Halpern, "Transformation and the Source of the Fundamentally New"

Esther Harding, *Woman's Mysteries, Ancient and Modern*

C. G. Jung, *Memories, Dreams, Reflections*

Louis Kampf, *On Modernism*

Malcolm X, *The Autobiography of Malcolm X*

Octavio Paz, *The Other Mexico: Critique of the Pyramid*

Howell Raines, *My Soul is Rested*

John Shockley, *Chicano Revolt in a Texas Town*

Leslie Marmon Silko, *Ceremony*

Ronald Takaki, *A Different Mirror*

Alice Walker, *Meridian*

EXAMPLES OF ASSIGNMENTS: BLOOD ON THE FORGE
AND THE CORE DRAMA OF TRANSFORMATION

Questions for Discussion

What are the archetypal stories that we find in this novel?

In the service of what way of life are these stories being enacted?

Why does Kentucky represent Act I, Scene 1 of the core drama for the Moss family? What destroys their fragile security?

Compare life in the North with life in the South for the Moss brothers, Melody, Chinatown, and Big Mat.

Describe the new stratification in the North.

Relate the story of the market society to the novel. Why were African Americans encouraged to come to the steel mills?

Why is the way of life of deformation so closely related to the way of life of incoherence in the novel and in American society?

What is the significance of the dog fights, drinking, whoring, and violence in the camps?

Why is Smothers important in the novel?

What is the initial relationship between Anna and Big Mat? Why and how does it change? What happened to Hattie?

What does Big Mat do with his masculinity?

Who are the Mr. Johnstons in the North and how do they co-opt Big Mat? Who does this remind you of?

At the end of the novel, why does Big Mat remember the riding boss?

Compare the ending of *Blood on the Forge* with that of *The Color Purple* and *One Flew Over the Cuckoo's Nest*.

Assignment

Explain fully Act II, Scene 2 of the core drama of transformation and apply it to *Blood on the Forge*. In your essays, relate the partial self, religion in the service of emanation, assimilation, the four faces of our being, Albert, the stories of tribalism, and self-veiling to Big Mat.

For purposes of this essay, the theory of transformation must be explicitly used. Your paper must reflect a knowledge of the entire novel. When applying theory to practice, make sure that you use quotes from the novel to substantiate your points.

Analysis of Blood on the Forge, applying the Core Drama of Transformation

The novel begins in Act I, Scene 1 of the core drama in Kentucky, where the Moss family is in emanation to the story of tribalism because they live enchained but enchanted as an embodiment of this mysteriously over-whelming story. Tribalism as an archetypal drama has taken over their lives. Because they experience it as God's will, they see this story as a mysteri-ously overwhelming source. Therefore they do not analyze the story of tribalism but practice self-veiling so that they can hide their anger, which is deadly in a situation of racism. It is Hattie who comes closest to criticizing the story of tribalism and to rebelling against it. For this reason she is a threat to Big Mat, who reads the Bible to assure himself that everything is all right. The way of life of emanation is fragile because everybody must agree to remain loyal, no matter how painful it is. In this sense Hattie represents Act I, Scene 2 because she is always criticizing and making Big Mat feel uneasy as Sofia made Celie feel nervous and as McMurphy made the men reluctant to admit what they were feeling. For this reason Big Mat slaps Hattie and Celie told Harpo to beat Sofia. They were getting too close to exposing their doubts and causing their world to crumble.

The four faces of Big Mat's life are as follows: His personal face is repressed because he refuses to deal with his anger and he acts out the role in the story of self-veiling that whites want him to play. Politically, Big Mat does not fight back but remains loyal to the codes of racial conduct that make him a "boy." His historical face continues to be shaped by the repetition of the story of tribalism that made him less than white people, and he copes with this humiliation by accepting a sacred face filled with sin, shame, and guilt that keeps him passive, quiet, and obedient to a vengeful God who cursed him. Since he feels cursed he cannot face fundamentally new questions. How can he resist if even God is against him? For this reason he desperately reads the Bible, looking for some sign of forgiveness. This is what religion in the service of emanation is all about.

But the anger remains, no matter how hard Big Mat tries to repress it through the use of religion or self-veiling. The constant pressure of this rage is a reminder that there is something wrong. Thus, in the second scene of Act I, a new inspiration, image, feeling gets hold of us. We can neither integrate it nor get rid of it. (Repression would turn it into a dangerous, unconscious force.) Big Mat's self-veiling fails because it is an attempt to repress the rage that he constantly feels. It is this anger that erupts as he responds consciously to this new emanational inspiration, and he enters Act II, Scene 1. The new emanational inspiration to which he responds is the memory of his recently killed mother, whom the riding boss ridicules. In the first scene of Act II, Big Mat breaks with the concrete manifestation (the riding boss and white people in general) of our earlier inherited form of emanation (the story of tribalism) because that relationship has become unbearable and unfruitful.

As a result of this attack, Big Mat and the whole family are in open defiance of white people. The self-veiling has now ended, and because they live in the dangerous situation of the segregated South, the brothers have to leave or they will be lynched.

Once the Moss brothers are in the North, they become caught up by the story of the market society, which takes them over in the service of incoherence in Act II, Scene 1. They assimilate into this story, especially Big Mat, who uses his strong body as a weapon in the competition against others. Big Mat hopes to become somebody in this way, but he remains angry and feeling cursed. He uses the work to expend his rage but he doesn't resolve the deeper issues in his life. When he learns that Hattie has had another miscarriage, he rebels against God and the last vestiges of his belief system that had allowed him to hang onto fragments of the way of life of emanation. His rejection of Hattie symbolizes how he is now in total rebellion against everything from his past. He demonstrates this freedom by rejecting the religion (the Bible) that had made him passive. He goes wild because there is no longer any belief in God to hold him back. At this point in the novel Big Mat enters into a romantic relationship with Anna that leads him into deformation. He unmercifully beats her in order to let her know that she belongs to him. He turns his masculinity into a fragment that becomes a total fantasy that takes over his life. In this way, Big Mat exits the core drama and practices deformation by making life fundamentally worse.

In the midst of all this there is trouble at the mill. The mill owners are living the story of the market society in the service of incoherence, arrested in Act II, Scene 1 of the core drama. But the way of life of incoherence is also fragile. People who live this way are always threatened by those they believe will lessen their ability to make more and more money. Because their main priority is money, they enforce brutalizing work conditions on the men. To get some relief from this relentless pressure, the men brutalize themselves, each other, and women. This is symbolized by the dog fights that bring shouts of approval as they grow bloodier.

Melody and Chinatown are caught by the story of the market society in the service of deformation and become victims of the mill owners, as do the rest of the men. Melody understands better than his brothers what is happening to them, but he feels powerless to do anything to help them. He feels guilty because he has betrayed Big Mat. When Big Mat needs him most and is trying to talk to Melody so that he can find his way, Melody cannot speak. When the trouble comes to the mill, the story of the market society is being openly challenged. The majority of the men are in the process of entering into open rebellion against their victimization in the service of deformation by organizing a union to protect their rights. But nobody must be allowed to threaten the power of the mill owners. They set out to divide the men on the basis of race and ethnicity, and so the story of tribalism, in alliance with the story of the market society that causes the men to compete with each other, is used to destroy the strike. Big Mat is faced with the most important decision of his life—the choice between deformation and transformation. Like Albert, Big Mat had the opportunity to turn his life around. Initially, Albert chose deformation; he became suicidal. But with the help of Harpo, Albert succeeded in emptying himself of the story of patriarchy in the service of deformation in Act II, Scene 2. Patriarchy was sent into the abyss and Albert and Harpo were able to create a fundamentally new and better story of mutuality and equality as friends in the service of transformation.

EXAMPLES OF ASSIGNMENTS: *BREAD GIVERS*

Analysis of Bread Givers: Applying Theory to Practice

If we respond consciously to this new emanational inspiration, we enter Act II. In Scene 1, we break with the concrete manifestation of our earlier inherited form of emanation because that relationship has become unbearable, untenable, and unfruitful. But unless we also enter the second scene of Act II of incoherence, we will not empty ourselves of the emanational force that empowered that concrete manifestation, and a new manifestation of it will soon possess us again. (All archetypal relationships and dramas can possess us, thanks to their emanational force. Only transformation as a drama cannot be enacted except with our conscious participation.

In Act II, Scene 2, we need to empty ourselves of the archetypal story that previously held us in its spell but has now become deeply problematical. We need also to empty ourselves of the way of life we served, if it was only a fragment of transformation as a way of life. (What makes transformation the core drama of our cosmos of being is that the other three ways of life freeze Act I, Act II, or the exit from the core drama and turn them into seemingly given, inevitable, repetitive overarching plays.)

Once we have emptied ourselves, we can count on being filled anew in Act III, Scene 1. And in the second scene of Act III, we no longer treat this new experience as only a personal and sacred renewal, but we reach out to the other two faces of our—and everyone's—being: the political and historical. We test our fundamentally new understanding and experience of love and justice with others, to discover whether it is in truth fundamentally better with respect to the problem at stake. (Manfred Halpern, "Notes on How to Analyze a Situation.")

Assignment

Papers should concentrate on Act II, Scenes 1 and 2, and Act III, Scenes 1 and 2. Provide evidence from the novel that Sara has succeeded or failed in emptying herself of the stories of patriarchy and romantic love and that she has created an alternative story that is fundamentally new and better. For example, Sara breaks with her father in Act II, Scene 1: "I'm going to live my own life. Nobody can stop me. . . . I leaped back and dashed for the door. The Old World had struck its last on me." Yet the most difficult task still lies ahead, in emptying herself not only of her concrete father but of the story lest she repeat this drama of patriarchy in collusion with the story of romantic love with another concrete manifestation of it, such as Max Goldstein. Sara's father also tries to seduce her back to Act I, Scene 1 and the story of patriarchy in the service of emanation. After graduation, Sara succeeds in relationship to one aspect of her life. But there is still unfinished business—her relationship to men and to her father.

As in the *Blood on the Forge* paper, you must explicitly use the theory of transformation and provide quotes from the novel when applying theory to practice.

STRATEGIES OF TRANSFORMATION: ISSUES RAISED BY STUDENTS

Questions for Discussion

How do you know transformation is present in your life?

Can you be in the service of emanation in respect to one aspect of your life and yet in the way of life of incoherence in regard to another relationship in your life?

What is the sacred all about? What are the four gods? How do the four gods relate to the deepest of sacred sources and the creation of the cosmos? Is the god of emanation an obstacle to the journey? Is organized religion always opposed to the core drama of transformation?

Once you have successfully realized transformation in one relationship, is it possible in this same relationship to regress to emanation?

How do we empty ourselves of an archetype and how do we know if we have accomplished this?

Is tribalism ever constructive?

Are the relationships of emanation, subjection, buffering, and direct bargaining always negative?

Why is romantic love always destructive?

Once you exit the core drama of transformation, how do you take up the journey again?

In regard to Act II, Scene 2, how do we empty ourselves of archetypal dramas?

Explain further "in the service of" and "the way of life of."

Do you break with someone only in Act II, Scene 1, or can you break with persons at other points of the journey?

Can you be crippled in any act of the core drama at any time?

What is the difference between the way of life of incoherence and the relationship of incoherence?

Does transformation discriminate against those in other acts of the core drama?

Why do people get stuck in the core drama at different places along the way?

Is deformation the only exit from the core drama?

Can you be in emanation to a particular ideal?

Can you achieve true autonomy in U.S. society if capitalism always contains subjection as an essential element?

What existed (if anything) prior to the theory of transformation?

How do you distinguish between different archetypal dramas?

Can you have more than one core drama at a time?

If you were raised with boundary management, will you still have to break away from your parents?

Can you skip an act or scene in the core drama?

Do the politics of liberation equal autonomy?

Do you need others/guides to practice transformation?

Why are there not more than nine relationships and four ways of life?

How can you have a sense of continuity and culture if you have to empty yourself?

What is liberalism?

Is power always negative? And why do we live in a society in the service of incoherence?

Is the theory of transformation based on religion and psychology?

How can we practice transformation in a power-hungry society?

Why don't people stop the deformation in our society?

How long does it take to travel the core drama in regard to one problem?

How can I determine where I am in relationship to the core drama?

Isn't it racist for a person to reject being an American in order to choose being a member of another ethnic group?

Can you have a relationship of transforming love and romantic love at the same time with the same person? Can romantic love become transformative?

If you have achieved transformation in your family life, why wouldn't that apply in all other relationships in your life?

Is deformation a journey?

If you don't assimilate, how do you make it or become visible in this society? How can you be educated without assimilation?

What is the god of transformation?

Can the powerful experience transformation?

Is transformation intuitive or do you have to go through analysis or take a course on transformation before you can know what it is all about?

Can you elaborate on the four faces of our being, especially the political? What does it mean to be political?

Please give specific examples of breaking with archetypal dramas.

How can subjection ever be positive?

How do you move beyond Act I, Scene 2 to Act II, Scene 1?

How do you distinguish between the way of life of incoherence and the way of deformation?

Explain the symbols that depict the core drama of transformation.

How does one overcome vulnerability in the way of life of incoherence?

Is it always possible to avoid deformation, especially when our decisions affect the lives of other people?

How do you analyze a situation?

How do the four faces of our being interrelate?

How can there be a relationship of incoherence in the service of emanation?

Is the relationship of emanation a form of deformation?

Why isn't it possible to express your freedom in the way of life of emanation, especially if security is guaranteed?

How can you have incoherence in the service of transformation?

How does all of this sacred language relate to groups in society?

Where did you get this theory?

What happens if you are not transforming? Is it possible to just exist as long as you are not hurting anyone?

What is an archetype?

What does it mean to say that we have found the "self?"

Give an example of a society, group, or individual who is currently practicing transformation.

Can you explain emanation in the service of deformation?

What about repression, suppression, and oppression?

Where are the people in relationship to the core drama who don't want us to break out of the container?

In buffering, what does it mean to mediate one's experiences through mental filters?

Where do archetypal dramas originate from?

Do you always feel sin, shame, and anxiety when you are stuck between two ways of life?

Discuss further the personal and political realms of our life.

What drives us to continue the journey after Act I, Scene 2?

Is a hero guide always necessary? Is this the only way to become your own guide and find your self?

Why is Act II labeled as incoherence?

Does everybody begin in the relationship of emanation?

If you are in a relationship of emanation and are happy and secure, why should you want to change?

How could a person with no self-confidence practice transformation? It seems irresponsible.

How do you know when the precise time has come to break with your father, mother, lover?

FINAL ASSIGNMENT

The topic for the paper is: Apply the core drama of transformation to Tayo as he confronts his life.

In the novel *Ceremony,* how does Tayo succeed in emptying himself in Act II, Scene 2? What two archetypal ways of life are primarily at stake in this novel, and how do you know this? Does Tayo avoid exiting the core drama of transformation? Give examples that describe fully what transformation is in Act III, Scenes 1 and 2, that is, the wholeness that Tayo achieves. In the second part of your paper, draw parallels between your own life and that of Tayo. For example, where are you now in relationship to the core drama? What story or stories are you living? In the service of what way of life are you enacting choices? How do the four faces of our being relate to you? *In this aspect of the paper, once again give examples directly from the novel and the theory.*

You are being asked once again to test the theory. In writing this paper you must explicitly use the language of the theory of transformation. Please be sure to quote both that part of the novel to which you are referring and the aspect of the theory that you are applying to your example.

The following are examples of ways to include aspects of the theory in your paper:

- The stories of our lives and how they wounded/helped the various characters in the novels.
- The nine archetypal relationships enacted in the service of a way of life.
- Apply the four faces of our being to Tayo and yourself.
- Explain fully why Act II, Scene 2 is so crucial. Find direct quotes that are examples of Act II, Scene 2 in the novel.
- *Ceremony* provides us with an understanding of what actual transformation looks like in Act III, Scenes 1 and 2.
- Chapter 2 of *Latinos in the United States* helps us to understand Tayo.
- Chapter 6 of *Latinos in the United States* relates to the story found in *Ceremony*.
- In regard to Chapter 7 of *Latinos in the United States*, on professionals: As their lives and ours go on, Tayo, Big Chief, Chinatown, and Melody will have to develop the relationship of autonomy in the midst of the market society.
- Relate the stories of the novels to your experiences, that is, where you are in the core drama, the story you are living, in the service of what way of life you are choosing to enact your life, the four faces of your being, and the character that best relates to your story or stories.

Teachers' Seminar:
Multicultural Education

Irvington School District
Spring 1992

COURSE DESCRIPTION

The purpose of this seminar is to provide us as teachers with an opportunity to redefine and reclaim our education and that of our students from a multicultural perspective. This means claiming and taking responsibility for our education, rather than merely passively receiving it. Multicultural education is above all an attitude, a spirit of openness, and inclusion; multiculturalism honors and celebrates the history and culture of all people.

Multicultural and gender scholarship has largely been the result of women and people of color re-envisioning and redefining their place in American history and culture. By discovering their own voices, people of color and women were empowered to tell their own stories. This new scholarship is not an attempt to diminish or to threaten the existing curriculum; on the contrary, multicultural education constitutes a corrective enrichment, a contribution to the understanding of our national heritage. Multicultural education has reopened a healthy and critical debate on how we see ourselves as a nation and seeks to help answer the question as to where we are going. In the process of this re-evaluation, we have discovered aspects of ourselves as a community that had been rendered invisible. This means, for example, that when the contributions of Asian Americans, African Americans, various European American communities, Latinos, Native Americans, and women to the development of this country are ignored or simply unknown, some of our students are rendered people without a history, without a face. That is, they are made invisible.

Thus to include multicultural and gender scholarship into the classroom/curriculum is to accomplish two things. It allows each student to see herself/himself as a person with a valuable culture and history as mirrored in the curriculum. In addition, multicultural education ensures that our students will also be enabled to go beyond their own specific heritage to see, as through a window, the parallels between their historical and cultural experiences and those of their fellow students. In this way, the curriculum as window and mirror allows all of us to rediscover ourselves and each other in new and rewarding ways. This mutuality helps to create an environment of respect and understanding of otherness.

Due to an attitude of openness and inclusiveness, multicultural education enriches the study of history, the social sciences, literature, art, music, math, and science. This is accomplished not only by introducing new scholarship into the classroom but also through an awareness of different learning styles that may vary according to culture. Thus, pedagogical changes are also a result of being sensitive to how students learn.

Ultimately, multicultural education, with all of its respect for diversity, is also grounded in the search for our common humanity. To see my story through the stories of others is to realign my emotions and to recognize myself and others in a fundamentally more human and compassionate way. In today's society, to be an educated person is to be multiculturally literate, diverse in our vision, and pluralistic in our attitudes. If we are to build a strong nation, we are required to build on our greatest strength—the diversity of our people united on the common principle that each person is sacred. A community is only worthy of respect when the individuals who make up the whole are inviolable.

Finally, we shall be retelling our story and those of our students and colleagues from the perspective of a theory/story of transformation. This theory is grounded on an understanding that each person is unique and that the task of culture and community is to enable each of us to travel the core drama of transformation time and again in a process of continuous creation.

Course requirements include

- Keeping a journal
- A multicultural project for your class
- Reading and discussion of *Blood on the Forge* by William Attaway
- Assigned readings on multicultural education

PROJECT

Here are some examples of projects you might undertake:

- Select three stories and analyze them for biases in regard to race, gender, class, ethnicity, religion, different abilities
- Develop an annotated bibliography of folktales from four cultures
- In what you are already teaching, infuse at least one or two other cultural perspectives

JOURNALS

Enter critical reflections in your journal four times a week. Ask yourself questions such as the following:

- Is my classroom conducive to creating a multicultural/diverse environment?
- Did I face a multiculturally sensitive issue today in my classroom?
- Are my students aware of multicultural issues such as differences based on culture, gender, race, ethnicity?
- In my teaching today was I able to include comparative and parallel material from another culture?

Bibliography

Abalos, David T. "The Personal, Political, Historical and Sacred Grounding of Culture: Some Reflections on the Creation of Latino Culture in the United States from the Perspective of a Theory of Transformation." In *Old Masks, New Faces: Religion and Latino Identities*, Vol. 3, Anthony S. Arroyo and Gilbert Cadena, eds. New York: Bildner Center, CUNY, 1995.

_____ . *The Latino Family and the Politics of Transformation*. New York: Praeger Press, 1993.

_____ . "Rediscovering the Sacred Among Latinos: A Critique from the Perspective of a Theory of Transformation." *Latino Studies Journal* 3:2 (May 1992).

_____ . "Multicultural and Gender Inclusive Education in the Service of Transformation." *Latino Studies Journal* 2:1 (January 1991).

_____ . "Latino Female/Male Relationships: Strategies for Creating New Archetypal Dramas." *Latino Studies Journal* 1:1 (1990).

_____ . *Latinos in the United States: The Sacred and the Political*. Notre Dame, Ind.: University of Notre Dame Press, 1986.

Acosta-Belen, Edna. *The Puerto Rican Woman*. New York: Praeger, 1986.

Acuña, Rudolfo. *Occupied America*. New York: Harper and Row, 1981.

Allen, Paula Gunn, ed. *Spider Woman's Granddaughters: Traditional Tales and Contemporary Writing by Native American Women*. New York: Fawcett Colombine, 1989.

_____ . *Grandmothers of the Light: A Medicine Woman's Sourcebook*. Boston: Beacon Press, 1991.

Alvarez, Julia. *How the García Girls Lost Their Accent*. New York: Algonquin Press, 1992.

American Council on Education and Education Commission of the States. *One-Third of a Nation: A Report of the Commission on Minority Participation in Education and American Life*. Washington, D.C.: American Council on Education, 1988.

Anaya, Rudolfo A. *Bless Me Ultima*. Berkeley: Tonatiuh-Quinto Sol International Publishers, 1988.

Anzaldúa, Gloria, ed. *Making Faces, Making Soul: Haciendo Caras, Creative and Critical Perspectives by Women of Color*. San Francisco: Aunt Lute Foundation Book, 1990.

Apodaca, Maria Linda. "The Chicana Woman: A Materialist Historical Perspective." *Latin American Perspectives* 4:1, 2 (Winter and Spring, 1977).

Appiah, Kwame Anthony. *In My Father's House*. New York: Oxford University Press, 1992.

Arabi, Ibn. *The Wisdom of the Prophets*. Aldsworth, Gloucestershire: Bashara Publications, 1975.

Asian Women United of California, eds. *Making Waves: An Anthology of Writings By and About Asian American Women*. Boston: Beacon Press, 1989.

Asturias, Miguel Angel. *Men of Maize*. New York: Verso, 1988.

Attaway, William. *Blood on the Forge*. New York: Monthly Review Press, 1987.

Avineri, Shlomo. *The Social and Political Thought of Karl Marx*. London: Cambridge University Press, 1968.

Baldwin, James. "Here Be Dragons." In *The Price of the Ticket: Collected Nonfiction, 1948–1985*. New York: St. Martin's Press, 1985.

Barrera, Mario. *Race and Class in the Southwest*. Notre Dame, Ind.: University of Notre Dame Press, 1979.

_____ . "The Barrio as an Internal Colony." In *La Causa Politica*, F. Chris García, ed. Notre Dame, Ind.: University of Notre Dame Press, 1974.

Bateson, Mary Catherine. *Composing a Life*. New York: Atlantic Monthly Press, 1989.

Beck, Mary Ann, et al., eds. *The Analysis of Hispanic Texts*. New York: Bilingual Press, 1976.

Bell, Derrick, *Faces at the Bottom of the Well*. New York: Basic Books, 1992.

Bellah, Robert, et al. *Habits of the Heart: Individualism and Commitment in American Life*. Berkeley: University of California Press, 1985.

Berger, Peter. *A Rumor of Angels*. Garden City, N.Y.: Doubleday, 1969.

Berman, Marshall. *The Politics of Authenticity, Radical Individualism and the Rise of Modern Society*. New York: Atheneum Press, 1972.

Birnbaum, Norman. "Critical Theory and Psychohistory." In *Explorations in Psychohistory*. R. J. Lifton, ed. New York: Simon & Schuster, 1978.

Blauner, Robert. "Internal Colonialism and Ghetto Revolt." *Social Problems* 16:4.

Bloom, Harold. *The Book of J.* New York: Grove Weidenfeld, 1990.

Bonilla, Frank, and Ricardo Campos. "Puerto Ricans in the New Economic Order." *Daedalus* 110:2 (Spring, 1981) pp. 133–176.

Bonilla, Frank, and Robert Girling. *Structures of Dependency.* Nairobi: Nairobi Books, 1973.

Boswell, Thomas D., and James Curtis. *The Cuban American Experience: Culture, Images, and Perspectives.* Totowa, N.J.: Rowman and Allanhold, 1984.

Branch, Taylor. *Parting the Waters, America in the King Years 1954–63.* New York: Simon and Schuster, 1988.

Brinkley, Alan. "The Western Historians." *New York Times Book Review*, September 20, 1992.

Brown, Joseph Epes. *The Sacred Pipe.* Baltimore, Md.: Penguin Books, 1972.

Brown, Norman O. *Life Against Death.* Middletown, Conn.: Wesleyan University Press, 1959.

Brown, W. McAfee. *Religion and Violence.* Philadelphia: West Minster Press, 1987.

Buber, Martin. *I and Thou.* New York: Scribner, 1970.

Burckhardt, Titus. *Alchemy.* Shaftsbury: Element Books, 1986.

Campbell, Joseph. *The Hero with a Thousand Faces.* Princeton, N.J.: Princeton University Press, 1973.

———. *Myths to Live By.* New York: Viking Press, 1972.

Castro, Americo. *The Spaniards*, translated by Willard King and Selma Margaretten. Berkeley: University of California Press, 1971.

Chan, Jeffrey Paul, et al. *The Big Aiiiieeeee! An Anthology of Chinese American and Japanese American Literature.* New York: Penguin Books, 1991.

Cisneros, Sandra. *Woman Hollering Creek and Other Stories.* New York: Random House, 1991.

———. *The House on Mango Street.* Houston: Arte Publico Press, 1987.

Clark, Kenneth B. *Dark Ghetto: Dilemmas of Social Power.* New York: Harper and Row, 1965.

Cooke, Michael. *Afro-American Literature in the Twentieth Century: The Achievement of Intimacy.* New Haven, Conn.: Yale University Press, 1984.

Corbin, Henri. *Creative Imagination in the Sufism of Ibn Arabi.* Princeton, N.J.: Princeton University Press, 1981.

Cordasco, Francesco, and Eugene Bucchioni. *The Puerto Rican Community and its Children on the Mainland.* Metuchen, N.J.: Scarecrow Press, 1982.

———. *The Puerto Rican Experience.* Totowa, N.J.: Rowman & Little Field, 1973.

Cortes, Carlos E., ed. *Cuban Exiles in the United States.* New York: Arno Press, 1980.

Craven, Margaret. *I Heard the Owl Call My Name.* New York: Dell Paperback Books, 1962.

Dixon, Vernon J., and Badi Foster. *Beyond Black and White: An Alternative America*. Boston: Little, Brown and Co., 1971.

Doi, Takeo. *The Anatomy of Dependency*. New York: Harper and Row, 1981.

Dorris, Michael. *Yellow Raft on Blue Water*. New York: Warner Books, 1988.

Dougherty, James E. *The Catholic Pastoral Letter on War and Peace*. Seattle, Wash.: Shoestring Press, 1984.

Dubois, W.E.B. *The Souls of Black Folk*. New York: Signet Books, 1969.

Elizondo, Virgilio. *Galilean Journey: The Mexican-American Promise*. Maryknoll, N.Y.: Orbis Books, 1983.

Ellison, Ralph. *Invisible Man*. New York: Vintage Books, 1972.

Emerson, Ralph Waldo. *Collected Essays*. Hartford, Conn.: Transcendental Books, 1993.

Erikson, Erik. *Gandhi's Truth: On the Origins of Militant Non-Violence*. New York: W. W. Norton, 1968.

Esquivel, Laura. *Like Water for Chocolate*. New York: Doubleday, 1992.

Evans, Sara, and Harry Boyte. "Schools for Action: Radical Uses for Social Space." *Democracy* 2:4 (Fall, 1982).

Fagan, Richard R. *Cubans in Exile*. Copenhagen: Gyldendal, 1988.

Fanon, Franz. *The Wretched of the Earth*. New York: Grove Press, 1963.

Fitch, Robert. "Tilting With the System." In *La Causa Politica*, F. Chris Garcia, ed. Notre Dame, Ind.: University of Notre Dame Press, 1974.

Flores, Juan, et al. "La Carreta Made a U Turn." *Daedalus* 110:2 (Spring, 1981).

Frazier, Edward Franklin. *Race and Culture Contacts in the Modern World*. Westport, Conn.: Greenwood Press, 1978.

Freedman, Samuel G. *Small Victories: The Real World of a Teacher, Her Students and Their High School*. New York: Harper and Row, 1990.

Freire, Paulo. *Pedagogy of the Oppressed*. New York: Herder and Herder, 1970.

Freud, Sigmund. *Future of an Illusion*. New York: Norton, 1975.

Friedlander, Paul. *Plato, An Introduction*. Princeton, N.J.: Princeton University Press, Bollingen Series LIX, 1973.

Fuentes, Carlos. "Writing in Time." *Democracy*, 2:1 (1982), pp. 61–74.

García, Cristina. *Dreaming in Cuban*. New York: Alfred A. Knopf, 1992.

García, F. Chris, ed. *La Causa Politica: A Chicano Politics Reader*. Notre Dame, Ind.: University of Notre Dame Press,1974.

García-Bahne, Betty. "La Chicana and the Chicano Family." In *Essays on La Mujer*. Vol. 1, ed. Rosaura Sanchez. Vol. 2, ed. Rosa María Cruz. Los Angeles: Chicano Studies Center Publication, UCLA, 1977.

Gates, Henry Louis, Jr., ed., *Bearing Witness: Selections from African-American Autobiography in the Twentieth Century*. New York: Pantheon Books, 1992.

_____ . *Loose Canons: Notes on the Culture Wars*. New York: Oxford University Press, 1992.

_____ . *The Signifying Monkey: A Theory of Afro-American Literary Criticism*. New York: Oxford University Press, 1988.

Ghiselin, Brewster. *The Creative Process*. New York: Mentor Books, 1963, pp. 33–42.

Giddings, Paula. *Where and When I Enter: The Impact of Black Women on Race and Sex in America*. New York: Bantam Books, 1988.

Gilligan, Carol. *In a Different Voice*. Cambridge, Mass.: Harvard University Press, 1982.

Gomez-Quiñones, Juan. *On Culture*. Los Angeles: UCLA, Chicano Studies Center Publications, n.d.

Gordon, David. *Theories of Poverty and Unemployment*. Lexington, Mass.: Heath, 1972.

Gray, Francine DuPlessix. *Soviet Women, Walking the Tightrope*. New York: Doubleday, 1989.

Griswold del Castillo, Richard. *The Treaty of Guadalupe Hidalgo: A Legacy of Conflict*. Norman, Okla.: University of Oklahoma Press, 1990.

_____ . *La Familia: Chicano Families in the United States, 1848 to Present*. Notre Dame, Ind.: University of Notre Dame Press, 1984.

Gutiérrez, Armando, and Herbert Hirsch. "The Militant Challenge to the American Ethos: Chicanos and Mexican Americans." In *La Causa Politica*, F. Chris García, ed. Notre Dame, Ind.: University of Notre Dame Press, 1974.

Gutiérrez, Gustavo. *A Theology of Liberation*, rev. edition. Trans. Caridad Inda and John Eagleson. Maryknoll, N.Y.: Orbis Books, 1988.

_____ . *We Drink from Our Own Wells*. Maryknoll, N.Y.: Orbis Press, 1984.

Guzmán, Ralph. "Mexican Americans in the Urban Area: Will They Riot?" In *La Causa Politica*, F. Chris García, ed. Notre Dame, Ind.: University of Notre Dame Press, 1974.

Hacker, Andrew. *Two Nations, Black and White, Separate, Hostile, Unequal*. New York: Charles Scribner's Sons, 1992.

Halpern, Manfred. *Transformation: Its Theory and Practice in Personal, Political, Historical and Sacred Being*. Unpublished manuscript, 1994. Chapter 14, "Archetypes as Sacred Sources."

_____ . "Notes on How to Analyze a Situation from the Perspective of the Theory of Transformation." Unpublished manuscript, Princeton University, 1993.

_____ . "Toward an Ecology of Human Institutions: The Transformation of Self, World and Politics in Our Time." Paper delivered at a national symposium, "Beyond the Nation State: Transforming Visions of Human Society," College of William and Mary, September 24–27, 1993.

_____ . "Why Are Most of Us Partial Selves? Why Do Partial Selves Enter the Road into Deformation?" Paper delivered for a panel on "Concepts of Self: Transformation and Politics," at the annual meeting of the American Political Science Association, Washington, D.C., August 29, 1991, p. 12.

———. "A Theory of Transformation and the Archetypal Drama of the Conquering Hero." Paper presented at the annual meeting of the American Political Science Association, San Francisco, September 1, 1990.

———. "Choosing Between Ways of Life and Death and Between Forms of Democracy." *Alternatives.* 12:1 (January 1987), pp. 5–34.

———. "Four Contrasting Repertories of Human Relations in Islam: Two Pre-Modern and Two Modern Ways of Dealing with Continuity and Change, Collaboration and Conflict and Achieving Justice." In *Psychological Dimensions of Near Eastern Studies*, L. Carl Brown and Norman Itzkowitz, eds., Princeton, N.J.: Darwin Press, 1977.

Heisenberg, Werner. *Physics and Beyond.* New York: Harper and Row, 1971.

Hesse, Hermann. *Narcissus and Goldmund.* New York: Farrar Straus and Giroux, 1972.

———. *Siddhartha.* New York: Bantam Books, 1971.

———. *Demian.* New York: Bantam Books, 1966.

Hijuelos, Oscar. *The Mambo Kings Play Songs of Love.* New York: Harper and Row, 1990.

Horno-Delgado, Asunción, et al. *Breaking Boundaries: Latina Writings and Critical Readings.* Amherst, Mass.: University of Massachusetts Press, 1988.

Huizinga, Johan. *Homo Ludens.* London: Maurice Temple Smith Ltd., 1970.

Hurston, Zora Neale. *Their Eyes Were Watching God.* New York: Harper and Row, 1990.

Ibsen, Henrik. *A Doll's House, The Wild Duck, The Lady from the Sea.* New York: Dutton, 1910.

Jacobi, Jolande. *Complex, Archetype, Symbol in the Psychology of C. G. Jung.* Princeton, N.J.: Princeton University Press, 1959.

Juarez, Alberto. "The Emergence of El Partido de la Raza Unida: California's New Chicano Party." In *La Causa Politica*, F. Chris García, ed. Notre Dame, Ind.: University of Notre Dame Press, 1974.

Jung, Carl G. *Answer to Job.* Princeton, N.J.: Princeton University Press, 1973.

———. *Man and His Symbols.* New York: Dell Press, 1966.

———. *Memories, Dreams, Reflections.* New York: Pantheon Books, 1963.

Kazantakis, Nikos. *The Last Temptation of Christ.* New York: Simon and Schuster, 1960.

———. *Zorba the Greek.* New York: Simon and Schuster, 1953.

Kesey, Ken. *One Flew Over the Cuckoo's Nest.* New York: Signet Books, 1962.

King, Martin Luther, Jr. *Why We Can't Wait.* New York: Signet Books, 1964.

Kingston, Maxine Hong. *The Woman Warrior.* New York: Vintage International Edition, 1989.

Kozol, Jonathan. *Savage Inequalities: Children in America's Schools.* New York: Crown Publishers, 1991.

Kuhn, Thomas. *The Structure of Scientific Revolutions.* Chicago: University of Chicago Press, 1970.

Lawrence, D. H. *The Plumed Serpent.* New York: Vintage Books, 1954.

LeGuin, Ursula K. *The Dispossessed*. New York: Harper and Row, 1974.

Lerner, Gerda. *The Creation of Patriarchy*. New York: Oxford University Press, 1986.

Lernoux, Penny. *Cry of the People*. Baltimore: Penguin, 1979.

Lessing, Doris. *The Summer Before the Dark*. New York: Alfred A. Knopf, 1973.

Levy, Mark, and Michael Kramer. *The Ethnic Factor: How America's Minorities Decide Elections*. New York: Simon and Schuster, 1972.

Lewis, Oscar. *Five Families*. New York: New American Library, 1959.

Lightfoot, Sara Lawrence. *Balm in Gilead*. New York: Addison-Wesley Publishing Co., 1988.

Lincoln, C. Eric, and Lawrence H. Mamiya. *The Black Church in the African American Experience*. Durham, N.C.: Duke University Press, 1991.

MacCorkle, Lyn. *Cubans in the U.S.: A Bibliography for Research in the Social and Behavioral Sciences, 1960–1983*. Westport, Conn.: Greenwood Press, 1984.

MacEoin, Gary. *Revolution Next Door*. New York: Holt, Rinehart & Winston, 1971.

Macklin, June, and Stanley A. West. *The Chicano Experience*. Boulder, Col.: Westview Press, 1979.

Mahfouz, Naguib. *Palace Walk*. New York: Doubleday, 1990.

Malcolm X. *The Autobiography of Malcolm X*. New York: Grove Press, 1966.

Maldonado-Denis, Manuel. *Puerto Rico: A Socio-Historic Interpretation*. New York: Vintage Books, 1972.

Marcuse, Herbert. *Eros and Civilization*. Boston: Beacon Press, 1966.

Marques, René. *La Carreta*. Rio Piedras, Puerto Rico: Editorial Cultural, 1971.

Márquez, Gabriel García. *One Hundred Years of Solitude*. New York: Harper and Row, 1970.

Martin, P. W. *Experiment in Depth*. London: Routledge and Kegan Paul, 1967.

Marx, Karl. *Economic and Philosophic Manuscripts of 1844*. New York: International Publishers, 1964.

Marx, Karl, and F. Engels. *On Religion*. Chico, Calif.: Scholars Press, 1982.

Mattheisson, Peter. *Sal Si Puedes*. New York: Random House, 1973.

Memmi, Albert. *The Colonizer and the Colonized*. Boston: Beacon Press, 1965.

Minnesota Humanities Council. *Braided Lives: An Anthology of Multicultural American Writings*. St. Paul, Minn.: Minnesota Humanities Council, 1991.

Mirandé, Alfredo. *Gringo Justice*. Notre Dame, Ind.: University of Notre Dame Press, 1987.

Moore, Joan W. "Minorities in the American Class System." *Daedalus* 110:2 (Spring 1981). Pp. 275–299.

Moore, Joan, and Harry Pachón. "Colonialism: The Case of the Mexican American." In *Introduction to Chicano Studies*, Livie I. Duran and H. Russel Bernard, eds. New York: Macmillan, 1970. Pp. 363–372.

Mora, Magdalena, and Adelaide R. del Castillo. *Mexican Women in the United States*. Los Angeles: Chicano Studies Research Center Publications, UCLA, 1980.

Morales, Alejandro. *The Brick People*. Houston: Arte Publico Press, 1988.

Morales, Armando. "The 1970–1971 East Los Angeles Chicano-Police Riots." In *La Causa Politica*. Notre Dame, Ind.: University of Notre Dame Press, 1974.

Morris, Walter F. *Living Maya*, photography by Jeffrey Jay Foxx. New York: Harry N. Abrams, 1988.

Morrison, Toni. *Playing in the Dark*. Cambridge, Mass.: Harvard University Press, 1992.

———. *Beloved*. New York: New American Library, 1987.

Neihardt, John G. *Black Elk Speaks*. Lincoln, Nebr.: University of Nebraska Press, 1961.

Neumann, Erich. *The Origins and History of Consciousness*. Princeton, N.J.: Princeton University Press, Bollingen Series, XLII, 1971.

Noble, David. *A World Without Women*. New York: Alfred A. Knopf, 1992.

Ogletree, Earl J. *Education of the Spanish-Speaking Urban Children*. Springfield, Ill.: Thomas, 1975.

Otto, Rudolf. *The Idea of the Holy*. New York: Oxford University Press, 1950.

Padilla, Elena. *Up from Puerto Rico*. New York: Columbia University Press, 1969.

Padilla, Felix. *Puerto Rican Chicago*. Notre Dame, Ind.: University of Notre Dame Press, 1987.

Pagels, Elaine. *The Gnostic Gospels*. New York: Random House, 1979.

Paton, Alan. *Too Late the Phalarope*. New York Charles Scribner's Sons, 1953.

Paz, Octavio. *Sor Juana Ines*. Cambridge, Mass.: Harvard University Press, 1988.

———. "Reflections: Mexico and the United States." *The New Yorker*, September 7, 1979.

Pifer, Alan. *Bilingual Education and the Hispanic Challenge*. New York: Carnegie Corporation, 1979.

Pitkin, Hanna F., and Sara Shumer. "On Participation." *Democracy* 2:4 (Fall 1982).

Piven, Frances F., and Richard Cloward. *The New Class War*. New York: Pantheon Books, 1982.

———. *Poor People's Movement*. New York: Pantheon Books, 1977.

Pixley, Jorge V. *On Exodus: A Liberation Perspective*. Maryknoll, N.Y.: Orbis Books, 1987.

Polanyi, Michael. *The Tacit Dimension*. Magnolia, Mass.: Peter Smith, 1983.

Portilla, Miguel Leon, ed. *Native Mesoamerican Spirituality*. New York: Paulist Press, 1980.

Poulantzas, Nicos. *Political Power and Social Class*. London: Humanities Press, 1975.

Raines, Howell. *My Soul is Rested: The Story of the Civil Rights Movement in the Deep South*. New York: Bantam Books, 1978.

Rich, Adrienne. *On Lies, Secrets, and Silence: Selected Prose, 1966–1978*. New York: W. W. Norton, 1978.

Riding, Alan. *Distant Neighbors: A Portrait of the Mexicans*. New York: Vintage Books, 1986.

Rivera, Edward. *Family Installments: Memories of Growing Up Hispanic*. New York: Penguin Books, 1983.

Rivera, Tomás. . . . *Y No Se Lo Trago La Tierra* (And The Earth Did Not Devour Him). Houston: Arte Publico Press, 1987.

Robbins, Tom. *Even Cowgirls Get the Blues*. New York: Bantam Books, 1976.

Rodriguez, Clara. *The Puerto Rican Struggle*. New York: Puerto Rican Migration Research Consortium, 1980.

Rodriguez, Richard. *Hunger of Memory*. New York: Bantam Books, 1983.

Rogg, Eleanor Meyor. *The Assimilation of Cuban Exiles*. New York: Aberdeen Press, 1974.

Rogler, J. "Intergenerational Change in Ethnic Identity in the Puerto Rican Family." *International Migration Review*, 14. Pp. 183–214.

Roszak, Theodore. *The Unfinished Animal*. New York: Harper and Row, 1975.

Rousseau, J. J. *The Social Contract*. New York: Free Press, 1969.

Said, Edward. *Culture and Imperialism*. New York: Alfred A. Knopf, 1993.

Sánchez, George. "Bilingualism and Mental Measures: A Word of Caution." In *Chicanos: Social and Psychological Perspectives*, Nathaniel N. Wagner and Marsha Haug, eds. St. Louis: C. V. Mosby Co., 1971.

Shockley, John. *Chicano Revolt in a Texas Town*. Notre Dame, Ind.: University of Notre Dame Press, 1974.

Silko, Leslie Marmon. *Almanac of the Dead*. New York: Simon and Schuster, 1991.

———. *Ceremony*. New York: Penguin Books, 1986.

Simonson, Rick, and Scott Walker, eds., *Multicultural Literacy*. St. Paul: Graywolf Press, 1988.

Simpson, Janet Madden, and Sara Blake. *Emerging Voices: A Cross-Cultural Reader*. Fort Worth: Holt, Rinehart and Winston, 1990.

Skolnick, Jerome. *The Politics of Protest*. New York: Simon and Schuster, 1969.

Slater, Philip. *The Pursuit of Loneliness*. Boston: Beacon Press, 1970.

———. *Earthwalk*. Garden City, N.Y.: Anchor Press, 1974.

Sowell, Thomas. *Ethnic America*. New York: Basic Books, 1981.

———. *Race and Economics*. New York: D. McKay Co., 1975.

Spong, John Bishop. *Into the Whirlwind*. New York: Seabury Press, 1983.

Steinbeck, John. *The Grapes of Wrath*. New York: Penguin, 1989.

Takaki, Ronald. *A Different Mirror: A History of Multicultural America*. Boston: Little, Brown and Co., 1993.

———. *Strangers from a Different Shore*. Boston: Little, Brown and Co., 1989.

Tan, Amy. *The Joy Luck Club*. New York: Vintage, 1991.

Tarnas, Richard. "The Transfiguration of the Western Mind." *Cross Currents* 39:3 (Fall 1989).

Thomas, Piri. *Down These Mean Streets*. New York: Alfred A. Knopf, 1970.

Turner, Frederick. *Beyond Geography: The Western Spirit Against the Wilderness*. New York: Viking Press, 1980.

Ulanov, Anne Belford. *The Feminine in Jungian Psychology and in Christian Theology*. Evanston, Ill.: Northwestern University Press, 1971.

U.S. Catholic Bishops. *The Hispanic Presence, Challenge and Commitment*. Pastoral letter. Washington, D.C.: U.S. Catholic Conference, 1984.

――――. *The Challenge of Peace: God's Promise and Our Response*. Pastoral letter. Washington, D.C: U.S. Catholic Conference, 1983.

U.S. Commission on Civil Rights. *Puerto Ricans in the Continental United States*. Washington, D.C: The Commission, 1976.

Villarreal, Roberto E., and Norma G. Hernandez, eds., *Latinos and Political Coalitions*. New York: Praeger Press, 1991.

Villaseñor, Victor. *Rain of Gold*. Houston: Arte Publico Press, 1992.

Wagley, Charles. *Latin American Tradition: Essays on Unity and the Diversity of Latin American Culture*. New York: Columbia University Press, 1968.

Walker, Alice. *Meridian*. New York: Pocket Books, 1986.

――――. *The Color Purple*. New York: Washington Square Press, 1982.

West, Cornel. *Race Matters*. Boston: Beacon Press, 1993.

Whitmont, E. C. *The Symbolic Quest*. Princeton, N.J.: Princeton University Press, 1991.

Wilson, William J. *The Declining Significance of Race*. Chicago: University of Chicago Press, 1980.

Wolin, Sheldon. "What Revolutionary Action Means Today." *Democracy* 2:4 (Fall 1982).

――――. "The People's Two Bodies." *Democracy* 1:1 (January 1981).

――――. "Political Theory as a Vocation." *American Political Science Review* 63 (December 1969).

Yezierska, Anzia. *Bread Givers*. New York: Persea Books, 1975.

Young, Iris M. *Justice and the Politics of Difference*. Princeton, N.J.: Princeton University Press, 1990.

Yourcenar, Marguerite. *The Abyss*. London: Weidenfeld & Nicolson, 1976.

Zaretsky, Eli. *Capitalism, the Family and Personal Life*. New York: Harper and Row, 1976.

FILMS

The Ballad of Gregorio Cortez. Directed by Robert Young. PBS American Playhouse, 1982.

The Blood of the Condor. Directed by Jorge Sanjines. Bolivia, 1969.

Camila. Directed by Maria Luisa Bemberg. Argentina, 1984.

Hopi Songs of the Fourth World. Directed by Pat Ferrero. New Day Films, 1985.

Like Water For Chocolate. Directed by Alfonso Arau. Mexico, 1992.

Lucía. Directed by Humberto Solas. Cuba, 1968.

El Norte. Directed by Gregory Nava. Independent Productions, 1983.

Nothing But a Man. Directed by Michael Roemer. Du/Art Cinema Video, 1964.

La Operación. Directed by Ana M. Garcia. Cinema Guild, 1982.

Operation Bootstrap. Directed by Carl Dudley. Universal Education and Visual Arts, 1964.

A Portrait of Teresa. Directed by Pastor Vega. Cuba, 1979.

Raisin in the Sun. Directed by Daniel Petrie. Columbia Pictures, 1961.

The Salt of the Earth. Directed by Herbert Biberman. Independent Productions Corporation, 1954.

The Sewing Woman. Anti-Defamation League of B'Nai Brith, 1986.

La Strada. Directed by Federico Fellini. Italy, 1954.

Yentl. Directed by Barbra Streisand. MGM, 1983.

Index

About the Author

DAVID T. ABALOS is Professor of Religious Studies and Sociology at Seton Hall University. He is the author of *Latinos in the United States: The Sacred and the Political* and *The Latino Family and the Politics of Transformation* (Praeger, 1993). In recognition for his work in the classroom, he was selected by the Council for the Advancement and Support of Education as one of the top ten university professors in the nation.

ISBN 0-275-95270-3

90000>

EAN

9 780275 952709

HARDCOVER BAR CODE